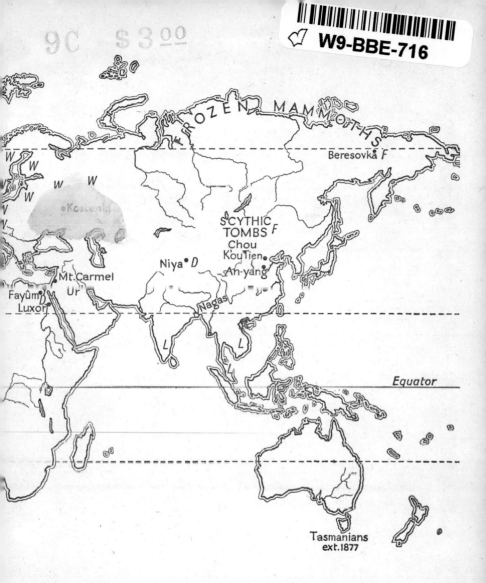

FROZEN MAMMOTHS

Beresovka F

W W
W W
W V
V

•Kostenki

SCYTHIC
TOMBS F
Chou
KouTien•
An-yang

Niya• D

Mt.Carmel

Fayûm•
Luxor   Ur

Nagas

L   L

Equator

Tasmanians
ext. 1877

CAL   SITES

D = Desiccated sites   L = Leached sites

ARCHAEOLOGY
AND SOCIETY

Early Bronze Age woman in oak coffin from Skrydstrup,
Schleswig-Holstein

(Text, pp. 92, 205)

ARCHAEOLOGY AND SOCIETY

RECONSTRUCTING
THE PREHISTORIC PAST

by

GRAHAME CLARK

*Fellow of Peterhouse and Disney Professor
of Archaeology, University of Cambridge*

1957

HARVARD UNIVERSITY PRESS
CAMBRIDGE · MASSACHUSETTS

First published in this edition 1957

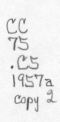
Printed in Great Britain by
Jarrold and Sons Ltd, Norwich

TO

MY WIFE

PREFACE

Since *Archaeology and Society* was first published in 1939 and reissued (with small changes) in 1947, considerable advances have been made along the lines advocated by its very title: archaeologists have become more and more interested in the history of the societies of which archaeological material is a detritus, and contemporary society has become much more aware of archaeology. When therefore I was asked to prepare a new edition I found that I had to write what was in effect very largely a new book, one that adhering in large measure to its original plan was able so to speak to advance beyond the territory already consolidated. In this preface it may be useful if I give some indication of the extent of the changes made.

Although by no means confined, either in its examples or its relevance, to prehistoric archaeology, *Archaeology and Society* in its present guise is directed primarily to the use of archaeology as a means of elucidating the prehistoric past, and Chapter I has accordingly been rewritten with this aim in view. On the other hand, chapters concerned with the actual recovery of archaeological data—those dealing with discovery (Chapter II) and excavation (Chapter IV)—have merely been modified to bring them up to date, and that dealing with the survival of archaeological material (Chapter III) has been left substantially as it was written eighteen years ago. Chronology is another of the permanent requirements of archaeology, but in this case advances have been particularly rapid and important; although therefore the basic framework of Chapter V has been retained, it has been found necessary to rewrite it almost in its entirety.

In Chapter VI of the old book I suggested that the object of locating, excavating, and dating archaeological material was to interpret it in terms of societies that once lived. Since then I have endeavoured to realize this in respect of the economic life of prehistoric Europe in my *Prehistoric Europe: the economic basis* (Methuen, 1952). The welcome given to this book—it has been translated into French, Russian, and Polish—has encouraged me to employ the same sequence of topics and to utilize several of the illustrations in Chapter VI of the present book, which deals with the way in which archaeological data can be used to reconstruct the economic aspects of life. In Chapter VII some attempt has been made to examine the much more difficult subject of the extent to which information can be won concerning non-material aspects of existence, and in writing this I have used the model (fig. 25) I constructed for my Albert Reckitt Archaeological Lecture on 'The Economic Approach to Pre-history', printed in the *Proceedings of the British Academy* for 1953.

The final chapter of *Archaeology and Society* was written in the angry era of Fascists, Nazis, and Stalinists—and revised during the hardly less difficult era that followed the end of the war. It is possible now to take a more detached view of the significance of prehistory today. Public appreciation, reflected not only in a spate of books of varying merit, but even more widely in the sound and television programmes of the B.B.C., has grown immeasurably since I originally wrote *Archaeology and Society*. Moreover, modern historiographers have come to recognize more and more explicitly the parochial character of what down to our own schooldays passed for History. In my final chapter (VIII) I have aimed to point the relevance of pre-history to men and women of today. Archaeology has been and still can be a retreat from harsh reality, but equally it can be and is coming more and more to be an exciting quest to satisfy deep-felt needs of contemporary society.

G. C. *Cambridge*

CONTENTS

9

ILLUSTRATIONS IN TEXT

PLATES

ACKNOWLEDGEMENTS

Of the line drawings figs. 2—11, 13, 14, 16—19, 29, 47 and 48 are taken over from the original edition of this book; figs. 30–34, 39–41 and 43–45 come from *Prehistoric Europe* (Methuen); figs. 25–28 from my Reckitt Archaeological Lecture 'The Economic Approach to Prehistory', by courtesy of the British Academy; fig. 1 from the *Proceedings of the Prehistoric Society*; fig. 12 from the *Berichten van de Rijksdienst voor het Oudheidkundig Bodemonderzoek*; figs. 23 and 37 from Dr. H. Godwin's *The History of the British Flora* (C.U.P.); fig. 46 from the *Historia de España* directed by Don Ramón Menéndez Pidal; fig. 49 from the *Transactions of the Lancashire & Cheshire Antiquarian Society*; fig. 42 from the late Sir Ellis Minns' *Scythians & Greeks* (C.U.P.); and figs. 50 and 51 from *From Savagery to Civilization* (Cobbett Press). Of the new drawings fig. 20 is based on an original in Dr. Johs. Iversen's *Landnam i Danmarks Stenalder* (Danmarks Geologiske Undersøgelse); fig. 21 on one from *The Antiquaries Journal*; fig. 22 on one from Miss D. A. E. Garrod's *The Stone Age of Mount Carmel*, vol. I (O.U.P.); and Fig. 52 on a photograph supplied by the National Museum, Copenhagen.

The half-tones are substantially those of the original edition, but Pl. IIIb is taken from the *Proceedings of the Prehistoric Society* and Pl. XXa from *The Antiquaries Journal*; and the original for Pl. VIII was supplied by the National Museum, Copenhagen.

Grateful acknowledgements are made to all concerned.

I

INTRODUCTORY:
Archaeology and Prehistory

Archaeology may be simply defined as the systematic study of antiquities as a means of reconstructing the past. For his contributions to be fruitful the archaeologist has to possess a real feeling for history, even though he may not have to face what is perhaps the keenest challenge of historical scholarship, the subtle interplay of human personality, and circumstance. Yet he is likely to be involved even more deeply in the flow of time. The prehistoric archaeologist, in particular, is confronted by historical changes of altogether greater dimensions than those with which the historian of literate civilizations is concerned, and has to face demands on his historical imagination of a commensurate order; further, at a purely technical level he is likely to be met with much greater difficulties of decipherment, difficulties which can as a rule only be surmounted by calling on scientists and scholars practised in highly specialized branches of knowledge.

Much of the fascination of archaeology indeed resides in its many-sidedness. One can safely say that there are few faculties, experiences, or fields of special knowledge that cannot contribute to or are not stimulated by its pursuit. The complete archaeologist, if such a being existed, would need to have a genius for travel, exploration, and reconnaissance; to be adept at business and administration, skilled at raising funds and obtaining all manner of permits from authorities and owners, few of whom can hope to gain from his activities, and capable of administering and directing excavations which may well turn out to be large-scale enterprises; to be a competent surveyor, draughtsman, and photographer, so that what he finds can be adequately recorded; to combine a gift for exact description and analysis with a power of synthesis and a flair for journalism; and to have the gift of tongues, or at very least an ability to digest the reports of his foreign colleagues without which his own will lack the authority that only wide reading and comparison can provide.

In addition to all these talents of the market-place, without which even the finest scholarship is likely to prove ineffective in this field, our paragon must be endowed with other qualities of a higher and a rarer order. The fruitful practice of archaeology involves to a unique degree an ability and a willingness to comprehend the aims, methods, and potentialities of fellow-workers in the most diverse branches of both humanistic and scientific study. To express the matter differently, the quality of the contributions an archaeologist is likely to be able to make depends on the degree to which he recognizes the limitations as well as the possibilities of his discipline in the elucidation of the past. The first step is to recognize that archaeology is in fact a discipline, but only one of the many disciplines needed to throw light on the more or less remote past, and the second that success is likely to depend not only on the rigour of its own proper methods, but also on the skill and sympathy with which its practitioners combine with those of cognate disciplines to solve common problems.

The discipline of archaeology imposes special requirements of its own. All archaeologists, whatever their precise field, have to depend primarily on the study of artifacts, and the classification and understanding of these call for a highly developed sense of style: the archaeologist has to rely in the first instance very largely on his appreciation of form, texture, and artistic convention if he is to distinguish correctly the products of separate cultures, discern stages of historical development, or detect the interaction of different traditions. Further, so soon as he concerns himself with attempting to reconstruct the lives of the societies responsible for the artifacts he studies, he is brought up against a new set of requirements. Even to appreciate ancient works of art it is necessary to combine with a capacity for aesthetic appreciation a wide knowledge of the techniques and history of architecture, sculpture, and painting. But the range of artifacts with the production and use of which the archaeologist has to be familiar is co-extensive with the life of society. Indeed, technical processes and the artifacts shaped by them can only yield their full historical meaning in relation to the economic and social systems of which they formed an integral part. This means that archaeologists need to be aware of the work, not merely of economic and social historians, but still more, in the case of those working on preliterate societies, of the findings of social anthropology.

Again, since artifacts are made by and for people and since societies are constituted by individuals, it is vital to study the mentality and actual physical characteristics of the bearers of his cultures, and this the archaeologist can only do indirectly, since in the case of the former he is often studying people without a literature and whose language is unknown to him, and in the case of physical type and condition he is as a rule confined to skeletal traces which may often be very incomplete: for his knowledge of mentality he will have to rely mainly on what he can infer from the way in which the people he is studying have utilized their environment, behaved to each other and come to terms with non-material, unseen forces, though where skulls are available he may get some help from the size and convolutions of their brains; and for physique, racial type, age, sex, medical history, nutrition, and deformation he will have to rely on anatomy and forensic medicine and, where ancient, fossil material is concerned, on human palaeontology, branches of knowledge which, if he is lucky, he will find combined in the person of a physical anthropologist. Further, the archaeologist, and more particularly the prehistoric archaeologist, must study his cultures in their geographical setting, if he is to bring them to life in all their dimensions or even understand their economic basis. It is not sufficient to study the relationship between traces of former stages of settlement and the present geographical situation: such studies may and indeed must be misleading, and the more so the older the cultures studied, since the geographical environment can no more be taken as a constant factor than can human settlement itself. What the prehistoric archaeologist has to study is the history of human settlement in relation to the history of the climate, topography, vegetation, and fauna of the territory in question. One of the greatest difficulties in such a study is to distinguish between changes in the environment brought about by purely natural processes and those produced, whether intentionally or incidentally, by the activities of human society, and this can only be resolved by intimate co-operation in the field with climatologists, geologists, pedologists, botanists, zoologists, and palaeontologists in the comradeship of Quaternary research. The archaeologist wants to know precisely what geographical conditions obtained at each stage of human settlement; the extent to which the economic activities of any particular community were limited by the external environment; and above all how far the economic activities of the people he is studying are reflected in and can be reconstructed from changes in the geographical surroundings. It is only by observing the human cultures of antiquity as elements in a changing ecological situation that it is possible to form a clear idea of even the economic basis of early settlement, see precisely how early man utilized his environment and so arrive at a fuller understanding of his intellectual, economic, and social progress.

Archaeological methods can profitably be applied to any phase or aspect of history insufficiently documented by written records, however recent in time; indeed, archaeology can not only be used to fill gaps in the documents, but also to check or corroborate them. In this respect archaeological evidence bears some analogies to the circumstantial evidence of the law courts. Human testimony, whether written or oral, has a directness of appeal that may at first sight seem to be lacking from the fragments and traces on which the detective relies for his circumstantial evidence, but the very humanity which appeals to us in literature or speech involves grave limitations. Human memories are fallible and the motives of witnesses, writers of state papers, and even historians are more mixed than they know themselves. Cross-examination in the courts and critical analysis in the study may do something to rectify or at least check the unveracities of human testimony, but they can hardly do more than reduce the area of uncertainty. Although the interpretation of scientific data by hired experts is notoriously liable to point to opposing conclusions, the value of circumstantial evidence can hardly be doubted as a check on personal testimony. In dealing with the past it is the gaps even more in many cases than the imperfections in the surviving written record that enhances the value of archaeological evidence. For instance, it has been found that more precise information about the proficiency of the men of medieval times can be obtained from a study of their scientific instruments than from their treatises alone. Similarly, excavation has recently been throwing more light on the history of medieval settlement in Denmark than could be obtained from the documents, and even in England, where the documentary record is relatively complete, there are large spheres of economic activity never or only incidentally recorded in writing.

As a general proposition it must be accepted that the value of archaeological evidence as a source of information about human history varies inversely with the extent and nature of documentary sources in the broad sense of the term. The more incomplete the historical record the heavier the reliance that must be placed on alternative kinds of evidence. Thus the value of archaeology is likely to be higher in relation at any rate to the earlier stages of the older oriental civilizations than to the classical or later European ones. Yet even in the study of the earliest literate communities archaeology is bound to play an ancillary, if not a subservient, role where any considerable bulk of inscriptions has survived, since these give an insight into the mentality and values of early societies more direct than material things can ever do. Conversely, it is in the reconstruction of prehistory, the unwritten history of all but a comparatively brief span of all humanity, that archaeology can render its greatest contribution to human understanding. Although in discussing the nature of archaeological evidence and the methods used to salvage this, I shall not hesitate to draw examples from the archaeology of literate societies, my main theme in this book will be prehistoric archaeology, the archaeology of the preliterate phase of humanity, a phase which over extensive regions of the world, many of them only now gaining control of their own destinies, lasted down till modern times.

No precise delimitation of the range of prehistory is likely to find wide acceptance, though it would probably be agreed by most English-speaking archaeologists that it is concerned with preliterate societies. At the lower end of the range no hard and fast line can be drawn between animal and human societies, but for practical purposes one may take the appearance of tools shaped in conformity with a recognizable tradition as a useful datum. As regards an upper limit one might accept the appearance of a more or less continuous written record as marking the end of prehistory and the beginning of what is conventionally regarded as history. Quite clearly, though, some difference of opinion is likely to exist as to precisely at what stage preliteracy gives way to literacy: attainment of literacy must in the first instance have been a slow process; and the spread of literacy was so uneven that it has taken about five thousand years for it to extend from the earliest centres over the world as a whole.

One of the results of this slow diffusion of literacy is that the prehistoric period lasted much longer in some regions than in others. Thus even in Europe marked differences can be noted as between different areas: over much of the Mediterranean coasts the prehistoric period was brought to an end by Greek and Punic colonization already by the middle of the first millennium B.C.; the extension of the Roman Empire during later centuries incorporated the rest of the Mediterranean and parts of the temperate zones within the sphere of history and, even if outlying provinces suffered a relapse into barbarism, the experience of Imperial rule was sufficiently profound to mark the end of an age; but extensive territories in the northern, central, and eastern regions of the continent remained prehistoric until gathered into the fold of Christendom in the course of the Middle Ages. Most of western and parts of southern Asia had already been drawn within the sphere of ancient oriental civilization long before Alexander's famous march, and the rise of an independent, if in part derivative, civilization in North China and its attainment of literacy soon after the middle of the second millennium B.C. had already brought prehistory to an end over extensive tracts of the Far East before direct contact was established with the West. Much of Africa on the other hand remained prehistoric until quite modern times; influences from ancient Egypt had early penetrated extensive areas of North Africa, but it was not until the establishment of Phoenician trading-stations on the coast that any part of the continent outside the Nile Valley and its immediate area passed into history; trade and commerce from the Indian Ocean must have opened up parts of the east coast comparatively early, and on the west the Portuguese extended their influence as far down as the Gold Coast before the end of the fifteenth century; but it was not until 1652 that the Dutch disturbed the prehistory of South Africa, and much of the tropical interior remained prehistoric until the middle of the nineteenth century. Australia remained for all effective purposes prehistoric until the founding of Sydney in 1788 initiated a process that was not to affect the greater part of the continent until well into the nineteenth century. When the New World was first effectively discovered by Europeans it is true that indigenous civilizations existed and that in certain of these historical records were maintained, but by far the great part of both the Americas remained prehistoric until opened up by exploration and settlement during the post-Columban era.

It follows from this not merely that there was a broad overlap in time between the later prehistoric communities and those recording their own histories, but that simpler cultures in proximate and even in quite distant regions would even in quite early times have been liable to more or less profound influence from civilized centres. This means that the later prehistoric cultures must needs be studied in the same context as their literate contemporaries. With characteristic clarity our French colleagues have long recognized that this necessity in turn serves to differentiate the phases of prehistory anterior to the rise of the early civilizations (or at least to their impact on the prehistory of whatever area is in question) and those which betray in metallurgy or other traits the impact of ideas deriving ultimately from literate communities: it is the former alone, running from the beginning of the Old Stone Age to the Neolithic, that for them comprise *la préhistoire*; the latter they consign to *la protohistoire*. British archaeologists have generally preferred to hold to the concept of prehistory as a unitary field. Yet it is important to recognize the existence of a polarity of interest as between those concerned with the primary evolution of culture up to the discovery and spread of an elementary farming economy and those whose main interest is with the secondary devolution of culture and the transformation of primitive farming communities under impulses from civilization up to the stage at which they were capable of beginning to record their own history: for some purposes it may even be useful to speak of primary and secondary prehistory.

The general aim of prehistory is to recover as much as possible about the history of preliterate societies which by their very nature were incapable of recording it. This makes it hardly necessary to emphasize that the kind of information to be won from the prehistoric past differs profoundly from that to be gained from the history of even partially literate societies. In a sense there is justice on the side of those who have claimed that, since prehistoric peoples have and can have no history, prehistorians are attempting the impossible in trying to recover it. The distinction we have to preserve is that between history in its rigorous, academic sense, which began only when it was written down, and history in its broader evolutionary connotation, the product of the last two centuries of scientific thought, which comprehends the whole story of mankind in society. The fact that we now recognize a continuity of development, and one that can only conventionally be restricted to human societies, should not prevent us from recognizing Natural History, Prehistory, and History as separate disciplines, disciplines which differ not merely in their procedures, but still more in what they can tell us about the past.

It is the glory of history that by means of it one is enabled not merely to check general trends by reference to a multitude of particularities—one can often do this for prehistory—but actually to study the relations of individual men to one another and to the circumstances in which they found themselves, and even to discover the motives that determined or at least influenced specific choices. The prehistorian, on the other hand, lacking documentary sources, is precluded from identifying individuals; so soon as the names even of the most prominent are known we sense ourselves on the threshold of history proper and begin even in the English-speaking world to qualify our studies as protohistoric. Prehistory, as I have written elsewhere,[1] is a social study: it deals 'not with individuals or with the relations of individuals to one another and to society in general, but with societies, including their internal stratification and their local organization, and their relations to one another

[1] *The Study of Prehistory*, Cambridge, 1953.

and to the world of nature of which in the final resort they form an integral part'. Yet, though the units with which it deals are larger and though it has to work at a higher level of abstraction than history proper, prehistory is nevertheless fundamentally historical in the sense that it deals with time as a main dimension.

Now, although, as will be further emphasized in the relevant chapters (VI and VII), archaeology is only one of many disciplines involved in the reconstruction of prehistory, it is nevertheless a central one, and one which happens to be the principal concern of this book. It may therefore be appropriate to devote the remaining part of this introductory chapter to considering in barest outline the history of archaeology[1] with particular reference to the idea of prehistory.

One may begin by making the point that, although hidden treasure has exercised its fascination on men's minds since men have made treasures worth finding, the idea of reconstructing man's past by discovering and interpreting material traces of his former modes of living is comparatively recent. It is true that the Greeks and the Romans appreciated the existence of a prehistoric age, but however engaging their speculations may seem to us they remained such, and they resulted in no ordered attempt to recover the material traces of past ages. The men of the Middle Ages, conscious of living in a divinely ordered present, were for the most part uninterested in the past, and in so far as they were it was with the traces of classical antiquity. The rediscovery of ancient civilization was mainly literary, but we know of at least one late medieval scholar, Cyriac de Pizzicolli, born at Ancona in 1391, who engaged in archaeological reconnaissance on the Greek islands and mainland, collecting coins, recording inscriptions, and visiting sites of classical antiquity.

This interest in the material remains of classical antiquity, which marked the effective beginnings of archaeology in western culture, was greatly increased with the revival of

_____
[1] See Glyn E. Daniel, *A Hundred Years of Archaeology*, London, 1950.

ancient learning in general that marked the transition to the modern period of our history, and which, significantly, found expression in a distinctive Renaissance style of art. The new taste drew its inspiration from monuments of classical antiquity. The desire to recover further models from the classical period led to the development of what may justly be termed archaeological quarrying in the soil of Italy and Greece, and the impact of this was felt wherever the new ideas spread. When Thomas Howard, Earl of Arundel, visited Italy in 1612 he not only initiated a habit that was for two hundred years to draw young Englishmen of the aristocratic class to the Mediterranean, but himself entered on a course of collecting that was ultimately to bring together a mass of classical sculpture from as far afield as Greece, the islands and western Asia; although dispersed and to a large extent lost, the Arundel marbles played a part in making Englishmen aware of the tangible remains of classical antiquity, and a residue survived to form the nucleus of the present Ashmolean collection. Another and much later tour of Italy, that made by Thomas Hollis and Thomas Brand between 1748 and 1753, led to the founding of the first chair of archaeology in Britain. The house built by the two travellers at Ingatestone in Essex to display their treasures was in due course purchased by John Disney, together with their collection. Before he died Disney published it in the three stately volumes of the *Museum Disneianum* (1846-9), handed the originals to the recently built Fitzwilliam Museum, and in 1851 endowed a Disney Professor, no doubt with the idea, fortunately not specified, of extolling the antiquities of Greece and Rome.

The revival of interest in classical antiquity was only one of several factors that led to the rise of archaeological studies. Another was the preoccupation with indigenous history, associated with the disintegration of medieval Christendom and the emergence of national states. To begin with, this interest was mainly literary, as we see from the commissioning by Henry VIII of John Leland (1506-52), Keeper of the King's

Libraries, to search for historical documents in the religious houses and colleges of England, or from the activities of later antiquaries like John Stow, William Lambarde, Robert Cotton, John Spelman, and William Camden (1551–1623), who with others formed the short-lived Elizabethan College of Antiquaries. The true aim of these Elizabethans was frankly patriotic. As Dr Joan Evans has recently written,[1] they sought above all 'to establish a "cultural longevity" for their country: Parliament had to date from the Roman era; the bearing of arms to go back to Caesar, and Christianity to have been brought to Britain by Joseph of Arimathea'. Their purview was limited to the historical period, and, though he displayed engravings of ancient British coins in the first edition of his *Britannia* (1586), Camden was firm that the true historian ought not to venture behind the Romans.

Yet, once embarked on the quest for antiquity, there was no logical reason to halt at this particular boundary, and this applied with even more force in territories beyond the frontier of the Roman Empire. The antiquarian interests of Germans and Scandinavians focused naturally on the free barbarians. Even so, it is characteristic that they should have turned in the first instance to references and descriptions in the Greek and Latin authors. German scholars showed an almost pathological interest in the *Germania* of Tacitus. The first printed edition issued from Nuremburg as early as 1473, and this was followed in 1535 by *Das Buchlein von der alten Teutschen Brauch und Leben*, the first of a lengthy series of works in the vulgar tongue that sought to describe the life of the Germans of antiquity: to begin with, the material was obtained largely from Tacitus, but as time went on this was supplemented more and more by the findings of archaeology. In yet more remote territories, classical references to which were correspondingly exiguous, antiquaries were driven almost of necessity to the monuments, as for instance Olaus Wurmius, Physician to the King of Denmark,

[1] *A History of the Society of Antiquaries*, 11, Oxford, 1956.

whose *De Monumentis Danicis* appeared in 1643. As might be expected, Wurmius concentrated on inscribed stones, but he nevertheless classified and indeed illustrated rude stone monuments, including megalithic tombs, and was not above referring to and even depicting objects dug out of tumuli.

Yet the transition from the study to the field that was necessary before archaeology could emerge from antiquarianism was a painfully slow one. John Aubrey (1626–97) appears to have been the first Englishman to make effective records of prehistoric field monuments at first-hand, and it is significant that his *Monumenta Britannica* should have had to wait for two centuries for publication. The first field archaeologist to make enough impression on his contemporaries to get into print was William Stukeley (1687–1765), whose survey work at Avebury and Stonehenge between 1718 and 1725 was a model for his day and has proved of permanent value, even though carried out to show that the Ancient Britons were confirmed Trinitarians. Stukeley opened the Preface to his *Itinerarium Curiosum* (1726) by informing the reader that 'the intent of this Treatise is to oblige the curious in the Antiquities of Britain', went on to add the significant qualification that 'it is an account of places and things from inspection, not compiled' and invited 'Gentlemen and others in the country, to make researches of this nature'. Stukeley certainly rode about the country and plied his survey instruments, but so far as we know he stopped short of excavation.

Archaeological excavation first got going on any scale during the later half of the eighteenth century. The early antiquaries, as we have seen, went to their classics for information about their early forebears, but no decisive advance came until the revulsion of taste symbolized by the Romantic movement in literature had brought about a change of attitude towards the rude material traces of barbarian societies. From being disregarded as failing to conform to classical standards the monuments and small objects of prehistoric times were sought after just because they were rudely finished. The excavation of burial mounds, easy to locate and liable to be productive of relatively intact finds, was undertaken on an increasing scale by pioneers like Fausset and Douglas in Kent, Cunnington in Wiltshire, and Borlase in Cornwall. No doubt the barrow-diggers of the late eighteenth and nineteenth centuries wrought great destruction, and by modern standards gained little knowledge, yet by disinterring a considerable body of material they helped to lay the foundations of prehistoric archaeology. Hardly less valuable was the collection of stray finds brought to light in increasing quantities as the Industrial Revolution spread its influence. The quickening of economic life, manifested, for example, in improved roads and in the construction of canals and in due course of railways, as well as in the intensification of agriculture to feed the growing town population, helped to bring increasing quantities of antiquities to light at a time when men were more prepared than ever before to recognize and salvage them.

The growth of public collections brought to the fore the problem of arrangement and so of classification, and it is significant that the Three Age system of C. J. Thomsen was published in a guide (*Ledetraad til Nordisk Oldkyndighed*, 1836) to the national collections at Copenhagen. Yet, though this system was designed to serve a practical purpose, it also enshrined an idea, that of progressive development: the succession stone, bronze and iron, long ago adumbrated by Lucretius, epitomized a progressive improvement in the effectiveness of tools, and thus in control over the natural environment. In this connexion it is significant that Sven Nilsson, who applied the same scheme to the collections at Lund, laid a special emphasis on stages of economic development in his *Skandinaviska Nordens Urinvånare* (1838–43), distinguishing: savages based on hunting; herdsmen or nomads; agriculturalists; and civilized communities marked by writing, coinage, and a relatively advanced subdivision of labour. Under the influence of such men as Buffon

(1707–88), Erasmus Darwin (1731–1802), and Lamarck (1744–1829) transformist ideas had already for some time pervaded biological studies, and what Thomsen and Nilsson were doing was to apply these to the field of human culture.

Yet, though it is true that the idea of evolution was in the air at this time, its implications for the antiquity and early history of man remained veiled. Thomsen may have been influenced by the transformist ideas of his time, but he had no inkling of the antiquity of man and was content to allot an age of 3,000 years to the Stone Age of Denmark. Even more revealing is the attitude adopted to discoveries bearing directly on what we would now term the Palaeolithic age. These were mostly ignored, but where they were noticed this was only to be explained away. John Frere's discovery of flint implements at Hoxne in a situation which, as he phrased it in 1797, 'may tempt us to refer them to a very remote period indeed; even beyond that of the present world' found no contemporary echo; Boucher de Perthes's discoveries in the Somme Valley were disbelieved or ignored; and the very notebooks recording MacEnery's excavations at Kent's Cavern were mislaid. One of the most instructive figures of his day was William Buckland (1784–1856), who combined the Readership in Geology at Oxford with the Deanery of Westminster. When one considers the implications of the full title of his *Reliquiae Diluvianae; or Observations on the organic remains contained in Caves, Fissures, and Diluvial Gravel and on other Geological Phenomena attesting the action of an Universal Deluge* (1826), the dedication of this work on Pleistocene Geology to the reigning Bishop of Durham loses its air of anomaly. Buckland was too good a geologist to miss the traces of early man, but he was quite unable to accept these at their face value because, as he frankly informs us in his *Geology and Mineralogy considered in relation to Natural Theology* (1836), of the 'great difficulty in reconciling the early and extended periods which have been assigned to the extinct races of animals with our received chronology'. When therefore he came upon the remains of the so-called 'Red Lady' in the Pleistocene filling of the Goat Cave at Paviland he was unable to accept the evidence of his own eyes, and took refuge in the notion that the burial with its ivory rods and bracelets and its covering of red ochre must relate to 'the remains of a British camp' that existed conveniently on the hill above the cave. Dean Buckland was an outstandingly able man and the leading expert of his day on Pleistocene caves, but he was subject to the preconceptions of his age.

It was possible under the old dispensation for archaeology to develop from antiquarianism, and even for the outlines of secondary prehistory to take shape in parts of Europe—after all, Thomsen's Three Ages could fit into the span of Archbishop Ussher's chronology with several thousand years to spare—but quite definitely there was no room for Palaeolithic man. It needed a revolution in men's conception of the nature and antiquity of man as an organism before the bare notion of primary prehistory could take birth.

Such a revolution was wrought by the publication in 1859 of Charles Darwin's *Origin of Species*. The idea of transformism had been current during the previous century, but it was not until Darwin formulated his coherent and to many scientists convincing theory of natural selection that the evolution of species became acceptable as a hypothesis. The relevance of this to the status of man was as manifest as it was challenging to old beliefs. In Huxley's words acceptance of Darwin's views made it essential to 'extend by long epochs the most liberal estimate that has yet been made of the Antiquity of Man'. The effect on those open to conviction was indeed dramatic. That same year the geologists Lyell and Prestwich together with John Evans made their famous pilgrimage to the Somme Valley, and returning, handsomely endorsed the previously neglected claims of Boucher de Perthes. Further, MacEnery's notebooks were sought and found; and five years later excavations were resumed at Kent's Cavern under the auspices of the British

Association. Meanwhile in France the disregard of Tournal's work in the Grotte de Bize in 1828 was compensated for by the notable series of excavations in the caves of the Dordogne carried out by Lartet and Christy in 1863-4. By one of those chances that enliven the history of any science the phenomenally low levels to which the Swiss lakes had fallen in the winter of 1853-4 had greatly expanded interest in the later prehistory of Europe by revealing for the first time details of the daily life of Neolithic and Bronze Age peasants. This made it all the more possible for Sir John Lubbock to write his *Prehistoric Times* only six years after Darwin's book, and yet to draw in it the fundamental distinction between the Palaeolithic and Neolithic eras, an illustration of how rapidly prehistory developed once the inhibitions that prevented Dean Buckland from appreciating the implications of his own discoveries had been swept away by the tide of biological science.

The vast extension in the range of human history implicit in the idea that man evolved from some antecedent animal species at a remote period of time emphasized the need to gather fossils illustrating his cultural as well as his biological development, and it is not surprising in the circumstances that both should have been conceived of in terms of unilinear evolution. Excavation of the caves of the Dordogne was pressed forward with such zeal that already by 1881 G. de Mortillet was able to present in his *La Musée préhistorique* a prototype of the classic French sequence of prehistory, a sequence which the Abbé Breuil was able to complete in 1912. The impulse to complete the chain of evolutionary development also involved the later stages of European prehistory. Yet here there is an important difference to be noted in that men like Oscar Montelius, Sophus Muller, and Joseph Déchelette were fully aware that the periods they distinguished, mainly on the basis of detailed typological studies, were valid only for the provinces for which they devised them. The greater duration and geographical extent of the Palaeolithic cultures and the fact that they were studied in association with and sometimes as mere extensions of geology and palaeontology all helped to obscure the fact that they, no less than those of later prehistoric times, were the product of human history rather than of biological evolution.

It was the expansion of prehistoric research from the west to central and eastern Europe, to Africa, and to Asia—which after all was only made possible by the achievement of the French pioneers—that destroyed the epochal validity of the classic sequence. The unilinear sequence began to break even for the Lower Palaeolithic in Europe itself, and already in 1916 Hugo Obermaier recognized in his *El Hombre Fosil* the existence of two contemporary traditions. The Upper Palaeolithic sequence was more finely drawn and even more vulnerable. Already by 1928 Dorothy Garrod, on the basis of her experience in Palestine and Kurdistan, was able to point out that de Mortillet's classification merely recorded 'the order of arrival in the West of a series of cultures, each of which ... originated and probably passed through the greater part of its existence elsewhere'. The more widely research has spread in western Asia, North Africa, and in Central Europe and South Russia the more complex the pattern of the blade and burin cultures of the Late Pleistocene has become, and the more certain it is that their history cannot be explained in terms of any simple line of development.

In the case of the later stages of prehistory, concerned to a greater or less degree with settled peoples based on farming, the regional validity of local sequences had been recognized from the beginning by leading European scholars. Even so, the emphasis rested almost entirely, as it was bound to do at this stage, on the establishment of periods: it was not until the second and third decades of the present century that much attempt was made to distinguish cultural groupings. In this respect Gustaf Kossinna (1858–1931) was a pioneer, because, vitiated though much of his work was by a preoccupation with Nordicism, he at least made clear his interest in the peoples rather than with the mere periods of prehistory, as well as by the use he made of distribution maps demonstrating the possibility of studying prehistoric settlement. The publication in 1925 of V. Gordon Childe's *The Dawn of European Civilization* showed the possibilities of the new approach, just as successive editions reflected its progress during the years between the two World Wars. Meanwhile the rapid, one might say sensational, progress made in the years immediately following the First World War in documenting the antiquity of settled life and even of literate civilization itself in Egypt and western Asia had made it evident that the later prehistoric cultures of Europe were secondary growths, relatively recent developments in a region which in those days was marginal and backward, so that Childe was able to show that many of the leading developments chronicled in his *Dawn*—such as the spread of farming and metallurgy—were the product of impulses emanating from the centres of ancient civilization.

Prehistoric archaeology, which grew up in Europe, has indeed ceased to be a European monopoly: like so much else of worth, it has been contributed by Europe to the world. One result of the extension of the field of research has undoubtedly been to force a recognition that European prehistory, like the prehistory of any other part of the world, is parochial. This has been all to the good: it has allowed Europeans to view their prehistory in perspective and it opens up the prospect of a real world prehistory. Great progress has already been made in realizing this, thanks first to the long-range activities of western scholars—American as well as European—operating through their own institutes or field expeditions, and latterly, and most encouragingly, to the full-time activities of indigenous archaeologists. Europe may still claim pre-eminence in the study of the higher hunting cultures of the Late Pleistocene, but for the earlier phases in the evolution of man and of his culture the decisive evidence is more likely to come from the broad zone from Africa to China and Java. Again, it is to the territories between the Nile and the Oxus that we look for the vital evidence concerning the origins of agriculture and of the world's most ancient civilizations, influences from which, as we have already noted, were responsible for the key developments of later European prehistory, as well as contributing to the genesis of classical civilization. Much has already been learnt by means of archaeology of the origins of the distinctive civilizations of India and China, the latter of which in turn influenced extensive regions in South-east Asia and the western Pacific region. No less important for their present inhabitants is the prehistory of some regions, which from the point of view of universal history have been relatively unproductive, such as Melanesia, Australia, and New Zealand. Apart from all this, we have to reckon with the newly discovered prehistory of the New World, posing problems of great theoretical importance and interest, among them: the original colonization by Stone Age hunters; the origins of New World farming and the rise of the civilizations of Middle America; and the movements of Eskimos between Alaska and Greenland, not to mention their relations with the Indians and the peoples of North-east Siberia.

Side by side with this great extension in the geographical field, which today embraces almost the whole world, has gone an increasing depth, an awareness of problems of interest to specialists in a wide range of knowledge. Whereas in the quite recent past prehistoric archaeology was virtually a branch of museology, a poor relation of antiquarianism, concerned with the classification of squalid monuments and unprepossessing bric-à-brac, it is recognized ever more widely today as a key to the understanding of prehistory, as an aid to economic history, as an integral part of Quaternary research, and as a significant contributor to anthropology in the broad sense. The modern prehistorian approaches his subject in the spirit of an ecologist, by which I mean that he seeks to study prehistoric communities as wholes, to observe the interaction of their activities and organs both with one another and with their environing habitats and biomes, and to do this in the context of time, paying special attention to the causes underlying the changes that together constitute prehistory.

Yet, ambitious though the aims of prehistory have become, the fact remains that, in so far as they are to be realized by means of archaeology, they depend on evidence that needs to be recovered from the soil. The prehistorian, like the detective, is concerned with tangible, visible clues. He has to locate and above all to select his site, taking account of the nature of the problem to be solved and of the physical state of the evidence, and then, with the same considerations in mind, to extract the information he needs by skilful excavation and by the application to the material data of all the resources of science and scholarship on which he can lay hands, not least in regard to the dating of his finds. Before going on to consider how the prehistorian endeavours to reconstruct prehistory, and why it is important that he should be enabled to do so, it is well therefore to consider these more elementary, even if vitally necessary matters.

II

AVENUES OF DISCOVERY

The element of luck is not least of the attractions of archaeology: rich finds, or clues to sites of the greatest scientific importance may turn up by merest chance, whereas the most elaborate and well-planned excavation may fail to yield results or alternatively may throw wholly unexpected light on related problems. Yet the archaeologist who seeks diligently is likely to find, and it must always be remembered that whether his concern is with the collection of raw material, its classification or its interpretation and the actual writing of prehistory, his work depends ultimately on the basic archaeological evidence.

The student of Medieval, Classical, or Oriental Archaeology may expect to have available a reasonable proportion of monumental structures, which though often ruinous can commonly be located without special difficulty. The peoples of prehistory, on the other hand, being poorer, generally used more perishable materials for building, and most traces of prehistoric antiquity are buried in the soil with little or no indication on the surface of the ground. There are of course notable exceptions; for instance, megalithic structures, burial mounds, and defensive earth-works—not to mention natural caves and rock-shelters—and it was on the investigation of these that the early excavators concentrated, but the progress of prehistoric studies depends on the discovery and investigation of a broader range of site, including in particular settlements, which, unless defended by strong earth-works, are too frequently invisible on the surface of the ground. Much can be done by means of carefully planned trial soundings, but it is hardly practicable to undertake these

until the most likely areas have been defined by observation of
stray finds, or slight surface indications. Field-work is particularly essential as a preliminary to excavation in the case of
prehistoric sites. Moreover, the prehistorian, lacking a background of historical information about the people he is studying, needs to build up from scratch his knowledge of their
geographical spread and of the detailed distribution of their
sites in relation to natural features and to the remains of other
cultures. For these reasons he needs to keep his eyes on the soil
even more intently than his colleague in other fields of
archaeology.

In the present chapter it will first be emphasized that much
of the raw material of archaeology is exposed by natural erosion
and still more by the normal activities of contemporary society.
Next, a survey will be made of the main agents that provide
surface clues to the prehistorian as he takes the field on foot or
in his aircraft in quest of sites. And last some consideration will
be given to clues that may work on his imagination as he takes
his case of a winter's evening and suggest further lines of investigation in the field. It can hardly be emphasized too strongly
that, whereas man and nature provide unwitting clues in
plenty, it is the instructed observer alone who can turn them
to advantage, and conversely that it is the formulation of problems, the desire to answer questions about the past, that leads
prehistorians to quest, to scan the soil, it may be from an altitude
of thousands of feet, and locate the very spot, perhaps in some
remote part of the world, best calculated to yield under excavation the historical information he seeks.

SOIL EXPOSURES

Natural agencies. Wherever the natural surface is broken by
erosion archaeological evidence is liable to be brought into
view. Of the various forms of natural erosion which come to
the aid of archaeology erosion by the sea is one of the most
important. The part played by the cliff exposures at Cromer

and elsewhere on the Norfolk coast in the development of Palaeolithic studies in Britain has been very great. One cannot forget, either, that industries of the Lower Palaeolithic 'Clactonian' flake culture were first exposed in Pleistocene deposits on the foreshore at Clacton and Lion Point, Essex. Incidentally, the same stretch of coast has yielded quantities of archaeological material dating from Neolithic times.

Where the sea is eroding rapidly land which once supported a relatively dense population, archaeological material is continually being exposed in the cliffs, washed on to the foreshore, and, unless rescued, destroyed by the waves. At Selsey Bill the process is in full swing, but fortunately a careful watch is kept there and an impressive collection of material has been salvaged in the last few years, including Mesolithic axes and microliths, a Neolithic cooking-hole full of pottery, two gold bracelets, and a number of cinerary urns of the Late Bronze Age, Early Iron Age pottery, numerous gold coins minted by the Regni, and an Anglo-Saxon settlement.

The fact that rivers have from the beginning of human history attracted settlement to their banks makes it easy to understand why their powers of erosion can so often be turned to good account by archaeologists. Thus we owe the discovery of Vinča, possibly the most famous prehistoric site in the Balkans, to the erosive action of the Danube, which, cutting into the tell, revealed a section of the successive settlements some nine metres thick. To quote a lesser instance from nearer home, one of the best preserved bowls of the British Neolithic Peterborough ware was noticed by an angler sticking out of a bank of the Thames near Hedsor.

Wind erosion, especially when operating on sand-dunes, is another friend of the archaeologist. When the surface of a dune overlying old land-surfaces settled by prehistoric man is broken and the wind starts to erode a hollow, the fine sand blows away and the heavier objects, including material left behind by early man, are left on the floor. This happened on a big scale on

Risby Warren, near Scunthorpe, a region densely settled by Mesolithic and by later prehistoric men. Collectors searching among the dunes have reaped a rich harvest of worked flints, bronzes and potsherds, and occasionally the blowing wind has left isolated, on a stretch of old surface, little stone-ringed hearths. Wind erosion has been responsible for the discovery of more Mesolithic sites over a wide stretch of north-western Europe from Britain to Poland than any other factor. Sometimes the blowing sands reveal more than just hearths and loose finds. It was a great storm in the middle of the nineteenth century that, sweeping away some sand-dunes at Skara Brae in Orkney, revealed the famous stone-built village about which I shall have more to say later (pp. 108f. and 202).

Exceptional droughts, by lowering the levels of lakes and rivers, have often revealed sites normally obscured from view. The extraordinary drought and prolonged cold of the winter of 1853–4 caused the rivers and lakes of the Alpine region to sink to their lowest recorded levels. On the banks of the Rhine, the Aar, and the Limmat wooden structures of Roman age were revealed, while at Meilen on Lake Zürich the remains of a lake-dwelling of much greater antiquity were fully exposed. As long ago as 1829 piles and other antiquities had been found near the site during excavations to deepen the harbour, but little attention was paid to the discovery at the time: the revelation of 1853–4 was far more striking, and interest in such matters was already much more advanced. The discovery of the Swiss 'lake-dwellings', coming as it did at a time when interest in archaeology was quickening all over western Europe, had an extraordinary effect. The completeness with which the wooden structures were found, thanks to their submersion beneath the lake waters, and the extraordinary state of preservation of food-waste and objects and utensils of all kinds, of materials rarely preserved from remote antiquity, captured people's imagination and stimulated the discovery of similar sites as far afield as Britain.

Human activities. Although Nature sometimes goes out of her way to help archaeology, the normal activities of human life create more opportunities than any other factor. It seems that the soil is so rich in history that man has only to scratch it to bring forth vestiges of his ancestors. From the earliest times the ploughman has been the un-witting discoverer of archaeological remains, and the practice of deep cultivation by means of tractor-drawn ploughs has resulted during recent years in an exceptional harvest of finds. To quote but one instance: when Ken Hill field, Snettisham, Norfolk, was ploughed twelve instead of the usual seven inches deep in November 1948, three hoards of Celtic metal-work (fig. 1) and coins, originally buried probably during the final quarter of the last century B.C., were brought to light on conse-cutive days; and, again, two years later plough-ing thirteen inches deep, turned up two further hoards. Since gold ornaments and coins were included and had presumably been buried with the intention of being recovered at some future date, both groups were declared treasure trove, and the tractor-drivers received £400 and £1,850 respectively. Archaeologically the treasure is important, not only for the out-standing quality of some individual pieces, but above all for the association of a range of objects with gold and speculum (tin) coinage; and historically it is interesting that rich objects

FIG. 1

Part of design on gold alloy bracelet from Snettisham, Norfolk originating from different parts of south-eastern and south-western England should have been committed to the soil of East Anglia at some time around the Birth of Christ.

Sometimes it happened in the past that, when new land was enclosed, 'obstructions' in the form of ancient monuments were removed, and on such occasions antiquities frequently came to light. This applies especially to stony countries like Wales and Scotland, where boulder cairns must often have presented tiresome and insuperable obstacles to husbandry. On chalk or gravel subsoils, where it was practicable to plough over barrows, these were commonly ploughed down gradually to the mere crop-marks observed by modern airmen. Although so often carried out, a piece of Lincolnshire folk-lore, attaching to a long barrow that once existed at Adam's Head in the parish of Ludford Magna, suggests that the proceeding was sometimes viewed with a certain apprehension; a passage recording the folk-lore runs as follows:

'Along the High Street above Adam's Head [the source of a certain beck is so called] runs a long detached mound called the Giant's Grave. After lying for generations in neglect a neighbouring farmer ploughed and sowed wheat upon it, but nothing came up; not to be beaten he next year sowed potatoes on it; not one ever grew. In despair it is now abandoned to the grass and moss with which it has for centuries been covered by Nature.'

Yet some farmer must have braved the qualms of his neighbours and ploughed the barrow flat, because no sign of it remains today.

Many of the methods employed to keep arable land in good condition have contributed their quota to archaeological discovery. The cutting of ditches and the laying out of drains are always worth watching. In regions like the East Anglian Fens, where draining is carried out on an extensive scale, its contribution has been especially notable. A large proportion of the fenland bronzes preserved at Cambridge were found in this way. Another important effect of drainage works in a fenland region is the general lowering of the surface due to contraction of the peat. This process, which is often a rapid one, has brought to light large numbers of Bronze Age settlement sites in the East Anglian Fenland as well as innumerable flint implements and bronzes. Sometimes the contraction of peat resulting from drainage works will even expose complete field monuments to view, as happened in the Kehdinger Moor, near Stade, Hanover, in 1913, when the lowering of the peat surface revealed some horizontal stone slabs. Excavations carried out after the First World War showed them to be the top stones of megalithic chambers dating from the Late Stone Age. In the same moor no less than a dozen round barrows were revealed through the same cause.

Another practice which has led to many discoveries in the fens is that of claying the land to fatten the peaty soil. As the peat directly overlies a thick bed of clay, popularly known in the fens as 'buttery clay' from its consistency, the method followed is to dig quite small bell-shaped holes at intervals, but the modern method of trenching is more favourable to archaeological discovery. Most of the bronzes from the fens not ploughed up or found during drainage operations have been recovered by claying gangs.

The excavation of coprolites[1] for manure has also yielded its archaeological harvest. In Cambridgeshire the coprolites lie at the base of the lower chalk, where they occur in a seam seldom exceeding a foot thick, so their extraction involves the removal of extensive areas of topsoil. It so happens that the Upper Cam Valley, one of the main centres of coprolite digging in the old days, formed the chief area of Early Iron Age settlement in the country. There is ample reason for thinking that only a fraction

[1] 'By origin the word coprolite signified petrified dung, presumably of enormous reptiles, but the term came to include phosphatized castes of vertebrate remains in general.'—*A Scientific Survey of the Cambridge District*, 126, London, 1938.

of the material brought to light has survived, but for what has come down to us we are indebted wholly to the watchfulness of local residents. One of the most interesting discoveries was made on a low hill, known as Bellus Hill, Abington Pigotts, between 1879 and 1884, when the whole site was turned over to a depth of twelve to eighteen feet in search of coprolites. From the notes very fortunately kept by the Rev. W. G. F. Pigott it is evident that the diggings destroyed an open village covering in all some twenty acres. A study of the material salvaged at the time testifies to a series of settlements from the pre-Roman Early Iron Age to Anglo-Saxon and medieval times. Had it been possible to organize an emergency excavation on modern lines much more could doubtless have been learnt of the houses and of the developments of the settlement, but without Mr Pigott's observations the site would have been destroyed without leaving a trace. In some parts of the country the digging of chalk for marling has been a means of bringing antiquities to light, especially when, as sometimes happened, barrows were quarried for their material.

As a rule farm buildings seldom require deep enough foundations to bring very much to light, but many finds of importance have been made in obtaining material for their construction. Excavations for brick-earth have been especially fruitful in results, not least among which must be counted Frere's discovery at Hoxne mentioned in Chapter I. In the highland zone of Britain the search for stones to build field walls often led to the destruction of burial cairns with the consequent discovery of urns and grave-goods. As long ago as 1540 we find Leyland writing:

'Mr Roulande Griffith tolde me that . . . in tyme of mynde menne usid not in Termone [i.e. Anglesey] to separate theyr grounde, but now stille more and more they digge stony hillokkes yn theyre groundes, and with the stones of them rudely congestid they devide theyre groundes after Devonshire fascion. In digging of these [they] digge up yn many places yerthen pottes with the mouthes turnid douneward, conteyning (*cineres et ossa mortuorum*).'

Many of the lesser activities of country life have contributed in their own small ways to our stock of archaeological knowledge. Peat-cutting for winter fuel has led to an enormous number of finds in the peat-bogs of Ireland, North Germany, and Scandinavia, dating from Mesolithic times onward. There is only space to cite a single find, that of a twisted torc of solid gold found in company with three bronze palstaves of Middle Bronze Age type, made by a poor man exercising his right of cutting peat in Grunty Fen in the Isle of Ely in the year 1844. According to a contemporary account he first of all came upon the three bronzes, and then, as he removed another foot of peat, the gold ornament sprang out of the soil. It was of pure gold and weighed 5 oz. 7·20 dwt. Evidently the turf-cutter happened to dig down on to the exact site of a votive offering deposited in the fen some 3,000 years ago. A large proportion of the Bronze Age gold objects, which make so glittering an array in the National Museum at Dublin, were found in similar fashion. To quote a further instance, the development of the egg trade played its part in the discovery of the Stone Age kitchen-middens of Denmark: pounded mollusc shells make an invaluable ingredient for hen food!

Another primary activity worth considering is fishing. When it is remembered that wide stretches of land in the Baltic and North Sea areas, as well as on the seaboard of Europe generally, have been covered by the sea only in comparatively recent times, the possibility of fishermen catching antiquities as well as fish is seen to be less remote than it might appear at first sight. Over many parts of the North Sea bed between the coasts of East Yorkshire and West Jutland, fishermen have found the remains of a great freshwater fen in the form of lumps of 'moor-log'. This fissile material, composed almost entirely of plant remains, occurs at depths ranging from twenty-two to twenty-three fathoms. Thousands of lumps must be thrown overboard by fishermen with no other feeling than dull annoyance, but one day in September 1931 something out of the ordinary occurred. Skipper Pilgrim Lockwood, master of the steam trawler *Colinda*, was night fishing in mid-channel between the Leman and Ower Banks off the coast of Norfolk, when his nets brought up a lump of 'moor-log' rather larger than he could easily manage. He broke it with his shovel and hit something hard; in his own words: 'I heard the shovel strike something. I thought it was steel. I bent down and took it below. It lay in the middle of the log which was about

FIG. 2
Barbed spearhead of stag antler from the North Sea

four feet square by three feet deep. I wiped it clean and saw an object quite black.' The 'moor-log' had yielded up what proved to be a finely barbed antler spearhead (fig. 2), closely similar in type to specimens known to occur over the whole extent of the (Mesolithic) Maglemose culture province from eastern Britain to Esthonia. Pollen analyses of the 'moor-log' in the immediate neighbourhood of the find show it to be contemporary with some of the bog formations on the North European plain that have yielded relics of the same culture.

Really sumptuous discoveries have sometimes been made by fishermen and sponge-gatherers in the Mediterranean lucky enough to strike the site of ancient wrecks. Many a treasure ship laden with works of art *en route* from Greece to Rome foundered in these waters with all its cargo. Only too often the bulk of the statues, candelabra, and the like were mere work-shop copies manufactured in bulk to satisfy the Roman craving for 'culture', but the fact that some of the former show clear traces of having been removed from pedestals suggests that a certain number of originals were also shipped to the Roman

market. As a rule the marbles have been sadly disfigured by
sea-creatures, which have not infrequently nibbled and bored
them to mere stumps, but apart from being coated with a
calcareous deposit and encrusted with barnacles, all of which
can quite easily be removed, the bronzes have survived a couple
of thousand years beneath the sea without the slightest ill-
effects. The development of the aqualung and of the technique
of free-diving by M. Cousteau and his associates has recently
made it possible to envisage submarine archaeology as a field
of purposeful research as well as of lucky finds; already submarine exploration has added to our knowledge of Minoan
harbours, as well as of Greek traffic with Massilia, notably in
the matter of wine.

Rich as are the opportunities afforded by rural economy to
the watchful observer, there is no doubt that these have been
enormously increased and intensified as a result of the Industrial
Revolution. The growth of urban life, the increased demands
of industry, and the immense development in communications
have each in their own way tended to extend and deepen all
manner of excavations and in so doing to bring antiquities to
light in unprecedented numbers.

The most obvious result of urbanization is an intensification
of building activity: not only do the areas trenched for foundations tend to spread, but at the centres increasing site values
make for taller buildings and ever-deepening foundations.
Moreover, the crowding together of great masses of people
has led to the development of all kinds of public services.
Water has to be accumulated in reservoirs and distributed by
a network of pipes, sewage must be collected and disposed of,
and gas and electricity generated and circulated, all of them
activities which necessitate excavation, sometimes on a gigantic
scale. On balance it may be that the progress of urbanization
and building development generally is a menace to archaeology,
since the clues it affords can rarely be followed up in a scientific
manner; although, even where the compulsory contribution

for the archaeological exploration of new factory sites obtaining in the U.S.S.R. is lacking, the voluntary organization of an emergency excavation can sometimes save the situation. In the case of built-up areas, on the other hand, the piecemeal accumulation of evidence from all kinds of excavation work is the only way of building up anything like an intelligible picture.

It is in the nature of things that most of the archaeology brought to light in modern urban centres relates to previous phases of town life, in this country Roman and medieval, rather than to prehistoric remains. London is a case in point. The foundations of our knowledge of Roman London were laid by a city chemist, Charles Roach Smith (1807–90), in his spare time. The collection of objects he obtained from city excavations is now housed in the British Museum, while his writings, all recording personal observations, form the permanent basis of research on Roman London. A close watch on all kinds of excavation by Smith and others has already revealed more than a score of the bastions of the Roman town-wall, three of them coming to light during the clearing of the Christ's Hospital site for the General Post Office (1908–9), one during the construction of the Inner Circle line near Tower Hill, and another in the course of widening the old London and Blackwall Railway (1800). The plan of the basilica of Londinium, which has been described as the longest Roman building north of Rome, has been pieced together from excavations of different kinds in and about Leadenhall Market. The importance of Londinium as a port adds to the interest of what is almost certainly a Roman boat, found in the course of laying the foundations of the County Hall at Westminster (1910). Many of the smaller finds relating to Roman London have come from the old channel of the Walbrook, into which foundations of the Bank of England and neighbouring buildings have been built. Among other interesting relics of daily life the wet mud has preserved masses of old shoes and cobblers' waste. The spread of 'modern civilization' to ancient provincial centres like Chichester has done much to stimulate the flow of discoveries in the field of Romano-British archaeology during recent years. The foundations of older buildings in such towns rarely penetrated much below the accumulation of medieval times, but the construction of chain stores and super-cinemas has often involved much deeper excavation.

Excavations connected with public services are more likely to yield results of prehistoric interest on the fringes of modern towns. The deep excavations required for gasometers have sometimes been fruitful. The 48-foot dug-out canoe, dating in all probability from the Bronze Age, found at Brigg, Lincolnshire, in 1886, and the bone fish-spear prong of Maglemose type from Hornsea, Holderness, both came to light in this way. The construction of filter-beds is also worth watching.

The importance of sewage farms as places of archaeological discovery is probably due to their frequent location on gravel spreads, to which prehistoric man was especially partial. However this may be, there can be no doubt about the correlation. The recently excavated Mesolithic site at Farnham, Surrey, remarkable for its evidence of semi-subterranean houses and easily the most prolific site of its period yet excavated in the British Isles, was found on the local sewage farm, as was the neighbouring Early Iron Age site at Wisley, perhaps the most important in the county. Examples, which could be multiplied indefinitely, will probably occur to the reader.

Another aspect of the Industrial Revolution of value to archaeology has been the immense increase in quarrying of various materials. The removal of overburden should reveal archaeological evidence on a grand scale, but only a small fraction is usually salvaged. The development in recent years of different forms of mechanical excavator has made it more difficult for watchers to observe antiquities when they are revealed, while the increased tempo that comes with machinery makes it less practicable to delay work for the examination of any features that may come to light. Nevertheless, the extension of quarrying during the nineteenth century tended to increase archaeological evidence in a remarkable way. The development of archaeology in the Kesteven division of Lincolnshire, for instance, is intimately bound up with the progress of ironstone working, which has, indeed, brought to light the bulk of the Bronze Age pottery from the entire county, if the sandy warrens north of Scunthorpe be excepted. During the prosperity of the nineteenth century, beakers and Late Bronze Age urn-fields must have been discovered in their scores to judge from the number that found their way into the museum of Grantham.

Chalk quarries, extensively worked for lime-making, are among the most productive. The clearing of overlying deposits often reveals the post-holes of structures, store-pits, silted-up ditches, and the like, as well as loose antiquities. It sometimes happens that the chalk required for lime manufacture is covered by thick deposits of Pleistocene age. In this case excavation of the overlying beds is liable to reveal Palaeolithic remains; indeed, two of the most famous Palaeolithic sites in Britain —Bolton & Laughlin's pit at Ipswich and the pits of the Associated Portland Cement Manufacturers at Swanscombe, North Kent, have been revealed through the quarrying of chalk.

Among the more specialized materials the digging of which has benefited archaeology, one may mention diatomite, a freshwater silt used for insulation purposes. Ever since diatomite has been extensively dug in the Bann Valley of North Ireland, quantities of flint implements, the leading form of which is a large tanged flake, have continually been coming to light. Bann River flints rapidly found their way into collections and museums and were early recognized as a feature of Irish archaeology. Recently test excavations were made by an expedition from Harvard University, and hearths left during seasonal visits of small groups of fisher-folk were found at different levels in the diatomite. Side by side with the flints were found polished stone axes and round-based Neolithic pots, which served to indicate the cultural background of the fishermen.

Few developments of the last 100 years have been more conducive to archaeological discovery than the extension and multiplication of means of transport. Railway construction is known to have played a role of real importance in the development of geology, owing to the sections it revealed, but in western Europe the main period of railway building came too early to benefit archaeology to any substantial extent. One find of outstanding importance, however, may be mentioned—that of one of the largest and richest Anglo-Saxon cemeteries of the pagan period ever found in England, which came to light during the construction of Sleaford railway station. Underground railways, on the other hand, have been developing up to our own day, and consequently more advantage has been taken of opportunities afforded by their construction.

In London they have contributed substantially to our knowledge of the Roman city, although only too often the evidence they brought to light has been destroyed. During the construction of the Inner Circle railway under Trinity Place in 1882 some seventy-three feet of the walls of Londinium were exposed and destroyed, and in 1935 excavations for a new sub-station in the same neighbourhood revealed a bastion. A careful watch was kept, and in the lower courses of the bastion an inscribed stone was found, obviously incorporated from a monument of earlier date. The inscription proved to be part of one, another portion of which had been recovered as long ago as 1852, belonging to the tomb of Julius Classicianus, who was sent to Britain in A.D. 61 as procurator after Boudicca's rebellion. A reproduction of the inscription has been set up in the station by the London Passenger Transport Board. A final railway anecdote shows that archaeological monuments sometimes hit back. It appears that on the outskirts of Rome in 1915 somebody noticed that ballast on the Naples line was disappearing down a hole and threatening the stability of the track: investigations revealed a basilica adorned in stucco-relief with scenes from Greek mythology executed in a style current during the first century A.D.

Roads lead to discoveries in two quite distinct ways, partly through new construction but mainly through the quarrying of material for maintenance. In Britain the former has all too little chance of operating, although bridge-building has produced many finds, an example being the hoard of thirty socketed axes dating from the Late Bronze Age, found in sinking caissons for the new bridge across the Trent at Keadby, Lincolnshire. What might be done in the event of a modern system of motor roads being built in this country is indicated by recent experience in Germany, where provision was made for the proper examination of sites met with during the construction of the *Reichsautobahnen*.

By far the most significant road metal, so far as archaeology is concerned, is gravel. Without gravel pits Lower Palaeolithic studies would be thrown back almost entirely on coastal exposures, and it is difficult to see how under such conditions they could have reached their present stage of development. The studies of Breuil and Kozłowski in the Somme Valley, which have formed a model for Palaeolithic-Pleistocene correlations the world over, were almost entirely dependent on the exploitation of gravels and sands for road work. Many a drama of excited discovery has been enacted also by amateur collectors against the golden background of a gravel face!

Gravel is only less important for what is to be discovered on its surface than for what it actually incorporates. Ever since its deposition it has been favoured for human settlement. Some of the chief Neolithic sites in England, among them the camp at Abingdon and the settlement at Fengate, Peterborough, have come to light in gravel-digging, not to speak of numbers of beaker burials, Late Bronze Age urn-fields and Early Iron Age settlements. Moreover, it was the need to salvage sites from the encroachments of gravel-working that led to the investigation of the remarkable group of Neolithic sacred sites at Dorchester, Oxon., including the cursus, mortuary enclosure, and group of proto-henge monuments.

Flint-digging on the South Downs has turned up a few sites, while it was stone-quarrying on the slopes of Penmaenmawr in North Wales that brought to light the famous stone-axe factory at Craig Llwyd, whose wares were traded as far as Wessex towards the end of Neolithic times.

Water transport has played an important part in archaeological discovery. The dredging of river-beds has recovered masses of archaeological material, much of it eroded from sites on their banks. Such finds have been made all over Europe for every period of prehistory since rivers have flowed in their existing beds. The Thames is a notable example, as a visit to the London Museum will show. Dredged finds suffer from lack of associations, although they sometimes group in a suggestive way; but individual pieces, especially those of bronze, are usually well preserved and among them are some of the outstanding examples of their kind.

The age of canal-cutting came too soon in England to benefit archaeology, but the excavation of the Kiel Canal revealed many sites, and the deepening of its approaches off Ellerbek in the Kiel Fjord produced the type site for North Germany of the Ertbölle culture—at a depth down to twenty-four feet below sea-level. During the construction of the Baltic-White Sea Canal by the Bolsheviks the excavations were carefully watched, and a number of investigations made by official archaeologists, in accordance with the accepted principle of watching the sites of new constructions for early remains.

The size of ocean-going liners has necessitated much excavation for docks and deepening of harbours. Dock excavations hold out promising possibilities of recovering material from many feet below sea-level, so allowing archaeological phases to be related accurately to their appropriate stage of geographical development. The discoveries at Barry Docks and Southampton Docks of peat-beds well below sea-level underline this possibility, which has been—for lack of observation —too seldom realized. Well-known Mesolithic finds from harbour dredgings are those from the free harbour at Copenhagen, comprising bone and flint objects characteristic of the Maglemose food-gathering culture and dating from the time of the *Ancylus* Lake. Similar material has been recovered from dredgings elsewhere in Denmark, e.g. from the fjords of Horsens and Kolding on the east coast of Jutland.

WAR

War is another form of human activity which brings antiquities to light incidentally, though conditions for observation are seldom ideal. Modern total war is more favourable because it involves increased disturbance of the soil. Even the trench warfare of 1914–18 yielded its quota of finds. On the German side the recovery of archaeological finds in the course of military activity was organized on an official basis. When discoveries were made in the field they were automatically reported to General Headquarters, who saw to it that museum authorities behind the lines were informed and given every facility for investigation. In this way, particularly on the eastern front, many useful finds were made and exploited. One of the best known was the cemetery dating from the first to the sixth centuries A.D., brought to light during the erection of defences near Lötzen, East Prussia, in which Hindenburg took a great personal interest. Professor Kossinna has recorded the following remarks of the Marshal made on one of his visits to the excavations: 'In the presence of the high-standing German culture of antiquity it behoves us to keep quite clear in our own minds that we can only remain German, if we know how to keep our sword sharp and our youth fit to bear arms.'

On the English side initiative rested with individuals, but official apathy no more stifled the private bent for archaeology in war than it does in peace-time. Many an English family treasures archaeological relics recovered from military works in the Gallipoli peninsula, and even the trenches of northern France yielded their spoil. The German offensive of 1918 caused the erection of a network of trenches behind the British lines at Coigneux, near Arras. The trenches were cut through a loess deposit into a clay bed at the junction of which Levallois implements occurred quite commonly. It so happened that the officer in charge of the 42nd Division Observers posted in the neighbourhood was a certain Captain Francis Buckley, later to make a reputation for himself as the chief investigator of the Mesolithic sites of the Pennines and already interested in flint implements. By searching the parapets of the newly excavated trenches Buckley managed to collect a good series of the palaeoliths, and to establish satisfactorily their true stratigraphical position. In the scientific paper recording his war-time discoveries he rather wistfully remarked that 'had it been possible to excavate the parapets at suitable places, no doubt much greater finds of implements would have been made. But for military reasons this was quite out of the question.' As it happened the Germans were thrown back and these particular trenches were never manned. The palaeoliths were sacrificed in vain.

Another feature of the First World War—the use made of aircraft—was destined to affect the future development of archaeological research profoundly. The application of aerial photography to archaeology can be traced directly to the experiences of war-time observers, among them the German pioneer, Dr Theodore Wiegand, who succeeded in tracing the eastern extremity of the Roman *limes* in the Dobrudja from the air. When peace came Colonel Beazeley was among the first to realize the archaeological value of a method since greatly furthered by another war-time flyer, Dr (Major)

O. G. S. Crawford. It may be noted also that the earliest experiments were made with British Army balloons. As long ago as 1880-7 Major Esdale's scheme for photographing ancient sites in the neighbourhood of Agra was being perfected. It was actually approved by the India Office, but official difficulties intervened and the scheme was never carried out. The first air-photographs of an archaeological site ever published were those of Stonehenge taken in 1906 by Lieutenant P. H. Sharpe from an army balloon. Since the First World War innumerable discoveries have been made in the ordinary routine of R.A.F. training, and thanks to the liaison maintained through the Ordnance Survey these are made available to the public.

The Second World War differed mainly in the emphasis laid on air-power. This involved not merely more air-fields, but much larger ones to cope with larger and faster aircraft. Many of the most important archaeological discoveries during the war were made in the course of air-field construction or of securing the materials needed for such works. Some were made in the course of rescue-excavations, organized in Britain by the Ministry of Works, when known ancient monuments had to be flattened, e.g. a chambered cairn at St Mary's, Scilly; Bronze Age barrows at St Eval, Cornwall, Northleach, Gloucestershire, and Beaulieu and Hurn, Hampshire; a broch at Watten, Caithness; and the 'Earthwork' at Heathrow, now under one end of the main runway, which proved on excavation to enclose a colonnaded Celtic temple. Other air-field discoveries, like the Neolithic house at Ronaldsway on the Isle of Man and the Early Iron Age settlement at Manston, Kent, were found by chance, though carefully excavated when once they had been recognized. One of the most interesting finds of all, that of the mass of Celtic metal-work from Llyn Cerrig Bach, Anglesey, was made when peat, needed for air-field construction, was dragged out of Cors yr Ynys bog by scoops drawn by wire ropes powered from cable engines. Indirectly, also,

bombing operations, by exposing for examination ground
previously obscured by modern buildings, have made possible
considerable advances in our knowledge of the towns of the
Roman province, through the systematic examination of
bomb-damaged sites in such cities as Canterbury, Exeter,
Leicester, and London; the discovery of the Temple of Mithras
in the last-named only served to dramatize what has in fact
been a prolonged and tedious but fruitful labour.

It would be easy to think of other ways in which natural
processes and the works of man conspire to expose antiquities
to those who care to observe them, and easier still, though
doubly tedious, to quote further examples. A more convincing
way of reinforcing my point is to consider how certain groups
of antiquities have in fact been discovered. So far as Lower
Palaeolithic discoveries in Europe are concerned, natural exposures and excavations of an economic character—mostly
quarries—account for all but an insignificant proportion. To
illustrate the causes operating for finds of later periods I tabu-
late the circumstances attending finds from different periods
from definite regions, details of which I happen to have by me:

Finds relating to the Maglemose (Mesolithic) culture in Britain:

Coastal erosion	2
Caught in fisherman's trawl	1
Sewage-farm works	1
Laying out recreation ground	1
Old war trenches	1
Gasometer excavation	1
Gravel-digging	3
River-dredging	2
Unknown (old collection)	1
Archaeological excavation	1
	—
Total	14

Gold bowls of periods III and IV of the Nordic Bronze Age:[1]

Coastal erosion	1
Ploughing	3
Under large stones (removed in course of agriculture)	3
Peat-cutting	1
Road-building	1
Sand-digging	2
Railway construction	1
House foundations	2
Unknown	3
Archaeological excavations	3
Total	20

SURFACE INDICATIONS

Other sites betray themselves through surface indications, whether by relief or by ecological differences. In either case these can usually be seen more readily to conform to a recognizable pattern when viewed from the high angle made possible by balloons or aircraft. Indeed the coming of the aeroplane and the development of air-photography have revolutionized the task of discovering archaeological and more especially prehistoric sites. Air reconnaissance not only makes it possible to survey unexplored or inaccessible territories with comparative ease, but when applied intelligently it is capable of adding greatly to our knowledge of areas closely investigated by generations of archaeologists. Experience has shown that to gain the best results it is essential that the photographs should be taken under the immediate direction of, if not by, an expert field archaeologist; the kind of standard cover taken by military air forces has its uses, particularly in archaeologically unknown

[1] Up till 1913 when Kossinna published his 'Der Goldfund von Messingwerk bei Eberswalde', *Mannus Bibl.*, no. 12.

areas; but to secure the kind of detail needed to advance knowledge in such a well-studied region as southern England, one
needs a Major Allen or a Dr St Joseph, aware of precisely the
right circumstances under which to photograph each particular
kind of site.

As regards sites visible on the surface by reason of their relief,
some, like the ploughed barrows and defensive works, are
readily recognized. Others—for example, the lynchets of
ancient field-systems—are less visible on the surface by reason
of their low relief, and were generally missed by the earlier
archaeologists. Observation of these low banks in recent years,
however, has told us much of ancient systems of cultivation,
especially on the chalk downs of southern England and on the
heaths of North Holland and of Jutland. In some areas careful
observation has revealed farmsteads, by the excavation of which
related field-systems have been dated. Thus Professor G. Hatt,
working chiefly on heather-covered heaths in the province of
Himmerland, Jutland, has brought to light a complete agricultural system with fields defined by low banks and nucleations
of farmsteads, dating from the Early Iron Age of Denmark.

In detecting and mapping such slight surface inequalities as
ancient field-systems generally afford, every advantage has to
be taken of natural conditions. The sun is most important.
With the shadows long in early morning or evening sites of
low relief are to be seen to their best advantage. In districts
where the field divisions are marked by stone walls a fall of
snow is often very effective in showing up the pattern. Snow
was also found of value by the Danish archaeologist Therkel
Mathiassen in tracking down old Eskimo house-ruins in the
North Hudson Bay region. Under certain circumstances
flooding by water helps to define superficial inequalities of
archaeological interest. The exceptional floods in the East
Anglian Fens during 1937 afforded several illustrations of this,
but even the normal seasonal flooding of restricted parts of the
fens can be relied upon to give results. Major G. W. G. Allen's

magnificent photograph taken in June 1937, and reproduced on Plate I, shows a portion of the Washes, a gigantic sump between the Old and the New Bedford Rivers designed to contain flood waters overflowing the lower inner banks of the two drains. Meandering across the Washes, and defined by the winter flood waters, can be seen the broad levee of an ancient river. On either bank of this watercourse during its final stage, marked by the narrow meander visible within the broad band of the levee, lived Romano-British peasants, who cultivated during the first four centuries of the Christian era the rich silt deposited by the river in its previous history. The ditches of their small rectangular 'Celtic' fields are in certain instances clearly defined by the flood water.

Many relief sites defined by shadows are likewise best observed from the height allowed by an aeroplane; from such a vantage-point low banks and ditches, which on the ground fail to attract attention because at that low angle they appear meaningless, achieve coherency and are seen to conform to some recognizable plan. Some of the best mapping of ancient field-systems has been done by means of air-photography, and it is worth noting that a photograph of such taken at 4 p.m. on 8 May 1922 from Old Sarum (Salisbury) aerodrome at a height of 10,000 feet was one of the first to draw attention to the archaeological possibilities of air-photography. Air-photographs of 'shadow-sites' have also told us much about the ancient 'camps' that crown so many of the eminences of the chalk downs of southern England. The great bank and ditch dating from the Early Iron Age on Trundle Hill, from which an excellent view can be had of Goodwood race-course, was well known to archaeologists, but until the site was photographed from the air in 1925 no one suspected the existence of a very much earlier camp, consisting of two rings of banks and causewayed ditches with an intermediate spiral of ditch segments, subsequent excavations by Dr E. C. Curwen proved that the earlier camp was of Neolithic age. Such is the prominence of the Early Iron Age hill-forts that the resources of air-photography might seem in their case superfluous, but observation of the minor relief revealed by shadow photographs has sometimes given information of great value. For instance, it was an air-photograph of the unfinished hill-fort on Ladle Hill, Hants (pl. II), that gave us the key to stages of construction in such works. Traces of a slight marking-out trench can still be seen on the causeways temporarily left between the deeper sections of the ditch proper to allow the passage of men and material, while well within the line of the rampart the tips of surface soil from the ditch-cuttings, thrown back so that the core of the rampart could be built of chalk blocks from lower levels of the ditch, are clearly visible. Minor internal features of hill-forts as well as phases in their construction may also be revealed by air-photographs which often assist an excavator to determine the most profitable situation for his key sections.

Where the traces revealed from the air are difficult to find on the ground it is sometimes possible to map ancient ditches by thumping the ground with a heavy rammer (preferably a navvy's implement fitted with a long handle) and listening for indications of hollowness. A chalk subsoil with a thin capping of mould is best adapted to the percussion method; to quote its discoverer, Dr E. C. Curwen, 'over undisturbed chalk or a bank of consolidated chalk rubble the note produced is high-pitched and dull; over mould or loose material filling a pit or ditch it is low-pitched and resonant. The two types of note may be compared respectively to the sounds "thud" and "thoomp".' Even stamping the ground with the foot will often give some indication of ancient disturbance. A windless day should be chosen for percussion if it is to be done alone, but with a companion stationed in a near-by hollow out of the wind equally good results can be obtained even on a windy day, owing to the readiness with which the vibrations are conveyed by chalk. Using this method, Dr Curwen has been able to plan the discontinuous ditches of Neolithic camps, invisible on the surface. It is also useful for locating store-pits in the interior of hill-forts. The accuracy of the method has frequently been tested and vindicated by excavation.

A more elaborate method is that of resistivity survey taken over from mineral and oil prospecting and from civil engineering. This depends basically on the amount of moisture the soil contains, so that the silting in a ditch or hollow, holding more moisture than the surrounding rock, will show less resistivity, and conversely, foundations overlying the natural soil will show more. By using a 'Megger' Earth Tester, and measuring resistivity at intervals, it is possible to contour degrees of resistivity and so to detect areas of ancient disturbance, in the form of ditches, pits or post-holes, and of buried foundations invisible on the surface. The method was used with conspicuous success by Mr Richard Atkinson in connexion with the examination of Neolithic sacred sites at Dorchester, Oxon. It may be added that mine-detectors have been used to locate metal objects in the soil, but owing to the quantity of iron in the form of horseshoes and portions of agricultural equipment it is seldom of any use on open sites.

Where the surface is ploughed ancient sites are often revealed by soil-marks. When pasturage covering an area of Romano-British settlement in the fens of northern Cambridgeshire is broken up for the first time in recent history, the peat-filled ditches of the ancient fields and droveways show up clearly against the background of the pale coloured silt. A few years of cultivation tend to obscure the clarity of the picture to the observer on the ground, but the pattern continues to be recognizable from the air for a very long time. In chalk regions subjected to heavy ploughing, soil-marks, especially when seen from the air, preserve the sites of ancient monuments, which have lost all or nearly all their surface relief, in a most amazing way. In following up Major Allen's photographs on the ground Dr O. G. S. Crawford was recently able to treble the number of round barrows known in the Royston district of northern

Hertfordshire and south-western Cambridgeshire; many of the barrows were revealed as soil-marks, a whitish halo indicating the chalk rubble round a turf core with a dark outer band to mark the ditch.

But bare soil is as a rule less eloquent of ancient remains than is its vegetable covering. A careful watch on plant life will often bring its reward to the archaeologist. As anyone who has noticed dense growths of nettles by disused middens or cattle sheds will appreciate, the addition of organic substances to the soil, such as might result from human settlement, is liable to find some reflection in the surrounding vegetation. There are, however, reasons for doubting whether vegetation can ever reflect human settlement of great antiquity through any such direct chemical cause. Thus Therkel Mathiassen, working at Disko Bay, half-way up the western coast of Greenland, found that the ruins of the most recent Eskimo settlement were marked by vigorous growths of sappy-green *Alopecurus* vegetation; the older ruins, on the other hand, were difficult to distinguish from the surrounding landscape with its covering of willow bush, dwarf birch, crowberry, and bilberry. In the Julianehaab district of southern Greenland the same worker was even able to recognize at a glance the relative antiquity of the house-ruins: those with very luxuriant grass vegetation proved to belong to the nineteenth and twentieth centuries, those with much vegetation to the seventeenth and eighteenth centuries, and those with little or no vegetation to the earliest stage of the Eskimo settlement in the region.

The clues afforded by vegetation are generally more indirect: in a very dry country disturbed ground will often carry more moisture, and so affect the local plant ecology. Miss G. Caton-Thompson succeeded in discovering and mapping the Ptolemaic irrigation channels of the Fayûm (Egypt) by observing the localized growth of desert plants mainly of the genus *Mysembrianthemum*. In Britain and western Europe generally vegetation also gives its clue to ancient disturbance as a result of

I   Air-photograph of Welney Washes, Norfolk

(Text. p. 61)

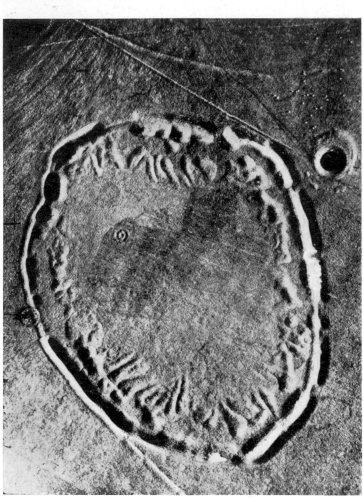

II   Air-photograph of Ladle Hill, Hampshire
(Text, pp. 62, 235)

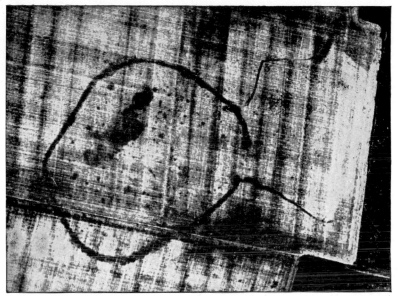

III (a) Air-photograph (crop mark) of Iron Age farmstead, Little Woodbury, near Salisbury, England

(Text p. 66)

Impressions of grain on Neolithic pottery from Windmill Hill, near Avebury

(Text, p. 193)

(a)

(b)

IV   (a) Wheat and barley from the Fayûm, Egypt
(b) Basket and silo in position
(Text, pp. 80, 193, 195)

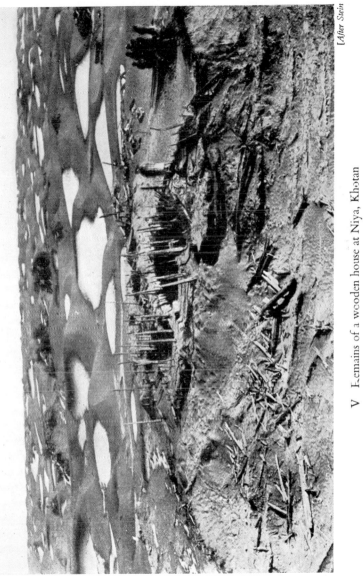

V Remains of a wooden house at Niya, Khotan

(Text, p. 81)

VI Human foot with sandal from a basket-maker cave at Kayenta, Arizona

(Text, pp. 84, 205)

VII   Man's kirtle and cloak from an Early Bronze Age oak coffin
burial at Borum, Denmark

(Text, pp. 92, 205)

VIII Panel from the Gundestrup Bowl, Denmark, showing mounted warriors, foot-soldiers, musicians and human sacrifice. Celtic work (first cent. B.C.)

(Text, pp. 206, 236)

differences in the moisture available for growth; where building foundations or the footings of ploughed-down ramparts are in the way crops will tend to languish, resulting in pale crop-marks; where on the other hand ancient trenches, store-pits, graves, or post-holes exist, the topsoil will tend to be deeper, and the crops will grow with extra luxuriance and so cause darker markings. Such crop-marks are generally visible but seldom intelligible from the ground: like shadow-sites and soil-marks, they are best observed from the air. Good results have been obtained from observing ordinary wild pasturage, but most discoveries have been made with such agricultural crops as wheat, peas, beans, roots, and clover. Chalk is a favourable soil, but silt and gravel are equally good. Much depends on the weather and on the state of crops. A dry summer is peculiarly favourable to crop-marks in that it tends to accentuate contrasts. On the other hand, too dry a summer is often fatal to grass sites. The 'henge' monument at Arminghall, Norwich, showed at the time of its discovery by Wing-Commander Insall, V.C., in the summer of 1929, two concentric ditches broken by an entrance giving access to a central area on which could be seen quite distinctly the socket-holes of great timber uprights arranged to form a horseshoe pattern open towards the entrance. In the spring of 1935 the ditches were quite distinct even on the ground, and slight traces could be seen of the post-holes; but by the summer the post-hole markings had vanished, and by the end of the excavations in early autumn the ditches themselves had faded appreciably. Markings may also vary on the same site according to the nature of the crop and according to its stage of growth. When dealing with a complex site with numerous tiny markings, therefore, it is very desirable if possible to obtain a series of air-photographs taken under varying crop and weather conditions.

Discoveries made in England during the past thirty years through the observation of crop-marks from the air have been numerous and in some cases of outstanding importance. Ancient field-systems, barrows, camps, and enclosures of all kinds (pl. IIIa) ploughed flat in modern times have been rescued from oblivion in large numbers, particularly on chalk and on gravel spreads. Among the most significant discoveries the so-called 'henge' monuments have a special claim to closer attention. The observation of the original Woodhenge at Durrington, Wiltshire, was made from a height of 2,000 feet by the same flyer who discovered the Arminghall site. The low circular bank had long been known locally from observation on the ground, but previous to Wing-Commander Insall's photograph the existence of an arrangement of six rings of post-holes within the enclosed space had not been suspected. Mrs Cunnington's excavations, which followed the discovery from the air, disclosed the former existence of a monument of the same general type as Stonehenge, only made of wood. Since that time a whole group of analogous monuments has been recognized, including that at Arminghall already described. In addition to helping in the first discovery of sites, crop-marks are often capable of aiding the excavator in laying out his trenches. For instance, the task of excavating the group of barrows close to Woodhenge was made very much easier by the fact that the actual graves, indicated by small dark spots in the middle of the circles, were distinctly visible on the photograph. In the case of extensive sites like Roman Caistor-next-Norwich, where the plans of buildings show up clearly as pale markings, crop-marks often save the excavator much dead work.

Animals can also play their part. Their positive activities as burrowing agents are too well known to require comment, but their failure to burrow in suitable ground may give an equally useful clue. One day in 1932 up on Easton Down, a few miles east of Salisbury, where for some years past he had been searching for early sites and excavating them, Dr J. F. S. Stone noticed an elongated patch of virgin turf untouched by moles or rabbits. His suspicions aroused, he removed the turf and found a layer of tightly packed flint nodules, sufficient to explain why they had neglected the area. On pulling up the flints he came upon a number of small cists cut into the underlying chalk, some containing urns with cremated remains, others just plain cremations. What he had found turned out to be a small urn-field dating probably from the latter part of the Middle Bronze Age (1400–1000 B.C.). As it happens, the cemetery, though a small one, proved to be of special interest owing to the beads of lignite, amber, and faience found with the cremations; recent work on trade routes makes it likely that the amber reached Wessex from the West Baltic region probably by way of North Germany and that the faience beads came from the East Mediterranean.

LITERATURE, MAPS, AND LOCAL LORE

It might at first blush seem a contradiction in terms to aver that reading books could ever lead to discoveries in prehistoric archaeology, but that it is true the story of Schliemann alone should suffice to prove. That we now know the city of Troy, which Schliemann took for Homer's Ilium, to have been something like a thousand years older, does not alter the reality of discoveries which, but for Homer, might never have been made. And Schliemann *did* find Homer's Troy, though experts now consider it to have coincided with the beginning of the seventh (VIIa) rather than with the second of the site's phases. At Mycenae he was equally mistaken in his identification, but the magnitude of his discovery is none the less for the fact that till his dying day he never realized he had made it. Had he not been inspired by Pausanias to dig for the tombs of Atreus, Agamemnon, and the rest, he would never have brought to light the splendours of Mycenaean civilization which changed all previous ideas as to the development of culture on the mainland of Greece.

But archaeological discovery has been influenced even more directly through the written record of archaeological exploration itself. In Europe and parts of the Near East, where archaeological research has had a history running into many generations, the works of pioneers, particularly those who like Aubrey and Stukeley were devoted to topography, have proved most suggestive, affording many invaluable, if sometimes unwitting, clues to modern field-workers.

Again, the maxim that discovery breeds discovery was never truer than when applied to archaeology. The publication of results almost invariably leads to fresh discoveries in the field. Demonstration of the authenticity of cave art in France and North Spain during the nineteenth century induced a veritable boom in Palaeolithic art, of which the effects spread far beyond the confines of western Europe to North and South Africa. The sudden revelation of moor- and lake-villages in Switzerland following the drought of 1853–4 led to the search for similar structures—and consequently to their discovery—all over Europe. Glastonbury is but one example. Arthur Bulleid had read Keller's book on the Swiss sites when he came as a young doctor to practice near the Somerset marshes. Consciously on the look-out for a likely site, he early fastened his attention on a group of low mounds in the Gedney marshes. His suspicions were given substance when, examining mole-hills on the site, he found bones and charcoal. Making inquiries among men employed in cutting drains in the marsh, he soon tracked down a dug-out canoe in the vicinity of the site. From this it was but a step to excavation, and he spent many seasons with his colleague, H. St George Gray, revealing the marsh village of his imagination.

Your true archaeologist is generally a lover of maps. Maps are not only an essential form of record for finds already made; intelligently used, they narrow down the field and sometimes even give the clue to new discoveries. Contour maps have their uses in a fresh country-side, but geological maps may be even more valuable. No one in his senses would prospect a new area for caves without verifying the distribution of limestone formations, or neglect sand in pursuit of microliths: conversely, it is generally a waste of time to look for prehistoric sites in heavy clay country.

There are even ways in which maps may give direct clues to early sites while the archaeologist is comfortably ensconced in his arm-chair. We owe it to General Roy that, ever since the first edition over 120 years ago, the one-inch sheets of the Ordnance Survey of Britain have had marked on them the positions of such antiquities as were observed during the Survey. It thus happens not infrequently that early editions of the Survey give exact clues to the whereabouts of barrows and other monuments, all surface indications of which have been ploughed away in the last hundred years. Larger scale maps (e.g. the six-inch O.S.) marking field and parish boundaries sometimes betray the presence of antiquities unwittingly. The apparently irrational behaviour of a field boundary may give the clue to an archaeological site, whose presence caused deviations to be made at the time of the enclosures: most of the new group of Long Barrows on the Lincolnshire Wolds were 'discovered' in this way during the revision of six-inch sheets at Southampton. Conversely, the unduly rational behaviour of an English lane has more than once betrayed a stretch of Roman road.

Place-names, particularly those in local use, are well worth watching. In the simple background of rural life burial mounds, camps, and dikes were almost bound to attract attention and acquire names—generic terms to express their outward form and, more rarely, specific names having reference to their supposed contents or associations. The generic terms vary widely from place to place. Even within the confines of Britain we find many equivalents for such a simple term as the English 'barrow': in the stony highland zone 'cairn' ('carn', carnedd', etc.) is most usual; 'how', 'howe', 'haw', and other variations of the old Norse *haugr* (mound or cairn) are common in Yorkshire, Cumberland, Westmorland, and Scotland;

in Derby, Cheshire, and Staffordshire you meet with 'low' (Saxon '*hlaew*'=earthern mound), in Gloucestershire with 'tump', and in East Anglia with 'hill'; elsewhere you may find 'cop', 'knoll', 'butt' (New Forest), 'mount', 'toot' (Somerset), and a string of others, all applied to ancient burial mounds and not unseldom to natural hillocks as well.[1]

Some of the commonest specific names attaching to barrows preserve memories of discoveries of bones when mounds were dug into for marl or other agricultural needs, e.g. such names as Deadman's Grave or Hills of the Slain, attached to long barrows in Lincolnshire. Names like Money Hill, Lucky Hill, etc., probably also hark back to finds made in barrows casually, or in course of treasure-seeking. The fact that some of the treasure-legends attaching to barrows have been confirmed by the results of archaeological excavation has led some enthusiasts for folk-lore into thinking that they carry back to the time of the original burials. It seems much more likely that they embody local memories of medieval treasure-seeking such as we know to have been carried on under royal licence. One of the legends often quoted was connected with a tumulus in Lexden Park, near Colchester, according to which an ancient king lay buried there wearing gold armour, with golden weapons at his side and accompanied by a golden table. When the barrow was opened in 1924 the excavators found in very fact the burial of a Belgic individual of high rank and among the grave-goods was chain mail, a bronze table, and gold tissue, possibly the remains of cloth of gold. It is significant that there were ample signs of previous disturbance having affected a good third of the burial area. Still, however we interpret them, local place-names and local tradition cannot be ignored as clues to discovery.

One further example of the value of place-names and local lore must suffice. Kostenki, on the Don, was so famous for its

[1] For further reading see L. V. Grinsell, *The Ancient Burial-mounds of England*, London, 1936.

finds of mammoth bones that it not only acquired its name thereby (Kostenki=bone village) but became the centre of many popular tales. By some the bones were attributed to the giant 'Inder' who lived underground, but whose bones came to the surface on his death. Others said that a giant was once passing through the village with his offspring. Finding the Don too deep to wade, he drank it dry. When he turned to call his young, his body failed to stand the strain and burst, his bones flying in all directions to the places where they are found today. The learned preferred to attribute the bones to elephants of Alexander's army, even as their British colleagues invoked Claudius and those of France and Italy, Hannibal. Reports of these stories ultimately found their way to the Czar, and in 1768 Catherine II sent Gmelin to investigate. Ever since, Kostenki has been known as a potential site for investigation. With the revival and intensification of prehistoric archaeology after the revolution, the place has become one of the leading Palaeolithic stations in South Russia.

There is no aspect of contemporary life which a keen archaeologist can afford to ignore. It is above all important to become fully acquainted with the behaviour and prejudices of the society in which one works. The most unlikely clue will sometimes lead to an epoch-making discovery. The Chinese dragon bones are a case in point. They gave the clue to two of the three or four most important archaeological discoveries made in China in modern times—Peking man and the oracle-bones of An-yang.

If the average Englishman ever gives a thought to dragons it is probably to connect them with St George. In China the dragon is a very actual being. In the days when an emperor yet occupied the dragon throne and the imperial standard still floated over his palaces, the dragon strode the land as guardian of its ruler, while today, as ever, he receives the offerings and prayers of countless millions as purveyor of rain in time of drought. The bones and teeth of so powerful a creature have not unnaturally been highly esteemed for their healing powers, and from the earliest times have formed one of the chief medicines stocked by Chinese apothecaries. Early writers have much to say as to the mode of their selection and preparation. Lei Hiao (A.D. 420–77) was of the opinion that 'Dragons' bones from Yen Chou, Tsang Chou, and Tai Yen are the best. . . . Those showing five colours are best; the white and the yellow are medium quality and the black ones are worst. As a rule it may be said that those in which the veins are longitudinal are impure, and those collected by women are useless.' His directions for preparing the medicine are reminiscent of Mrs Beeton in her most ruthless mood:

'To use dragon's bone first boil some aromatic herbs. Wash the bone twice in the hot water, then reduce it to powder and place it in bags of thin stuff. Take two young swallows and after removing their entrails, stuff the bags into the swallows and hang them over a spring. After one night take the bags out of the swallows, remove the powder and mix it with a preparation for strengthening the kidneys. The effect of such a medicine is as if it were divine.'

Dragons' bones can still be bought in Chinese drug-stores, the modern prescription being to pulverize and take with tea.

In 1899 a German naturalist bought numerous samples of dragons' bones from apothecaries' shops in various Treaty Ports, and took them home for investigation. Professor Max Schlosser, a well-known palaeontologist of Munich, examined the material closely and found it to consist of fossil mammalian bones, among which he distinguished no less than ninety species. His monograph, *Die fossilen Saugethiere Chinas*, was for many years the standard work on the Tertiary and Pleistocene mammals of China. It was partly under the influence of Schlosser's book that towards the end of the First World War the Chinese Geological Survey determined to trace some of these dragons' bones to their source. In the course of this search the Swedish scientist, J. Gunnar Andersson, at that time acting as Mining Adviser to the Chinese Government, discovered in 1921 the extensive bone-deposits in the cave of Chou K'ou Tien. Five years later further work on the 'dragon-bone' deposits produced the first human tooth. Subsequent years saw the discovery under the direction of Davidson Black and Pei of the whole group of fossil hominids with an associated bone and stone industry, which has since become world-famous.

The oracle-bones came to light in the following way. It appears that whenever a certain patch of ground in An-yang, North Honan, was ploughed, bones were brought to the surface. A certain farmer called Li formed the profitable notion that these were undoubtedly dragons' bones. The apothecaries to whom he used to sell them noticed that some of the bones were marked with un-dragon-like characters, but thinking little about it merely scraped them clean to make them saleable. In 1899, however, some marked specimens got into the hands of Chinese scholars. Decipherment showed them to constitute the earliest written records of China, dating from the time of the Shang dynasty (1765–1123 B.C.). This discovery quickly had the effect that, instead of inscribed bones being scraped clean, plain ones began to be supplied with fake inscriptions in such numbers that doubt began to attach to the whole group. The genuineness of the original finds has since been fully confirmed by the scientific excavations at An-yang begun in 1928. The inscriptions on the bones record questions asked of gods and ancestral spirits between three and four thousand years ago. To obtain an answer the diviner used to apply heat and study the behaviour of the cracks so formed. The inscriptions give us a unique insight into the hopes and fears of Chinese people in a period for which there is no other written history.

III

SURVIVAL OF THE EVIDENCE

What an archaeologist finds when he sets spade to earth depends to some extent upon the methods he uses and the powers of personal observation he brings to bear; but the possibilities of any site are limited fundamentally by what has survived the passage of time. And so in this chapter I am going to examine the main factors which regulate the preservation of early remains. The subject is one of supreme importance for three reasons: it largely determines the kind of site to be investigated when particular types of information are sought and the proper method to be followed in the actual work of excavation; and it affects profoundly that ultimate task of the archaeologist—the interpretation of his finds.

VARYING SURVIVAL-VALUE OF DIFFERENT MATERIALS

Inorganic materials. It is sufficiently obvious—although the consequences are not always fully appreciated—that, other things being equal, objects will tend to survive according to the material from which they are made. By and large, organic materials are more likely to decay than inorganic, although even these are by no means immune. Stone masonry in general survives well, but the marks of surface tooling, even engraving, or relief carving may easily be destroyed or gravely impaired by exposure to weathering or the attacks of an acid soil: thus, until the bases of the stone monoliths at Avebury were examined by excavation and clear traces of dressing revealed, it has always been supposed that they were erected in a rude and untouched state. Kiln-fired bricks are among the most

74

enduring remains, but those fired in the sun, such as are usual in parts of the Near East, may disintegrate rapidly under adverse conditions. Flint and stone implements are the most imperishable of antiquities, and for that reason bulk unduly large as 'type fossils' of early culture, but even these, although they seldom disappear completely, often undergo serious sur-face changes: exposure will facilitate the onset of patination, soil movements connected with glaciation will score them with striae, while carriage in water, in a river, or on the sea-shore, will sometimes roll them so effectively as to reduce them to unrecognizable pebbles.

Metals vary greatly in their powers of resistance. Gold is wellnigh imperishable, as we are reminded by the recovery in faultless condition of countless treasures found under the most diverse conditions in many parts of the world. Silver, on the other hand, although, when not too debased, it retains its form moderately well, usually tarnishes badly. Of the more useful metals lead and bronze survive much more satisfactorily than iron, which is rapidly reduced to rust. Bronze and copper objects from bogs and river-beds are sometimes as good as new, but so often do they come down to us with a bright green patina that we are sometimes in danger of forgetting that in their bright, burnished sheen lays one of their principal attractions. Adverse conditions will sometimes disintegrate the surface of a bronze so badly as to remove all trace of decoration, and where sufficiently severe they may even reduce bronze objects, especially thin blades, to mere greenish stains. Iron objects are more frequently reduced to discolorations of the soil, although sometimes where the core has disappeared its form will be preserved in a kind of rust-impregnated matrix.

Although its fragility ensures that pottery only survives complete under exceptional circumstances, individual sherds are extremely long-lived when adequately fired. Prehistoric pottery fired in an open kiln, however, tends to lose its surface rather easily, especially when a thin outer slip has been applied, and abrasion of the edges of sherds often makes the rebuilding of pots a difficult matter. Badly fired pottery is sometimes found in a softer state than its enclosing matrix, in which case it can be removed only after treatment. Really acid soils may even devour prehistoric pottery without leaving so much as a trace.

Organic materials. Organic substances, although as a group they decay more easily than inorganic, nevertheless show many gradations. Of animal products antler, bone, and ivory are by far the most resistant, although hair is capable of enduring under conditions and over a length of time that would surprise some people. Ligaments and skin (natural or prepared as leather) are neither of them very enduring, although capable of long outlasting flesh and the soft parts of the body. Animal fat can survive in residual form over very long periods, although rarely in more closely identifiable form.

Vegetable remains as a class have very low powers of resistance, although even here there are gradations. Wood, bark, nuts, and seeds tend to outlast leaves, flowers, and delicate stems: cereals, for instance, are more likely to be represented by bare grains than by grains replete with their tell-tale ears and husks. It hardly needs stressing that such remains survive as a general rule only when carbonized or as impressions on burnt clay.

CLIMATE AS A FACTOR IN PRESERVATION

One of the most important factors to be considered is climate, which varies in its effect from destroying every trace of organic material to conserving it as freshly as though just removed from a refrigerator.

Very warm, moist climates. Possibly the most deleterious climate from the archaeologist's standpoint is that of the equatorial and tropical rain-belts, where hot, moist conditions and insect pests combine to destroy rapidly all trace of organic substances, and rank vegetation overgrows and even dislodges the strongest masonry. Maudslay and Joyce and other explorers of the Maya civilization had to hack the massive temples of Honduras and Yucatan free of their entangling growths. On every side they found signs of collapse, due in part to the pressure of vegetation, in part to the decay of supporting timbers. Thomas Gann, writing of ruins in British Honduras, describes how 'the roots of large forest trees, finding their way into the interstices between the stones, have, in the course of ages, left hardly a single piece of the original masonry *in situ*'.[1] Excavations have habitually disclosed a bewildering variety of burnt clay and stone objects, including masks, crystal skulls, and flints worked to the most fantastic shapes; but not a trace of the woodwork in which the art of the stone-carvers was cradled, no wooden utensils or basketry, and none of the extravagant wearing apparel depicted on the stelae were found. The same is true of regions in South Asia potentially of great archaeological wealth, viz. South India, Indo-China, Malaya, Java, and the islands: only the hardest residue of material culture remains—all else has been ruthlessly purged away by the warm rains.

Very dry climates. Within the sub-tropical desert belt of the northern hemisphere are zones of scanty rainfall where conditions exist for the preservation of perishable substances to a degree unknown anywhere else save in the realms of perpetual refrigeration on the margins of the habitable earth. The classic zone of desiccation is, of course, Egypt, with parts of Inner Asia, and the south-west parts of the U.S.A. and the coast of Peru as good secondary examples.

(i) Egypt. Papyri are in some ways the most astonishing of all the remarkable things that have come out of Egypt. As the Egyptians, Greeks, and Romans wrote their books on fragile papyrus, made from the pith of a Nilotic water-plant, we would

---

[1] *Discoveries and Adventures in Central America*, 120, London, 1928. Other useful references include the *British Museum Guide to Maudslay Collection of Maya Sculpture from Central America*, 1923, and T. A. Joyce's *Maya and Mexican Art*, London, 1927.

have been compelled, but for the conserving sands of Egypt, to rely for our knowledge of their literature almost entirely on vellum documents dating from later times.

The first discovery of papyri of which any record survives was made in the Fayûm in 1778, when natives found a bundle of them in a pot. Most of them were burnt as rubbish, but one passed into the hands of Cardinal Borgia and was published ten years later. From this time onwards a steady stream of papyri found their way to Europe, but it was not until 1891 that public interest was really aroused, when a remarkable group was edited by Mr (later Sir) Frederick Kenyon of the British Museum. This single collection included the lost treatise on the constitutional history of Athens by Aristotle, the 'mimes' of the little-known poet Herodas, part of a previously unknown oration of Hyperides, and early versions of writings from Homer, Demosthenes, and Isocrates. About the same time a number of papyri, dating from the third century B.C. and including fragments of Homer and Plato, and of a lost tragedy of Euripides, were recovered from the cartonnage of a mummy excavated by Flinders Petrie. These and the subsequent discoveries, which came in ever-increasing numbers, have added 600 years to our knowledge of Greek writing, restored to us lost portions of many of the greatest Greek authors and versions of known works earlier by some centuries than any previously found, given us manuscripts of the Bible earlier than any yet known, and, not least, have told us all we know of the literature of ancient Egypt. All this we owe to the dry soil and climate of Egypt: elsewhere in the ancient world papyrus documents have rarely survived.

The tombs of the Pharaohs furnish another eloquent testimony to the virtue of a dry climate. The treasures of Tutankh-Amen's (c. 1345 B.C.) tomb at Luxor,[1] the furnishings and trappings, the textiles and flowered garlands, that took ten

---

[1] Howard Carter and A. C. Mace, *The Tomb of Tut-ankh-Amen*, London, 1923.

years and £44,000 to deal with, are familiar enough, but it is not always realized that judged by Egyptian standards physical conditions were by no means ideal. Quite apart from the deleterious effects of the unguent, the excavators complained of damp, which at different periods in the past found its way in through fissures in the limestone. The damp appears to have reduced leather-work to a black viscid mass, to have dissolved adhesive glues, causing objects to fall apart, and to have resulted in a certain amount of warping in some of the wooden objects. That such a complaint should be made only serves to show how normal in a country like Egypt is a perfect state of preservation among objects three and four thousand years old and often made of highly perishable substances. Any archaeologist digging in England would give his head to find grave-furniture in anything approaching such a state of preservation as that in the young Pharaoh's tomb.

The survival of the Pharaohs themselves in their golden coffins is admittedly due in the first place to the practice of mummification, but, as more than one writer has pointed out, the mummies themselves could not have endured save in air as dry as that of Egypt. The conserving powers of climate in respect of human bodies are well displayed in the burials of pre-dynastic times, which were placed without embalming or the protection of any form of coffin directly in a shallow grave scooped in the warm desert sand. The rapid desiccation that ensued, aided by the draining properties of the sand, may well, as Eliot Smith insisted, have suggested the practice of mummification to the people of dynastic times.

Less spectacular, but of deeper significance in human history, are what were at the time the oldest granaries in the world, discovered by Miss G. Caton-Thompson in the open desert of the Fayûm.[1] There were two distinct granaries, each comprising some scores of small silos (from 15 to 62 inches in diameter) of coiled basketry, one on the higher, the other on the lower

[1] *The Desert Fayûm*, London, 1934.

slopes of the beach of a lake of Palaeolithic days. Although close to the surface—the rims of the silos were only a few inches below the desert floor—the higher of the two was wonderfully intact. Clearing them, their discoverer found a delicately made basket, a wooden reaping-knife with the flint teeth still held in position with mastic (fig. 3), and grains of wheat and barley (pl. IV). What is chiefly remarkable is that this, the oldest cultivated grain in the world yet found, is so perfectly preserved, albeit in carbonized form. Describing barley from one of the

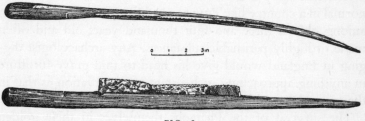

FIG. 3
Wooden reaping-knife inset with flint flakes, the Fayûm, Egypt

silos an expert has stated that it was 'in practically perfect state of preservation. Even the hairs on the rachis and rachilla and the tiny "prickles" on the nerves were clearly to be seen and, except for . . . having a curious mahogany tinge and being very light and brittle, it might have been harvested yesterday.'

(ii) Inner Asia. The ancient kingdom of Khotan is cut off from moisture-bearing winds by the great arc of the Himalaya, Pamir, and Tien Shan mountains. Human settlements in such a region are restricted to oases which, when abandoned through some political mishap or in response to some more fundamental natural cause, are rapidly engulfed in desert sands. The Takla-makan Desert has been a good friend to archaeology.

Although remote and inaccessible by modern standards, Khotan was once traversed by devout pilgrims from China, who from the fourth century onwards passed through on their way to the Buddhist shrines of India. Some of the descriptions written by returned pilgrims have survived, and their study has helped to convince Western scholars that Khotan lay on the route by which Buddhist teaching and worship spread from India to China and the Far East. The first tangible evidence from the soil of Khotan came to light in 1890 in the form of inscribed birch-bark leaves brought back from Kucha by Captain Bower. The survival of documents written on such perishable material implied conditions of preservation of quite exceptional character. One of the first to realize the possibilities was Aurel Stein, who within ten years was to lead an expedition of discovery with the backing of the Government of India.[1]

The richest finds of the 1900-1 expedition were made in the eastern part of the country on the fringe of the Taklamakan Desert, some sixty miles due north of Niya. Here, following up the clues of native 'prospectors', Aurel Stein came upon the ruins of an ancient settlement abandoned some time towards the end of the third century A.D. Around the houses, which wind erosion had often exposed as terrace-like features (pl. v), he found the gaunt and desiccated remains of gardens, drives with their rush fences, avenues and arbours of poplar trees and orchards of peach, plum, apricot, and mulberry (fig. 4). The houses themselves were built on massive timber foundations into which were set square wooden posts to carry the roof and provide a framework for the walls. These were made of a kind of matting of diagonally woven tamarisk branches covered on either side with frescoes. When the settlement was abandoned by its original inhabitants they carried away the best of their movable possessions, but left behind an assortment of discarded odds and ends, not to mention several promising rubbish-heaps. Most important of all, they abandoned quantities of official memoranda and other documents inscribed on wooden tablets and leather.

As he cleared room after room of sand, Stein recovered just

[1] Aurel Stein, *Ancient Khotan*, Oxford, 1907. Also, *Sand-buried Ruins of Khotan*, London, 1903.

the kinds of things an incoming caretaker might find in an abandoned house handed over to her care by outgoing tenants. In one room, evidently an office, he found wooden tablets, inscribed and blank, tamarisk pens, wooden eating-sticks, and a large hammock of tamarisk rushes. In another, a small closet, he came across a tamarisk bow, a bundle of wooden spear-shafts, part of a wooden shield, wooden spindles, and a wooden

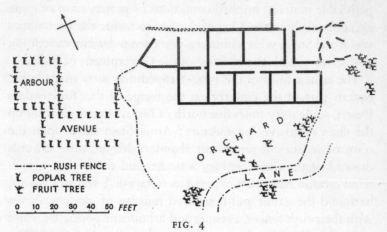

FIG. 4

Plan of ancient house at Niya, Khotan, with orchard and grounds

walking-stick in such fine condition that he was able to make good use of it. In other rooms his loot included a broken guitar, still retaining some broken strings, a wooden chair elaborately carved, a number of brooms, a wooden mouse-trap, and a wooden shoe-last. Felt, cotton textiles, and patterned rugs were found in somewhat tattered condition, but retaining their colours remarkably. It is, indeed, difficult to believe that the pale blues and greens and the dull Chinese reds were delighting the people of Niya more than a century before the Roman legions left the shores of Britain.

Though his fingers were numbed by a bitter north-east wind and his nostrils assailed by a smell which had retained its pungency through the centuries, the explorer, like a true archaeologist, delved patiently through all the rubbish-heaps he could find. Among the potsherds, straw, pieces of broken lacquer-work, and rags of felt, woven fabrics and silk, he was rewarded in finding a series of documents inscribed on carefully prepared sheepskin in the same script as the wooden tablets, and folded into neat little rolls.

All the documents dug up at Niya were written in Kharosthi, the script of North-west India during the first centuries A.D., so testifying to the importance of Indian influence in a territory politically subject to China. Stein's investigations indeed furnished the first tangible evidence of the spread of Buddhism from India to China, probably the most remarkable of India's contributions to the general development of mankind. The seal impressions on the wooden tablets reflect also contacts between China and the West, some of them being purely Chinese in character, others representing Athene, Eros, Heracles, etc., and plainly derived from classical sources.

Sir Aurel Stein's discoveries in Chinese Turkestan rank as one of the epics of archaeology. It is a chastening thought that in a temperate climate not one of the documents, none of the textiles, and little of the wooden structures and their furnishings would have survived more than a few years. Yet in the desert sands of Khotan they endured for seventeen centuries, for all the world as though they had been abandoned yesterday.

(iii) America. The preservative powers of desiccation are well illustrated in North America by the so-called Basket-maker culture of the south-western states.[1] Although its absolute age has recently been drastically reduced[2] the culture is recognized to belong to an early spread, substantially antedating in origin the Pueblo cultures of the same and neighbouring districts. Yet

[1] S. J. Guernsey and A. V. Kidder, 'Basket-maker caves of north-eastern Arizona', *Papers of Peabody Mus. Am. Arch. and Ethn., Harvard Univ.*, VIII, no. 2, 1921; also *Bull. Bur. Am. Arch.*, no. 65, 1919.

[2] Until recently the last millennium or millennium and a half B.C. was regarded as reasonable. Dendrochronology favours a period from the middle of the fourth to the end of the ninth century A.D.

in the shelter of dry caves and overhanging rocks, to which the Basket-maker people repaired for occasional refuge, for the storage of their crops and the disposal of their dead, many organic remains have survived.

The bodies of the dead are found as well preserved as those

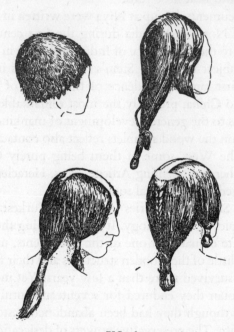

FIG. 5
Hairdressing styles of the Basket-maker people of Arizona

of the pre-dynastic people in the sands of Egypt, and like them they owe their survival entirely to natural desiccation. It has even been possible to make a close study of the often intricate styles of hairdressing (fig. 5). The Basket-makers probably needed but little clothing because of the high temperature, but women's aprons and cord sandals of several varieties have survived intact. To show how well objects are preserved in the caves of this region I illustrate (pl. VI) a human foot with its sandal still in position. Coiled basketry in the form of trays, bowls, carriers, water-containers (with the inner surface pitched with gum), and trinket-boxes, often beautifully decorated, form the bulk of the grave-goods. Feathered ornaments, decorated textiles, netting, rabbit-snares, leather bags and pouches, and wooden spear-throwers, feathered darts with stone heads in position, clubs and planting-sticks are among the other objects normally found. In one cave in the Kayenta region of Northeast Arizona a large dog was excavated; its body was dried up, but its long white hair was quite intact. Even the bodies of the flies which hatched out after the burial of the poor beast were found in a good state of preservation. The excavators hoped to deduce therefrom the exact season of the burial, but *Caliphora coloradensis* is one of those hardy flies which flourish from spring to autumn.

South America can show very remarkable examples within the territories of the Incan Empire. It is known from the descriptions of Spanish writers from the first century after the discovery that Incas of note were arrayed in splendour, yet the most careful excavations in the neighbourhood of their headquarters at Cuzco have failed to disclose more than a few bare fragments of textiles. Only in the arid coastal tract of central and southern Peru have conditions been favourable for the preservation of textiles, and here in such cemeteries as Ancon, Pachacamac, Ica, Nasca, and Arica splendid finds of Inca and pre-Inca Age have been made.[1] So well preserved are some of the mummies that patterns of conventionalized birds and fishes tattooed on legs and forearms can plainly be discerned. Ambitious basket-work head-gear in the form of tapered cylinders, the tops decorated with feathered mosaics, the lower and broader ends wrapped round with patterned textiles, also testify to highly favourable conditions. But above all it is the textiles that make Peru famous. The greatest care seems to have been lavished on the tunics of the notables, which were spangled

[1] Gosta Montell, *Dress and Ornaments in Ancient Peru*, Goteborg, 1929.

with gold and silver, embroidered, decorated with feather mosaic, and coloured by the tie-dyeing method, their varied hues surviving almost as fresh as when they were worn centuries before the New World had been rediscovered. Recent excavations by Junius Bird in midden deposits in the arid tract of the coast of North Chile have brought to light quantities of knotted wool bags.

Temperate conditions. The properties of a temperate climate which make it pleasant for Europeans are generally inimical to the lengthy survival of perishable materials. Relatively warm but variable temperatures and a sufficiency of precipitation combine as a rule to accelerate decay and dissolution. The one redeeming feature of such a climate from an archaeologist's point of view is its ability to maintain lakes, bogs, and fens; and, under propitious circumstances, to generate waterlogged conditions in the interior of barrows.

(i) Lake villages. The Alpine region, embracing Switzerland, the French Jura, Württemberg, and the northern frontiers of Italy, has given us more tangible evidence of the perishable aspects of the material culture of Neolithic man than all the other sites of Europe put together. It was believed by Ferdinand Keller that the wooden houses were built on platforms raised on piles over the open waters of the lakes and linked by bridges to the dry land, but recent research has shown that they were sited on lake-side marshes and during periods of low lake-level on the very beds of the lakes. In so far as the structures survived they were preserved by being incorporated in waterlogged deposits. Some were built directly on horizontal sleeper beams laid criss-cross on the marsh, others on piles driven into the firmer subsoil: at Riedschachen, one of several Neolithic sites on the shore of the Federsee in Württemberg,[1] two large pile-dwellings were overlaid by eleven smaller ones resting on sleeper beams, no doubt a reflection of changed conditions.

[1] H. Reinerth, *Das Federseemoor als Siedlungsland des Vorzeitmenschen*, Augsburg, 1929.

The two houses were rectangular in plan with gabled roof and were subdivided into two rooms, the pile-dwellings being differentiated by their greater size and the extensive development of their fore-porches. The clay hearths and baking-ovens were often preserved in perfect condition (pl. xiii).

The survival of organic materials, particularly those from the ancient lake-beds, has told us much of the habits of Neolithic man for which evidence is either lacking, or at least scarce in other parts of Europe. So far as animal remains are concerned the Alpine area is admittedly not particularly outstanding, since the calcareous lake deposits being alkaline no traces have survived of leather or wool, both of which have been preserved in the northern bogs. Nevertheless, the bones of cattle, pigs, sheep, goats, and dogs testify to the domestication of animals, while the presence of red deer, fallow deer, roe deer, elk, brown bear, wild pig, aurochs, fox, hare, chamois, hedgehog, stork, swan, wild duck, heron, pike, salmon, and carp show that hunting and fishing were also practised.

For vegetable remains, on the other hand, the Alpine sites are pre-eminent. Among the wooden objects which have survived must be reckoned clubs, hammers, handles of all kinds, shuttles and other weaving appliances, ladles and scoops, dishes, bows and fish-net floats. Basketry, net-work, mat-work, and linen textiles have come down to us in fragmentary condition, it is true, but still sufficiently well preserved to reveal an astonishing variety in techniques of plaiting and weaving. It seems likely that many of the embroidered cloths were designed as wall hangings for the timber houses. None of the textiles retain artificial colouring, although the presence of remains of weld suggest that yellow was a favourite colour. In comparison with the meagreness of the evidence from other parts of Neolithic Europe tangible remains of vegetable food are pleasantly abundant. Barley, wheat, oats, rye, millet, and peas, together with such common weeds of the cornfield as darnel, goosefoot, burdock, campion, chickweed, spurry, creeping crowfoot, and others, confirm the existence of agriculture, for which querns and sickles (their teeth still set in wooden handles) would otherwise have been the only evidence—evidence, it should be added, by no means conclusive. That the lake-dwellers collected wild fruits is known from the occurrence of remains of plums, sloes, bird cherries, apples, pears, raspberries, blackberries, and strawberries, as well as of beech- and hazel-nuts. Caraway and poppy seeds were probably used to give relish to the gruel, which formed the principal food of the peasants and of which the carbonized residues in the form of rounded 'buns' moulding the forms of the interiors of the bases of pots have so often been mistaken for bread. Mosses were evidently used to plug cracks and holes in the wooden houses, and timber fungi were collected for use as fire-lighters.

During the closing phases of the Bronze Age a new type of building, constructed of horizontal timbers interlocked at the corners on the block-house principle, came into use in Central Europe. A notable settlement of farmsteads, built in this way and enclosed within a timber stockade, has been completely excavated in Württemberg (fig. 6): it was once thought to have been constructed on an island in the lake—hence its name Wasserburg Buchau, but it seems likely that it was in fact built on a low hillock in a marsh. When the excavators cleared away the peat they found indications of two successive occupations, one dating from c. 1100 B.C. and represented by thirty-eight small rectangular houses, the other from c. 900 B.C. and comprising nine farmsteads, each enclosing three sides of a yard (fig. 7). The edges of the hillock were protected by a stone facing, reinforced on the north side by timber stakes. An outer palisade, consisting of some 15,000 pine stakes, served as an outer defence to which access was gained from the hillock by light bridges.

The lake-village at Glastonbury, in the Somerset marshes,[1] is famous as having, with its close neighbour, Meare, contributed

[1] A. Bulleid and H. St G. Gray, *The Glastonbury Lake Village*.

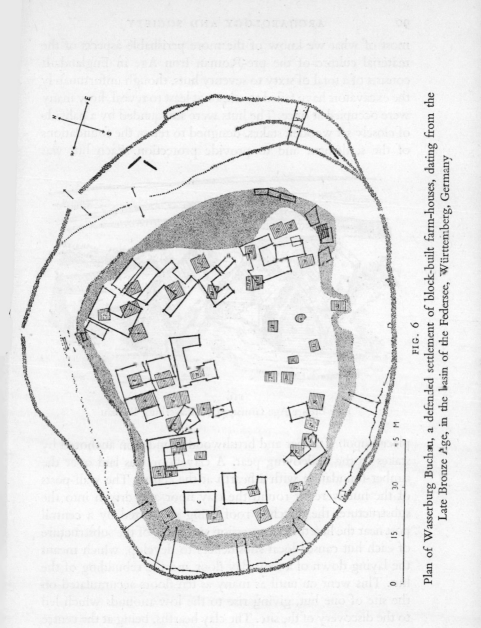

FIG. 6

Plan of Wasserburg Buchau, a defended settlement of block-built farm-houses, dating from the Late Bronze Age, in the basin of the Federsee, Württemberg, Germany

most of what we know of the more perishable aspects of the
material culture of the pre-Roman Iron Age in England. It
consists of a total of sixty to seventy huts, though unfortunately
the excavators have failed to ask, or at least to reveal, how many
were occupied at once. The huts were surrounded by a palisade
of closely set wooden stakes, designed to retain the foundations
of the settlement and to provide protection. Each hut was

FIG. 7
Late Bronze Age farmstead at Wasserburg Buchau

placed upon a timber and brushwood foundation anchored by
stakes to the underlying peat. A clay floor was laid over the
timber foundation with a hearth at the centre. The wall-posts
of the hut were set round the clay floor and driven into the
substructure, the thatched roof being supported by a central
post near the hearth. Compression and decay of the substructure
of each hut caused local subsidences to develop, which meant
the laying down of a new clay floor and the rebuilding of the
hut. This went on until as many as ten floors accumulated on
the site of one hut, giving rise to the low mounds which led
to the discovery of the site. The clay hearths, being at the centre
of the huts, sank more rapidly and had to be removed at more

frequent intervals; as many as thirteen were found superimposed in one hut.

In particular the woodwork from these lake-villages invites admiration for its wonderfully accurate turnery and joinery. The cups and tubs, both stave-made and cut from the solid, the loom-frames, ladles, handles, and above all the masterly wheel-hubs and spokes, all serve to underline what has been lost on the ordinary 'dry land' site. As in the Neolithic and Bronze Age villages of the Alpine zone of Europe, evidence for the sources of food is exceptionally rich. It is safe to say that the lake-villages at Glastonbury and Meare, thanks to their being permanently waterlogged, give us more insight into the daily lives of people living during the latter stages of the pre-Roman Iron Age than any other sites yet excavated in England.

(ii) Oak-coffin burials. The oak-coffin burials under round barrows, dating from the Early Bronze Age in northern Europe and mostly found in the area from northern Schleswig to Central Jutland, constitute some of the most remarkable instances of survival in the temperate zone.[1] Their preservation is due primarily to the waterlogging of the barrows, the inner cores of which were formed of stones packed round the wooden coffin.[2] Excavators have found on reaching the heart of such a barrow that water gushed out. It has recently been noted also that concreted bands (orstein) occur near the outer surface of the mounds. These, especially where they have been duplicated by the enlargement of the barrow (as in the well-known one at Skrydstrup, Hadersleben, excavated in 1935), had the effect of insulating its core from the evaporating effect of winds, and may well have helped to maintain it in waterlogged condition.

The stagnation of the water in such barrows set up acid

[1] For a summary and references see H. Shetelig and Falk, *Scandinavian Archaeology*, Oxford, 1937.

[2] A similar stone packing helped to preserve the Oseberg viking ship (pl. xix).

conditions peculiarly favourable to the survival of certain organic substances. The coffins themselves, consisting of half a hollowed-out oak trunk enclosed in an outer shell of two halves fitted together, survived intact in many instances. It was noted that some had holes at the bottom to allow the escape of moisture set up by putrefaction. The bodies, whose skin, hair, and ligaments were comparatively well preserved, were laid in their coffins fully dressed and accompanied by ornaments and other personal possessions. Among these latter must be included many highly perishable remains—wooden sword scabbards and palstave handles, a horn dagger handle and combs of the same material, birch-bark pails, cups and bowls of carved wood, a folding stool covered with otter's skin and strongly recalling in its form the type used in ancient Egypt, and, above all, a series of woollen textiles which give remarkably complete evidence for the dress of Nordic people over 3,000 years ago.

Although essentially a sheep's wool fabric, the material incorporates a certain proportion of red deer hair. The reason for this admixture may in part have been aesthetic, the hair giving an appearance of added depth and texture, but the desire to render the material more impervious to rain may have been more important. The men seem to have worn kirtles reaching to the knee, with leather shoulder-straps and woollen belts; over these were thrown long cloaks (pl. VII). There is no evidence for the use of trousers such as were worn by the horse-riding Scythians. The men's caps were round affairs with a shaggy exterior made up of innumerable loose threads knotted at the end. Shoes were made of leather or cloth. The women wore close-fitting jackets with sleeves reaching to the elbow. Their skirts were sometimes heavy, reaching down to the ankles and gathered in at the waist by a tasselled belt; but sometimes they were light, being made entirely of woollen fringes extending little below the knee. The Skrydstrup woman (frontispiece) wore a pad under her blonde hair, a wig, and a hair-net of horsehair (fig. 8).

(iii) Stray bog finds. Wherever peat-bogs are present these should be closely watched, because they are capable of adding greatly to our knowledge of early cultures by preserving features which have normally long since disappeared. Finds from peat-bogs in northern Europe range from human bodies with hair and skin intact—the North German 'moorleichen' (pl. xiva)—to fish-nets, boats, ploughs, skis, sledge-runners, and all manner of handles, sheaths, scabbards, and

FIG. 8

Hair-net worn by Danish women in the earlier part of the Bronze Age

receptacles. The body of a man found not long ago at Tollund in Jutland and dating from the Early Iron Age is especially interesting, because he was wearing a conical cap of leather and a rope noose pulled so tightly round his neck that we can only assume he was hanged by it, not to mention the fact that his intestines and their contents were so well preserved that it was possible to discover the exact nature of his diet or at least of his last meal.

Very cold climates. The most perfect climatic conditions for preservation are to be found in the circumpolar regions of the northern hemisphere from northernmost Russia and Siberia to Alaska, northern Canada, the sub-arctic archipelago, and the coasts of Greenland. In the permanently frozen soil of parts of this vast tract remains of early man and of some of the animals he hunted are preserved as though in a giant refrigerator, the process of decay held permanently in check.

(i) Mammoths. The frozen mammoths of north-eastern Siberia, more than twenty of which have been recorded, are effective illustrations of what an intensely cold climate can accomplish in the way of conservation.[1] Most of the discoveries have been made in the New Siberian Islands, or comparatively close to the Arctic Sea. The circumstances under which they were found suggest that they fell through surface layers of snow into deep crevasses, bringing snow down upon themselves in their struggles, so putting themselves neatly into cold storage. A few rhinos have been found in similar conditions, but none of the other quarries of Upper Palaeolithic huntsmen seems to have been heavy enough to meet a like fate—and it remains to find early man himself frozen and intact.

The best preserved—or at least the most expeditiously investigated—of the Siberian mammoths was found at Beresovka by a Lamut tribesman, who chopped off a protruding tusk. The story he told of a great hairy devil, when he came into Sredne-Kolymsk to sell the ivory, so stimulated the interest of those in authority that in the following year (1901) an expedition was sent out by the Imperial Academy of Sciences under the leadership of Dr Otto F. Herz accompanied by the zoologist E. V. Pfizenmeyer. The mammoth was found in a silted-up crevasse in a cliff overhanging the River Beresovka. The pelvis and right fore-leg were fractured as a result of his fall, which the presence of half-masticated food on his tongue and in his teeth shows to have been as sudden as it was unexpected. The position of the fore-legs, well displayed in the mounted specimens (pl. IX), shows that he died while still trying to extricate himself. When originally discovered the trunk—a succulent morsel

[1] Bassett Digby, *The Mammoth and Mammoth-hunting in North-East Siberia*, London, 1926.

—was already missing,[1] and in the course of the expedition wolves had devoured the fleshy covering of the top of the head. The rest of the body was remarkably preserved. The epidermis, it is true, had rotted, but the hair, although loose, was perfectly intact. When the skin was lifted in the process of dismemberment, Herz tells us that: 'The flesh from under the shoulder, fibrous and marbled with fat, was dark red and looked as fresh as well-frozen beef or horse-meat. It looked so appetizing that we wondered for some time whether we would not taste it. But no one would venture to take it into his mouth and horse-flesh was given preference.' The dogs apparently ate ravenously whatever was thrown to them. It was even possible to identify remains of the creature's last meal, traces of which were found in the mouth and many pounds in the stomach: his diet seems to have included fir cones and branches, larch and pine, sedges, mosses, wild thyme, Alpine poppy and buttercup, and various grasses. It is interesting to find that seeds were attached to many of the plant remains, showing that the mammoth's tragedy occurred in the autumn, presumably after the first snowfall had bridged the mouth of the crevasse sufficiently to conceal the danger.

(ii) Eskimo archaeology. The Danish explorers Therkel Mathiassen and Kaj Birket-Smith and the expeditions sent out from Cambridge have combined to throw a flood of light on the earliest settlement of the circumpolar region.[2] Thanks to the favourable conditions a great deal is already known of the

---

[1] The trunk of a young mammoth was found by Volosovitch in 1908. Another was obtained by a Tungu hunter in 1924 in the Kolyma district of Siberia. He sawed off the tip, which was dried and used as a table ornament by a Mme Kondratiev of Sredne-Kolymsk, in whose house it was noticed a few years later. The bi-lobate structure of the extremity of the trunk confirms the accuracy of such representations as those at Combarelles made by Upper Palaeolithic man. The absence of trunks from most of the mammoths found is due to their succulence; in nearly every case they were gnawed away by wild beasts prior to the discovery of the mammoths (see pl. IX).

[2] Therkel Mathiassen, *Archaeology of the Central Eskimo*, Copenhagen, 1927.

winter culture of the Thule people, who during this season lived in semi-subterranean earth-houses roofed by wood or whalebone heaped over with turf. Had we to depend on the hard residue, such as would have survived on a normal site in the temperate regions—in this case a few flint and stone implements, blubber lamps, and a few heads and blades of meteoric iron—our knowledge would not have reached its present stage so early, if ever at all. Fortunately, however, animal remains, highly perishable as a general rule, have here survived to an astonishing extent.

Over such an extensive area great local differences can naturally be observed in the completeness of refrigeration. In Greenland archaeological remains tend to be found in a more intact state as one travels north, since whereas in the Julianehaab district at the extreme south the January isotherm is 20°F. and the July figure as high as 45°F., farther up the west coast in the Melville Bay region the corresponding temperatures are as low as —15°F. and 37°F. At Melville Bay and even at the intermediate Disko Bay refrigeration is sufficiently effective all the year round to preserve all manner of objects made of wood, bone, and baleen—harpoons, arrows complete with shafts, gullhooks, leister-prongs, ice-scoops, sledge-runners and shoes, parts of umiaks and kayaks and their paddles, knives with their handles, bow-drills, needle-cases, thimble-holders, bodkins, wooden scraping-benches, trays, bowls, dippers, combs, trinkets, drum handles, dolls and toys of all kinds. In more southerly districts, on the other hand, the alternation of frost and thaw for part of the year is fatal to the preservation of many of these things, only the flint and stonework surviving at all completely. On Plate x I illustrate a sealskin boot and a stone axe with handles and lashing of baleen from an old Eskimo house at Qilalukan, East Baffin Land, dug by Mathiassen.

Another circumstance of which excavators have to take account is that the completeness with which organic materials survive in such a region may vary in the same hut according

IX   Mammoth from Beresovka, Siberia

(Text, p. 94)

Note the attitude of the beast as though endeavouring to extricate itself

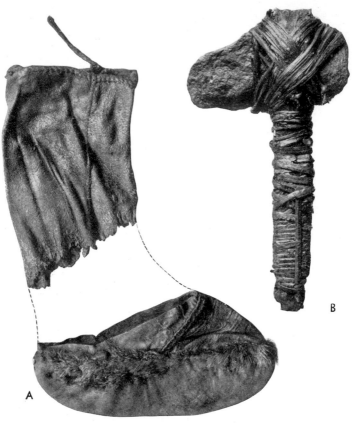

[*After Mathiassen*

X   Sealskin boot (*a*) and stone axe with Baleen handle and lashing
(*b*) from frozen house-sites at Qilalukan, East Baffin Land
(Text, p. 96)

[*After Childe, photo. Thomas Kent*]

XI   Excavated stone-built hut at Skara Brae, Orkney

(Text, pp. 193, 199, 200, 202)

[*After C. A. Nordman*

XII Passage-grave at Mejls, Jutland, with its covering mound removed

(Text, p. 109)

[*After R. R. Schmidt*

XIII   Neolithic timber house at Aichbühl, by the Fecersee, Württemberg

(Text, pp. 87, 109)

(a)

(b)

XIV (a) Early Iron Age corpse from a North German bog
(Text, pp. 93, 239)

(b) Cast of an asphyxiated man from Pompeii
(Text, p. 113)

XV View of excavations at Maiden Castle, Dorset, showing the Roman 'Priest's House'
overlying an early Iron Age hut and store-pits

(Text, pp. 114, 127)

XVI Dutch palisade barrow (Wessinghuizen I) in course of excavation

(Text, p. 117)

Note old surface line with turves heaped over it; also graves and traces of timber palisade in plan and section to the depth in the infilling. Easily perishable remains may be entirely absent from superficial layers affected by thawing, but be found almost intact in the permanently frozen layers below. Describing the excavation of a refuse heap left by people of the Thule culture on the coast of Repulse Bay, north of Hudson Bay, Therkel Mathiassen says that in the top layer he found hardly anything other than stone objects, lower down bone and baleen also occurred, while the lowermost stata were rich in 'wood, feathers, flakes of walrus hide, bunches of hair, canine excrement, egg shells, ashes, slag, heather, all saturated with blubber'. We can well believe him when he tells us that 'on a quiet summer day when the mosquitoes swarmed and the effluvia of the refuse heap was thick, it was anything but pleasant to be at the bottom of an excavating hole!'

(iii) Scythian tombs in the Altai. As a final instance of what cold can accomplish I cannot do better than quote some of the fascinating discoveries brought to light in Central Asia during the last thirty years or so.[1] I refer to the great tumulus burial grounds excavated by Colonel Kozlóv (1924–5) on the slopes of the Noin-Ula Mountains south of Lake Baikal and by M. P. Griaznov near Pazirik in the eastern Altai. In both cases the burials, of which only a small number out of hundreds have been excavated, are those of leaders of groups of steppe nomads, of a kind who move with their herds over immense though well-defined tracts of country, maintaining traditional burying-places, to which their leading men would be carried, if necessary, for hundreds of miles. The burials were enclosed in wooden chambers placed at the bottom of square pits twelve feet and more in depth. The low stone cairns which cover them appear to have acted as condensers of moisture, which found its way down into the chambers. At the same time the loosely

[1] M. P. Griaznov, 'The Pazirik Burial of Altai', *Priroda*, no. 11, 1929, and *Am. J. Archaeology*, vol. XXXVII, 1933; Camilla Trever, 'Excavations in Northern Mongolia, 1924–5', *Mem. Acad. Hist. Mat. Cult.*, vol. III, Leningrad, 1932; W. Perceval Yetts, 'Discoveries of the Kozlóv Expedition', *The Burlington Mag.*, April 1926.

heaped stones, being poor conductors of heat, allowed cold air to penetrate to the lowest layers of the pits—a process made easier by the vertical disturbances caused by tomb-robbers. The combined effect was to cause the formation of ice in the chambers during the severe winter months, sufficient to withstand the heat of summer. The tombs and their contents were thus maintained in permanently freezing condition.

Only one of the ten kurgans examined by the Kozlóv expedition has been satisfactorily excavated (by S. A. Teploukhov and G. J. Borovka). Nevertheless, and despite the previous attentions of robbers who ripped off the coffin-lids and plundered the bulk of the gold objects, the expedition found a wonderfully rich and varied collection of grave-goods. As well as objects of relatively enduring materials, such as gold strips and rosettes from the coffins, a bronze mirror, censer and cauldron, iron arrows and horse-bits, ornamented jade plaques, amber beads and wheel-made pots, the tomb contained many highly perishable substances. These included wooden and leather saddles and carved wooden bridle hangings, lacquer bowls (red within, black outside, and decorated with animal figures in gold lead), harness ornaments of horsehair, a number of queues of black hair (some of them encased in scalloped silk covers, decorated with charms), as well as a splendid series of felts and textiles. Among the latter were articles of clothing, some intact, e.g. a silken robe trimmed with sable and a silk cap, but mostly damaged by tomb-robbers; thick felt shoe soles embroidered with silk; silk damask hangings, felt carpets and woollen cloths embroidered with silk, and many other hangings, bags, and flags.

The presence of a Han mirror and of Han inspiration in some of the textile designs suggests that the Noin-Ula graves may in some instances date back to the first century B.C. From his study of the grave-goods as a whole, but particularly of the embroidered designs, W. Perceval Yetts detects the presence of Scythic-Sarmatian (e.g. the motive of the fabulous beast attacking his prey in the rear), Siberian, Iranian, Hellenic, and Chinese elements. The chief interest of the discovery lies in the light it throws on the breadth of the cultural contacts achieved by the nomad peoples of Central Asia nearly 2,000 years ago—and the most important evidence for this was such that under normal conditions in a temperate climate all traces would long since have disappeared.

We owe it to Griaznov that the Pazirik barrow was scientifically excavated and adequately recorded. The grave lay by a stone cairn 2½ m. high and 50 m. in diameter. Three-quarters of the pit were occupied by two rectangular wooden chambers, one within the other. Griaznov says that 'the inside appearance of the burial gave the impression that hardly a year had passed since its construction. The very timber out of which the burial chamber was built had not only preserved its original shape and quality, but had retained its fresh smell of pitch.' Robbers had removed the corpse for stripping, but on the wooden coffin the *appliqué* decoration of bird figures cut out of leather was intact, and on the walls of the chamber a black felt carpet with *appliqué* decoration of tigers' heads in thin felt still hung from its nails of wood and copper. The ten chestnut mares, thrown into the portion of the grave unoccupied by the wooden chamber, were possibly its most remarkable feature: in Griaznov's words they 'were preserved so well that not only skin and hair, but muscles, and entrails with the remains of undigested food were found in them'. Evidently they had been killed by a blow from a sharp axe on the forehead and then heaped into the open grave in disorder. So perfectly were they preserved that their smallest features were easily recognizable: their coats were free from chafing and showed no signs of their use for any form of work; their manes and the upper portions of their tails were seen to be clipped; and the ownership marks on their ears were found to be distinct in each case, suggesting that they may well have been offered by faithful retainers to their dead lord. Not the least interesting part of the find was the harness, of which each horse was provided with a complete set. The perfection of its preservation was astounding. The saddles, which were placed over a square piece of felt to prevent chafing, each consisted of two soft pillows of felt and finely tanned leather stuffed with reindeer hair. Each was provided with belly-, breast-, and tail-strap and each had a fine thin felt cover decorated in *appliqué* work with scenes of animal combats. The breast-straps in their turn were decorated with plaques of cedar, carved into animal forms and gilded or silvered. The bridles, attached to simple iron or bronze bits, were covered with wood carved in low relief and likewise gilded or silvered. The trappings of two of the horses were distinguished by several extra features: leather cases for manes and tails; masks for foreheads made of leather, felt, fur, and gold-leaf worked to represent animal forms; and provision bags of fur.

We can see in our mind's eye the dead leader borne on an ox-drawn cart—the remains of the cart and yokes were found heaped over the wooden chamber—to the traditional burial-place of his forebears high up on the mountain slope. We can almost assist at the building of his tomb and smell the timber as those who fashioned from it the coffin and the double chamber. The funeral hangings, the horse harnesses for the pleasure of the great one in the next world, we can see them all, so fresh that, as their excavator remarked, it seems incredible that it all happened some 2,000 years ago.

GEOLOGICAL CONDITIONS

The nature of the soil in which antiquities are found is a factor of importance. Indeed in a temperate climate it is often decisive. It may be true, for instance, that the viking ships of Norway owe their preservation in the first instance to the dampness of the climate, but this would not have sufficed of itself, as is shown by their disappearance in other parts of Scandinavia with a similar climate. It was the clay in which the Gokstad, Tune, and Oseberg ships were buried, supplemented in the last-mentioned by the packing of stones and the sealing layer of peat that ensured their survival.

Occasionally it happens that the soil has positive properties that make for the preservation of organic substances without reference to climate. An extreme instance is that of the oil-bearing Miocene beds of the Ropizcze (*rope*=crude oil) district of South-east Poland. Here at a place called Starunia a woolly rhinoceros of the type hunted and sketched by Upper Palaeolithic man was found by oil prospectors in an almost perfect state of preservation. All the circumstances suggest that it had been carried away by water after death. Probably the creature had been feeding in a deeply eroded valley when it was overtaken by swiftly rising flood waters and borne away by a strong current. By good fortune this particular specimen (and others along with it) seems to have been swept into a pool, beyond the normal reach of the river and saturated by salt and crude oil from the Miocene beds. The chemistry of the preservation process remains to be worked out, but oil literally poured from the broken bones and salt accumulated on the skin as the body was dried after excavation; possibly the condensed crude oil vapours helped to exclude the activity of bacteria, and by permeating the skin the salt may have helped to preserve it.

Whatever the cause, there is no denying its remarkably perfect condition. The two horns and the hoofs are missing, but except for parts of one side, damaged while transported in the water, the skin is almost intact. The actual hairs were found embedded in the silt adjoining, but their original position on the body was shown by the cavities of the skin. The woolly rhinoceros evidently had long hairs at the back of the head rather like a wild boar, while his tail, broad and flat near the base but almost circular in section towards the tip, was provided with a broad tuft at its extremity with which to swat flies and other insect pests in the neighbourhood of the stomach. Examination of the skin revealed numerous scars, relics of fights with others of its kind. The eye region with all its numerous folds was beautifully preserved and even one of the eyeballs. Tongue, throat, and palate and intestines had been washed out through a hole in the front part of the stomach; parts were recovered from the silt at a distance of some five feet. Round about the body were found the leaves and fruits of the typical tundra vegetation on which the rhinoceros thrived in lifetime, odds and ends washed in by the current—dwarf birch, small-leaved willow, various shrubs and *Dryas octopetala*, as well as numerous land and water beetles.

One instructive result of finding the Starunia rhinoceros is that in certain details, such as the shape and carriage of the tail, modern restorations can be shown to be less accurate than representations made by Palaeolithic man in the cave art. But perhaps the artist who painted the woolly rhinoceros so boldly on the walls of Font-de-Gaume in the Dordogne was in some ways better equipped than the most learned of palaeontologists.

The preservation of Pompeii and Herculaneum under the mud and ashes rained down by Vesuvius in the eruption of A.D. 79, described by Pliny, is a dramatic event for which no immediate parallel can be advanced from prehistoric archaeology. Yet the gradual accumulation of geological deposits over early sites has certainly preserved to posterity much that would otherwise have been lost or at least gravely impaired. The mantle of loess which stretches intermittently from the Rhine to the Ordos Desert has sealed down the open stations of Upper Palaeolithic hunting tribes, in South Russia even preserving the plans of their houses, the oldest artificial dwellings in the world. Rapidly forming peats and silts have served to enclose remains of the earliest post-Glacial cultures of Europe, stratifying them at different levels, and in some cases preserving such organic substances as wooden artifacts and even fishing-nets. Peat, by overgrowing and obscuring barrows, has saved many of them from destruction by ploughing, or mutilation by quarrying. The chambered tombs on Carrowkeel Mountain, County Sligo, and the Stripple Stones of Cornwall probably owe their survival to this cause, as certainly do the group of Bronze Age barrows and megalithic tombs discovered just before the First World War in the Kehdinger Moor in Hanover. Rapid peat formation has also played a big part in the preservation of wooden structures, such as the lake-villages of parts of Europe and of the British Isles.

Blowing sand, by covering sites in early times, has often been the means of preserving them. Aurel Stein had cause to bless the encroaching sands of the Taklamakan Desert, just as British archaeology has to thank the dunes which engulfed Skara Brae in Orkney (pp. 44 and 108f, and pl. XI).

SOCIAL BEHAVIOUR IN THE PAST

That the behaviour of people in the past has influenced the degree to which their material culture has survived is sufficiently obvious, although too often ignored by archaeologists. Probably no single factor has been of greater assistance to archaeology than the care lavished on his dead body by early man. The burial with the dead man of implements, weapons, and adornments is responsible for the 'grave goods', without which it is hardly possible to conceive the development of prehistoric archaeology. The construction of elaborate tombs, partly no doubt to commemorate the departed but in large measure to safeguard his equipment from plunder, has served, rather ironically, to ensure a portion of the material to modern excavators. Inhumation burial with plenty of grave-goods is the ideal from the archaeologist's standpoint: some cremations are accompanied by little more than cinerary urns, and they imply, besides, the destruction of evidence for reconstructing human physical types. For most early cultures we know little or nothing of the burials of ordinary people, and for some we have no burial evidence whatever: this is no wonder when we recall the many methods of disposing of the dead which, like tree-burial, cannot be expected to leave traces in the soil.

If the excavation of burials gave archaeology its flying start, it is settlement sites with their manifold social implications that provide the most promising material for the future. Clearly the nature of early man's settlements and dwellings affects profoundly the kind of material remains available to archaeology, as they go far to determine the aspects of his culture most likely to be represented among excavation material.

The cold winters of Late Glacial times, which in the limestone areas of Europe drove hunting tribes to the shelter of overhanging rocks, greatly aided the development of Upper Palaeolithic archaeology. Frequent returns to the same shelter aided by crumbling of the overhanging rock have combined to make easy the observation of stratigraphy; the properties of the limestone have favoured the preservation of quantities of antler, bone, and shell objects, in such condition that surface markings are well preserved; and inner recesses of the caves have sheltered from weather and human interference the engravings and paintings which give us so extraordinary an insight into the feelings and mentality of Palaeolithic hunters living 20,000 years ago.

Thanks to their habit of camping in the summer months by rivers, lake margins, bogs, and other wet places, the material culture of the Maglemose food-gatherers, who spread far and wide over the North European Plain from eastern Britain to the Urals, has survived in a remarkably complete form.[1] In addition to the 'hard residue' of flint and stone, all manner of perishable materials have come down to us—antler and bone axe and adze sockets and blades, leister-prongs, harpoons, arrow-heads, net-making needles, bodkins and fish-hooks, wooden clubs, handles, sockets and paddle-rudders, string nets and bark net-floats. At Star Carr, Yorkshire,[2] were found recumbent birch-trees felled by the proto-Maglemosians, part of a birch-wood paddle, quantities of birch-bark rolls, and

---

[1] J. G. D. Clark, *The Mesolithic Settlement of Northern Europe*, Chap. III, Cambridge, 1936.

[2] J. G. D. Clark *et al.*, *Excavations at Star Carr*, Cambridge, 1954.

numerous specimens of a bracket fungus (*Fomes fomentarius*) with the outer skin peeled off for tinder. The contrast with what we know of the contemporary microlithic cultures of the more southerly parts of Europe is instructive. Since these people dwelt predominantly on sand formations hostile to the survival of organic remains, our knowledge of their material culture is limited almost entirely to objects of flint or stone. As for the Maglemose culture itself it is worth noting that only the sites chosen for summer settlements seem to have been favourable to the preservation of organic substances: the winter culture is still almost an unknown quantity.

With the development of a food-producing economy conditions tended to favour the survival of a higher proportion of the material side of early cultures. The tells which reflect the growth of city life in the Near East, the eastern Mediterranean, and parts of south-eastern Europe are one example. Formed gradually by mere accretion of the debris of human existence, such sites not only give fine stratigraphical sequences, but by sealing the different levels preserve their contents to archaeology. Tells have played a role as important as have caves in another sphere.

In North-west Europe the 'terps' of northern Holland and the 'wurts' of North-west Germany offer the closest analogies, but they differ in their mode of origin. Unlike tells, these mounds have been heaped up deliberately in successive stages, possibly to cope with the onset of coastal subsidence, which is thought by some geologists to have affected the North Sea coast at that time. By excavating such sites van Giffen and his colleagues in Germany have not only obtained invaluable stratigraphical information, but have also been able to reveal in the lower levels timber and wattle houses, preserved almost intact by overlying deposits and the moisture of the subsoil (pl. XXIII). The habit of living by lake margins is another for which archaeologists have to be thankful.

It is a paradox that the best chance of organic material

surviving in the ordinary way is that it should be destroyed by fire, but such remains, in being converted into carbon, acquire enormously enhanced powers of resistance. Clay daub, a material much used in primitive structures, also gains by a good firing. It was certainly the experience of Professor Hatt digging Early Iron Age houses in Jutland that, only in the case of those destroyed by fire, could he hope to recover details of the structure. Those abandoned to the processes of natural decay disappeared so completely that only the barest outlines were recoverable by excavation. Burnt houses, on the other hand, were clearly defined by charred stumps, traces of roofing materials would be found lying charred on the floor, and indications of wattle impressed on the burnt daub. Even wooden utensils were recovered in charred fragments. It is amusing to compare with this the testimony of an excavator of Pueblo ruins in the south-western states of North America, who wrote of a burnt house in Colorado:

'the mud was baked to a brick-like consistency which thus far has withstood the actions of erosion to which it has been subjected during the centuries . . . had it not been for this firing the adobe [mud] would have melted back into the earth from which it was taken and the unprotected poles would have decayed and fallen into dust. In many instances the timbers are no longer present, it is true, but their imprints are ineffaceably preserved in the hardened plaster.'

So, it may be concluded, do archaeologists, by disinterring the dead and by uncovering the ashes of burnt-out habitations, turn to profit the tragedies of past ages. Yet it is through death and destruction that generations of men remote beyond the verges of history have come to life again in the consciousness of humanity, and it is the spoiling hands of the archaeologists that confer immortality upon them.

IV

EXCAVATION

Excavation is the central stage in the process of archaeological research, forming an essential link between
discovery and interpretation. There is thus a very real
sense in which the spade is the trade-mark of archaeology.
In practice there is a tendency for archaeologists to specialize,
it may be in field-work, it may be in interpretation; but
the archaeologist with little or no experience of excavation
is ill qualified to interpret the results of other people's
digging.

In any case, whatever the historical problem involved, the
excavator is always concerned at a technical level with two
primary tasks: to recover and record the form of an object or
site, and to trace stages in its development. If it is convenient
to consider the two aspects of his work separately, it must be
remembered that in practice these are indissolubly linked
together.

MORPHOLOGY

Certain obvious principles apply to all types of archaeological excavation, such as the paramount importance of
accurate methods of survey and record, but their successful
application depends upon full appreciation of the conditions
obtaining at particular sites. Different soil conditions, varying
degrees of preservation, and a hundred and one local factors
connected with the state of the site help to determine the way
in which the excavator will have to solve his problem. Rigid
adherence to some theoretical 'excavation technique' is hardly
likely to bring success any more than will the most earnest

perusal of this or any other book to anyone not possessed of the saving qualities of observation, pertinacity, and adaptability.

In the final analysis excavation methods, as applied to the elucidation of morphology, fall into two main classes: those which consist essentially in isolating what, owing to its enduring material or to the existence of conditions peculiarly favourable to preservation, has survived more or less intact, and those which aim to recover the shape of what has ceased any longer to exist in tangible form.

Well-preserved sites. As a general rule these are the more straightforward, often involving little more than the removal of overlying material and the exposure of easily recognizable features. Yet, within this category there are obvious gradations of difficulty. Buildings of brick and masonry, like those of the ancient civilizations of the Near East (pl. XXII) or of the Classical World, including Roman Britain, are from the morphological point of view the easiest to excavate. Much of the superstructure will, as a rule, have disappeared, but the recovery of the ground-plan, where walls have not been seriously robbed, should present few difficulties. Even where extensive robbing has taken place the regularity of such buildings tends to make easier the reconstruction of what has disappeared.

Dry-stone constructions, on the other hand, such as abound in prehistoric Europe where suitable material is available, and in certain backwaters persist to the present day, offer slightly greater difficulties. In the absence of any form of cementing material the collapse of walls and other features is more general, while the frequent absence of any form of dressing increases the difficulty of reconstruction and may even make it hard to distinguish between stones in their natural position and those relating to a ruined structure. The innumerable hut-circles and fortified sites of the Highland Zone of Britain have, however, been excavated chiefly by the simple process of isolating structural features composed of hard and enduring rock. An outstanding example is the Stone Age village of Skara Brae in

Orkney.[1] Here by the mere removal of overlying sand were recovered not only the form of the houses but, thanks to the extensive use of stone, many details of their furniture. The huts themselves are sub-rectangular in plan, having rounded corners. As a rule they have only one door and no windows, being connected with each other by roofed passages. The hearth is set in the middle of the floor and is kerbed by low stone slabs (pl. xi). On either side are the beds, box-like structures formed by stone slabs, once filled no doubt with grass or heather bedding. Recesses above probably served as receptacles for personal possessions and trinkets. At the rear end of the huts are elaborate stone dressers with two tiers. Cubical boxes let into the corners of the floors may once have contained limpets.

In some ways the most interesting constructions of un-mortared stones in prehistoric Europe are the megalithic tombs of the western Mediterranean and the Atlantic seaboard (pl. xii). Here the successive attentions of tomb robbers and antiquarian diggers have created some of the chief difficulties in the way of modern investigators. The burial chambers are as a rule formed of comparatively few large slabs, so that their form may be affected profoundly by the movement or destruction of even one or two stones. It is thus necessary when researching on megaliths to recover the early history of investigation of the monument on which one is working and in particular to examine successive plans. In the field one has to decide how far the existing arrangement of stones is original, how far it has been subject to disturbance. Where stones have been removed one can often recover their exact positions by finding their socket-holes through excavation.

When wooden structures survive, as they do by the Federsee or the Swiss Lakes, they offer little difficulty so far as the ground-plan is concerned (fig. 9 and pl. xiii). Sometimes even the walling and roofing material can be found collapsed on the

[1] V. G. Childe, *Skara Brae*, London, 1931.

floor, but usually the superstructure has to be inferred from the arrangement of posts and the footings on the ground (fig. 10 and pl. XIII). Wooden remains which owe their survival to waterlogging have, however, one serious drawback: they may, when uncovered, appear to be as fresh as if they were new, but

FIG. 9
Neolithic house in course of excavation, Aichbühl, Germany

they tend on drying to deteriorate rapidly. The excavators of Glastonbury wrote that:

'After a few hours' exposure a pile was scarcely recognizable; its fresh light colour was soon transformed to an inky-grey, and in proportion to the rapidity with which the moisture in the wood evaporated, so did the post crack longitudinally, shrink and warp, until it was about one-third of its original diameter and size.'

It can readily be imagined how serious these processes would be if they were allowed to attack such objects as bows, wooden vessels, or furniture. The remedy is, of course, appropriate treatment in the field. Conservation has literally in such cases to go hand in hand with excavation.

Methods have naturally to be adapted to local conditions. In dealing with mammoth remains at Upper Palaeolithic sites in Moravia, Absolon found by experience that it was best first of all to remove the loess soil in such a way as to leave the bones exposed on supporting pillars. Then, having treated them with a hardening mixture (Mollison's tincture), it was a simple

FIG. 10
Reconstruction of Neolithic village, Aichbühl, Germany

matter to saw them off and pack them in cases for transit to the museum laboratory. Wooden objects, so long as they are kept moist, can be made to retain their shape almost indefinitely. But for exhibition purposes, especially when it is desired to fit several pieces together, it is necessary to dry and harden them in such a way as to avoid shrinkage and cracking. A notable example of what can be done in this way is afforded by Professor Gustafson's treatment of some of the wooden objects from the Oseberg viking ship, familiar to many visitors to Oslo (pl. xix). By boiling objects in a solution of alum and then drying them and impregnating them with linseed oil, he succeeded in preserving them without loss of shape or volume so effectively that he could rebuild them to their original form and dimensions. This task was not a light one. It is difficult to believe that one of the finely carved sledges consisted, when excavated, of no less than 1,068 pieces of soft wood, each of which had to be treated separately. The restoration of this one sledge alone took over a year. Despite the experience of the staff, the authorities of the museum at Oslo have still thought it wise to preserve some of the finest carvings in water, suitably treated to discourage organic life. No amount of skill can eliminate all chance of disaster, and where very precious remains are in question, preservation in a liquid is still the safest method to adopt. Where, as so often happens in Egypt and the Near East, one has to deal with elaborately inlaid objects, the mastic of which has been dissolved by moisture or shrunk by dryness, special treatment such as the application of wax has to be improvised in the field so as to get them to a museum reasonably intact. Elaborate arrangements of beads, the original threads of which have of course long since vanished, impose a further strain on the patience and ingenuity of the excavator. One can only emphasize that, whatever physical means are adopted to solve such difficulties, there can be no substitute for detailed notes made while the finds are still in position as found.

The excavation of sites where archaeological remains are on the whole well preserved has its own special problems, although these are mainly of a practical nature. Where all tangible remains of actual structures, bodies, material objects, and the like have disappeared, leaving behind them only the merest traces, the archaeologist has, however, to rely on his powers of detection: for want of concrete remains he has to be content with such indications of their former existence as his technique is able to demonstrate. There is an element of art in the excavation of the average prehistoric site, which is lacking in the case of a Roman villa with its four-square walls and hard floors. Perhaps it is this, more than anything else, which makes the average prehistorian so scornful of his Romano-British or Gallo-Roman colleagues, who in turn pride themselves on a scientific accuracy beyond the reach of their benighted brethren!

The difference of outlook is determined in large measure by the difference in the nature of the problems to be solved. It is rather like the contrast between driving a lorry on the open road and driving an engine on rails.

'Ghost' sites. The indications available to the excavator of a 'ghost' site naturally vary according to the nature of the soil and the character of what he is after. Where the subsoil is solid or relatively compact he will rely mainly on casts. Sometimes it is possible by pouring in plaster to obtain an exact cast of what has decayed. Visitors to Pompeii will probably remember in the museum there a number of gypsum casts made by pouring liquid plaster into the moulds formed by volcanic ash raining down on to the corpses of asphyxiated men and dogs (pl. XIV). Sir Leonard Woolley used the method to advantage at Ur, where the conditions of preservation were rather poor. One of his triumphs was to recover the number of strings in the harp buried in one of the royal tombs with Queen Shub-ad.

As a general rule, however, the excavator will have to be content with such indications of former structures as are betrayed by the holes dug to receive posts and the slots cut to contain wall-footings. Where the subsoil is sufficiently solid, as in chalk and, under favourable conditions, gravel, the usual method is to remove the topsoil and expose the virgin rock; ancient disturbances will then reveal themselves owing to the different colour and consistency of their infilling. If any difficulty is found in distinguishing such features, exposure to the weather will often prove effective, but no general rules can be laid down. Local conditions are of such predominating importance that personal experience is the only real guide. When post-holes or sleeper-trenches have been revealed it is important in excavating them to note any variations in their infilling; it is often possible to discover by careful observation the actual diameter and form of timbers as distinct from the holes made for their reception. A good idea of the appearance of a chalk surface stripped of its topsoil is given by Plate XV from a photograph taken at Maiden Castle, Dorset, in 1934. Ancient excavations, including rain-water gullies (?), storage-pits, and the post-holes of a hut, dating from the Early Iron Age, have been cleared of their filling. The contrast between the pre-historic hut, all tangible traces of the walls and even main posts of which have long since vanished, and the well-preserved wall-base of the rectangular stone-built dwelling, probably the house of the priest of the nearby temple, is strikingly illustrated.

To the casual visitor it may sometimes look as though excavators spend most of their time digging holes on their own account, and the rest speculating about the meaning of grubby little markings which seem incapable of conveying anything to anyone. If such a person, instead of standing on the edge, got down and lent a hand at the work, he might, after a few weeks, grow less sceptical. But perhaps it is simpler to give archaeologists some credit for knowing their business. After all it is not everyone who can identify finger-prints; the interpretation of archaeological traces is equally a matter of skill and training. No one in his senses would pretend that, working on a chalk site, from which every vestige of organic material save a few bones and charcoals has disappeared, even the most expert excavator could hope to find out as much about timber houses, for example, as he would if he were digging a lake-village. Still, with a knowledge of the real thing, such traces as a chalk surface is capable of revealing are often sufficient to give a fair idea of what formerly existed. This can be illustrated neatly by comparing the timber houses uncovered at Aichbühl (pl. XIII; fig. 11B) on the shores of the ancient Federsee with the traces exposed at the famous site on the Goldberg,[1] near Neresheim, Württemberg (fig. 11 A). The post-holes and wall-slots cut in the chalky subsoil were easily defined after the removal of topsoil by the different colour of their infilling. When planned they were found to indicate houses of the same general type as those at Aichbühl, having

[1] G. Bersu, *Germania*, 1936, pp. 229–43.

the same rectangular form, the same central row of posts indicative of a gabled roof, and the same internal division. Moreover, a careful examination of the infilling of the wall-slots showed that, as at Aichbühl, the convex sides of the timbers were facing outermost. Although not a scrap of timber was found at the Goldberg, there can be no reasonable doubt about

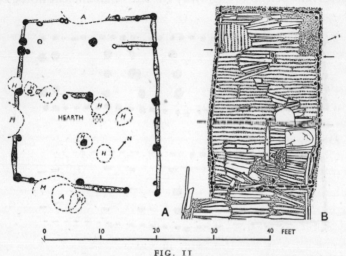

FIG. II
Neolithic houses as revealed on dry ground (Goldberg) and in
waterlogged soil (Aichbühl)

the character of the dwellings. In confirmation it can be said that pottery characteristic of Aichbühl was found associated with the 'ghost' houses on the Goldberg.

Working in soft, fine-grained soil like the loess of Central Europe and South Russia or the glacial sands of Holland, Denmark, and North Germany, the method of excavation calculated to yield the best results is naturally somewhat different. Instead of clearing out post-holes, wall-slots, and so on, as one would do in chalky country, these are now revealed in plan as discolorations by removing topsoil and shaving away the surface of the virgin soil. The implement used is the ordinary spade of the country, mounted at a low angle on a long handle, which allows one to shave the surface clean and flick away the shavings almost without effort. The character of the surface markings, which result from the replacement of timber or bone by soil, is of course to be tested by sectioning them vertically. It will be appreciated how easy it would be for an unobservant person to dig away the site of an ancient house or

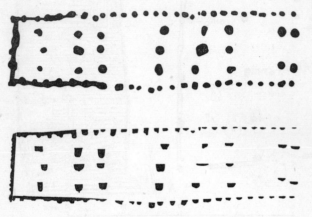

FIG. 12

Neolithic Danubian house defined by soil-marks, Sittard, Holland (1:250), Plan (upper) and section (lower)

fail to notice the existence of a former timber structure in a barrow. There is nothing so tangible as a post-hole cut in solid chalk; it is all a matter of colour. Under such conditions destruction is a necessary accompaniment of excavation and adequate recording becomes more than usually important.

The excavations carried out by Haberey and Buttler at Köln-Lindenthal,[1] a settlement of 'Danubian' (Neolithic) peasants on a loess patch near Cologne, showed what can be done by shaving down to the natural loess over an area of some 35,000

[1] W. Haberey and W. Buttler, *Die Bandkeramische Ansiedlung bei Köln-Lindenthal*, Berlin, 1936.

square metres, but they are equally interesting as showing that technical excellence will not make up for lack of judgement and erroneous interpretation. The excavators failed to recognize that the long rectangular structures, of which they recovered the plans so meticulously, were the houses in which the Neolithic peasants lived, rather than the squalid little hollows filled with discarded refuse, hollows which were really

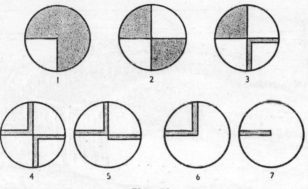

FIG. 13

The quadrant method of excavating round barrows

only the quarries for wall material filled with discarded refuse. Since Oscar Paret pointed this out, the long peasant houses of the Danubians has been recognized at many other German sites, as well as in Czechoslovakia, Poland, and Holland (fig. 12).

The ideal at which the excavator should aim is to expose as many sections as possible while gradually revealing the plan. For dealing with round barrows with internal structures of timber Dr A. E. van Giffen of Groningen has evolved what he terms the 'quadrant method'.[1] The first stage consists of removing the mound in such a way as not only to reveal but to retain sections while the plan is being recovered; successive stages in the process are shown in fig. 13, while Plate XVI

[1] A. E. van Giffen, *Die Bauart der Einzelgräber*, Leipzig, 1930.

illustrates the appearance of a barrow after removal of one quadrant. As the reconstruction of this particular barrow shows (fig. 14), an astonishingly adequate idea of the structure of the mound has been obtained, although nothing more tangible than colour differences remained.

An experienced barrow digger in such a region will not, however, stop short at this stage. He will endeavour by

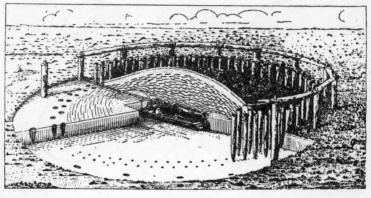

FIG. 14
Reconstruction of palisade barrow, Wessinghuizen, Holland

examining the graves to discover as much as possible about the burial. The Early Bronze Age people of Holland who heaped the mounds with timber palisades over their dead, buried them in oak coffins, presumably fully clothed. But, whereas the coffins and their contents have survived in astonishingly fresh condition in southern Jutland and Schleswig, conditions have been so much less favourable in Holland that nothing of the coffin survives beyond a dark smudge in the sand. Such traces of wooden coffins have been found again and again under Dutch barrows. Needless to say, the clothes have left no trace, but skeletons, whether buried extended in a coffin or contracted without one, have frequently been observed as dark silhouettes showing up clearly against the pale sand. The contrast between a contracted skeleton and a sand profile in the same attitude is illustrated by Plate xvii; in the former case all the excavator had to do was to brush the bones free, taking care only to avoid disturbance; in the latter he had delicately to shave away the sand, keeping a sharp look-out for suspicious markings. It is important to establish the attitude of burials, not only as an end in itself, but also with a view to establishing how ornaments, buttons, and pins were worn.

Intermediate sites. At the vast majority of sites remains of buildings and of smaller objects are neither so intact that they have only to be isolated from their encompassing material, nor so completely decayed that nothing tangible remains. Sometimes one and the same site will exhibit a complete range of states of preservation, requiring widely different modes of excavation. A famous instance is the wooden settlement at Hedeby, near Schleswig, which in viking times served as an entrepôt for the trade between western Europe and Scandinavia. The houses in the lower part of the town, near the shore of the vik, being well preserved, were dug by the straightforward isolation method. Those on the 'high and dry' portions of the site, however, had so far decayed that excavation by the shaving method, such as was used at Köln-Lindenthal in the Rhineland, was the only one available. Between the two extremes was a wide range calling for numerous variations in the mode of excavation.

Again, it very frequently happens that both buildings and loose antiquities are made partly from perishable, partly from imperishable substances, so that both methods have to be employed in their excavation. Stone constructions, if intelligently examined, will often give indications, it may be in slots or socket-holes, of wooden components which have since disappeared. Conversely, wooden structures, especially in such countries as Denmark where there are plenty of glacial pebbles and boulders, often have stone-built features, such as paving before the entrance, post-hole linings, and wall-footings (pl. xviii). Even when the timbers have vanished completely a few stones arranged in this way may give the clue to the general form and dimensions of a structure.

The same principle applies to the wooden ships in which important people were buried during the Dark Ages of northern Europe: the timbers decayed, but the iron parts have remained to preserve the form of the ship. The aim of the excavator must be to observe such colour traces as exist, and above all to note the relationship to these of any metal parts which have survived. An outstanding example of what can be done in this way is given by the excavation of a viking ship at Ladby in Fyen, the only one yet discovered in Denmark. Thanks to the munificence of Mr P. H. Mikkelsen of Odense, the 'ghost' ship of Ladby can still be viewed under its original mound. To anyone who has gazed on the Oseberg ship (pl. xix) and its rich furniture it is something of an experience to see what the skill of excavators has achieved at Ladby. Of the timbers of this rapid boat, 22 metres long but only 3 metres wide, only a few slight traces can be seen, but some 2,000 iron nails are still in position. The mast had long since gone, but iron shroud rings in position on the gunwales showed that it must have been somewhere amidships. The dragon-head prow itself has gone the same way as the hull, but a dozen iron spirals arranged along the crest of a dark marking in the soil show the line of its 'mane' (pl. xxb). Although robbers dragged away the viking before stripping off his finery, the skeletons of eleven horses and the bones of several dogs remain as witness that he was sent on his last voyage with the companionship of his favourite beasts. As for the wooden and textile furnishings of the ship, these must be restored in the imagination nourished with memories of the Oseberg and other ships found under happier conditions. Or one might quote an earlier example, the great open clinker-built rowing-boat of the pagan Anglo-Saxon period from Sutton Hoo, Suffolk. The boat with its rich grave-goods had been placed in a trench and covered over by a mound. The sandy soil had eaten up the wood and preserved the iron, but careful excavation revealed the clench-nails, which, together with the ribs, held the strakes together, as well as the pins that secured the tholes for the oars on to the gunwales (pl. xxa). By observing the metal parts and making the most of the dis-colorations of the soil, it was possible to reconstruct the plan of this boat almost as well as if the wooden hull itself had been preserved.

What is true of larger monuments applies equally to smaller objects: implements and weapons tend to lose their handles, shafts, and sheaths, beads their strings, and clothing everything but its fastening pins or buttons. Sometimes it is possible to recover in the form of a hollow cast or a soil-stain the actual shape of what has perished. Failing this, observation of the exact positions of surviving parts will sometimes be equally effective; this applies with special force to grave groups where the relationship of ornaments to skeletons or their surviving earth-stains will sometimes give the clue to their use. It cannot, indeed, be urged too often or too strongly that in excavation the positions in which objects are found and the records made of them are liable to be of far more importance than the objects themselves.

SEQUENCE

Whenever settlement sites or burial places were used over any length of time they were liable to undergo a process of development which it is the archaeologist's business to unravel. He must try and find out, not only what a hill-fort or a burial mound looked like in its final form, but the stages through which it passed in its life's history. In so doing his guiding principle will be the elementary geological law of super-position, by which younger deposits overlie older ones.

Caves. This is exemplified in its simplest form in the excava-tion of inhabited caves or rock-shelters. Having ascertained by preliminary trial trenches the whereabouts of the richest deposit —normally in or near the cave mouth—and having established the general sequence of deposits, it is then a comparatively simple matter to remove them one by one, and so obtain a series of industries from the youngest to the oldest immediately above bed-rock (pl. xxi). Theoretically, that is, it is a simple matter. Actually every cave will turn out to have its own peculiar snags and difficulties, not to speak of the discomforts of working in a confined space, not unseldom exaggerated by damp and darkness. One has to beware against the disturbing effects of burrowing animals, of early man himself, and of previous explorers. Careful removal of badly mixed deposits layer by layer would be a serious waste of time, while their interpretation as a true stratigraphical sequence would land anyone in a difficult position. To obtain really definitive results the aim should be to account for the formation of the cave and of all the various deposits that fill it, and then to establish the precise context in this natural sequence of the successive appearances of early man.

The ideal cave is one in which many archaeological levels are present, each being clearly separated from its neighbour by undisturbed natural deposits, preferably stalagmite or some other hard substance calculated to discourage burrowing animals. These conditions were perhaps better fulfilled at Castillo, near Santander in North Spain, than anywhere else. When first discovered the cave was so filled with debris that a normal person could hardly stand upright; early man had lived in it until his rubbish had, together with natural accumulations, reached very nearly to the ceiling of what had once been a lofty cave. When Obermaier and Wernert and their assistants removed the contents layer by layer (1910–14), they were gratified to find almost every stage of western European prehistory represented from Eneolithic down to Lower Palaeolithic. In all they removed deposits to a maximum depth of fifty-nine feet. The final section was as follows:

ENEOLITHIC	Modern
	Stalagmite
	Eneolithic
	Stalagmite
MESOLITHIC	Azilian
	Stalagmite

	Upper Magdalenian
	Loam
	Lower Magdalenian
	Loam
	Solutrian
	Loam
UPPER PALAEOLITHIC	Upper Aurignacian A
	Loam
	Upper Aurignacian B
	Loam
	Upper Aurignacian C
	Loam
	Middle Aurignacian
	Stalagmite

	Mousterian A
MIDDLE PALAEOLITHIC	*Loam*
	Mousterian B
	Stalagmite
LOWER PALAEOLITHIC	Acheulian
	Loamy breccia
	Limestone rock

(After Burkitt)

Tells. Somewhat analogous conditions exist at the sites of many of the earliest villages and cities of the higher civilizations of south-eastern Europe and the Near East, inhabited through centuries and even millennia, often with little break. But, whereas caves were visited sporadically by food-gathering groups between whose visits geological deposits often had time to form, the material composing the tells consists almost entirely of the debris of settled communities. That is not to say that settlement on such sites was entirely uninterrupted; on the contrary, it is episodes in their history, destruction by fire, or razing by an enemy that give the clearest evidence for making divisions in their stratigraphy. After a major disaster the site would be prepared for rebuilding by levelling the debris and so a new city might arise on the ruins of the old. This, together with the day-to-day accumulation of rubbish (at Troy some of the houses had as many as nine superimposed floors, entailing a raising of the roof—one alternative to sweeping the floor!), caused the gradual heightening of level and the formation of the mound. Where a site was fortified its growth naturally entailed successive rebuildings of the defences, often on entirely new alignments. It is by using such indications as these, together with superimposed buildings, layers of burning and of refuse, and the like, that Dörpfeld was able to distinguish the famous 'Nine Cities of Troy'.

In excavating a huge site like Ur it is naturally impracticable to remove the whole mound, although, as the R.A.F. airphotograph taken early in 1930 shows (pl. xxii), Sir Leonard Woolley and his associates managed to uncover an astonishing extent of building. By planning the uppermost level of the Temenos, digging down and planning again, they were able to trace the modifications and rebuildings of the chief temples up to 530 B.C. For four years much labour was expended on the excavation of the Royal Cemetery (3500–3200 B.C.), some of the principal tombs of which yielded a wonderfully rich assemblage of grave-goods. But most impressive from the stratigraphical viewpoint was the shaft sunk down to the pre-flood level.[1] The full significance of the section so revealed can be appreciated from the fact that it was dug at a point where the deposits of the historical period had been eroded. Yet approximately fifty-nine feet of archaeologically productive deposit

[1] *Ant. J.*, 1930, p. 329.

had accumulated prior to the First Dynasty of Ur (3100 B.C. ± 100 years). The following gives a simplified version of the succession:

Depths	Strata	Correlations
	Ground-level	
+17 m.	Building levels	1st Dynasty
	A ⎫	
	B ⎬	Royal tombs
	C ⎭	
	D	
	E	
	F	
	G	
	H	
+10 m.	Ash stratum with successive kilns and quantities of sherds: 11·2 to 12·2 m. to 4·5 m.	Jemdet Nasr al-'Ubaid II–III
+4·5 m.	Flood stratum of clean water-laid sand, with graves sunk from higher levels.	
+1·5 m.	Refuse layer with habitations of brick and wattle and daub.	
o	Sea-level. Mud with 'scatter' of sherds from neighbouring island.	al-'Ubaid I
—1 m.	Stiff green clay with reeds: the floor of the marsh.	

'Terps'. Settlement mounds or tells are a commonplace feature of Greek and Middle Danubian prehistory, but seem to call for no special comment. The 'terps' and 'wurts' of the low-lying coastal fringe from North Holland to western Schleswig-Holstein are, however, of rather special interest, since they seem to have been heaped up by throwing clay, turves, or dung over the abandoned level, possibly to offset the effects of subsidence. One result of their rather special position has been that in excavating them widely varying methods have to be used. For the uppermost levels it is a case of shaving the soil to discover colour markings; lower down traces of timber-work will survive; while at the base the excavator has only to clear the floors and lower courses of well-preserved timber houses and barns. The most famous of these sites yet investigated is the large terp on a fifth of which the present village of Ezinge stands. Dr A. E. van Giffen, who dug part of the site between 1931 and 1934, was able to distinguish six main phases from the top downwards:[1]

I a b } Clay.		Thirteenth cent.–Ottonian Early Med. and Late Carolingian
c	Burnt layer with pit dwellings.	Anglo-Saxon
II	Clay with dung on the outer margin. Large rectangular houses.	Merovingian–Late Roman
III	Clay. Long houses divided into three by two rows of posts.	Early Roman–Late La Tène
IV	Dung. Similar, but smaller houses.	Late–Middle La Tène
V	Primary mound of turf. Numerous small rectangular houses.	Middle–Early La Tène
VI	Settlement on virgin soil. Dwelling-house and pile-built granaries enclosed by fence.	Early La Tène

The original mound, a reconstructed view of which is given in fig. 15, only attained a height of 1·2 m. above the general level of the water-meadows and did not exceed 35 m. in diameter. As the terp grew it covered a progressively bigger area, until by the thirteenth century it reached a height of 5·5 m. and a diameter of 450 m. Some idea of the conditions revealed by excavation can be obtained from Plate XXIII, taken near the centre of the Ezinge site on which

[1] *Germania*, 1936, p. 40.

the church of the modern village now stands. The lowermost
house (A) belongs to phase VI. The low section exposed immediately behind it gives the thickness of the original turf mound,
on which were built the houses of period V (B). In the right
background the upper levels of the terp can be seen in section (c).

Open settlement sites. Over the most of western Europe prehistoric sites from the Neolithic and later periods tended to

FIG. 15
Reconstruction of Iron Age 'terp' village, Ezinge, Holland

develop on rather different lines, through the enlargement,
diminution, elaboration, or simplification of their plans. In
seeking to establish the main stages in their growth the archaeologist will not, indeed, neglect stratigraphical evidence, but this
he will utilize mainly as a subsidiary to his study of the general
layout of the site. For instance, the pronounced kink in the
outline of Maiden Castle, Dorset, would suggest to anyone
looking at the plan for the first time a stage in its history when
the hill-fort was more or less confined to the eastern knoll of
the hill-top. The low bank joining the two kinks would confirm this impression in the case of anyone visiting the site. It is
not surprising that, when Dr (now Sir) R. E. M. Wheeler started

digging in 1934, this was one of the first things he did.[1] He was soon able to show that the earliest Iron Age settlers had contented themselves with enclosing by a single bank and ditch the eastern knoll of the site, some 16 acres in extent. Later the enclosed area was extended to embrace the western knoll as well, a total extent of some 45 acres. Finally, the site was brought to its present formidable appearance through the multiplication of its defences and the elaboration of its entrances. In working out such a development an excavator is able to date individual ditches in terms of the pottery recovered from their primary silting; the sequences of ditches he can sometimes confirm by observing how they intersect; cross-sections through ramparts will give him the main phases in their construction; intersections of post-holes and the pottery types contained in them will enable him to evolve the history of the entrances; and superimposed hut-floors and intersecting store-pits in the interior will help to round off the picture. Thus he will avail himself of such direct stratigraphical evidence as comes to hand, but running like a thread through his whole work is the pottery, which will often allow him to date features never coming into direct contact with one another.

Barrows. In digging barrows the first interments met with will generally prove to belong to a late phase, having been inserted from the surface at a time when the mound had been appropriated as a convenient cemetery. Scores of Late Bronze Age cremations may be a trial indeed to the conscientious excavator who though anxious to get to the core of the barrow yet feels obliged to record them with scrupulous care. When he does reach it, he may find it stratified in such a way as to imply two or three phases of construction. Often the original barrow will have been quite a small mound; then, when later burials were made, a thick blanket of soil would be thrown over it to create a more imposing appearance. Where material for the mound was obtained from the ditch, increases in the size

---

[1] *Ant. J.*, 1935, pp. 265–75; 1936, pp. 265–83; 1937, pp. 261–82.

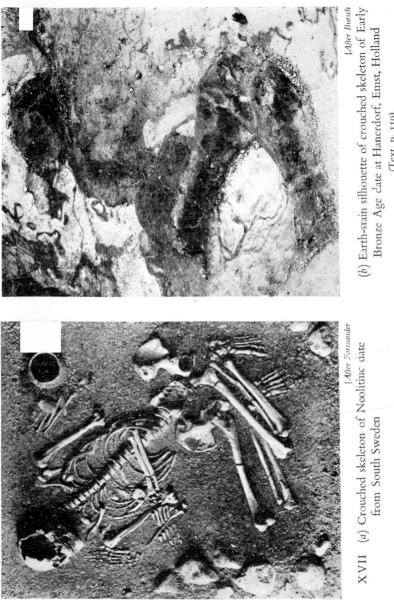

[*After Bursch*]

(b) Earth-stain silhouette of crouched skeleton of Early Bronze Age date at Hanerdorf, Emst, Holland

(Text, p. 119)

[*After Forssander*]

XVII (a) Crouched skeleton of Neolithic date from South Sweden

[*After Hatt*

XVIII Early Iron Age house at Skørbæk, Jutland, showing wall-slots, post-holes, and paving

(Text, pp. 120, 201)

XIX Viking ship at Oseberg, Norway, during excavation
(Text, pp. 111, 120)
Note some of the stone packing still in position

XX (a) Anglo-Saxon ship, Sutton-Hoo; port side showing iron rivets, thole pins and impressions of planking (*Ant. J.* xx (1940), pl. xxxiia)

(Text, p. 121)

(b) 'Ghost' of Viking ship at Ladby, Denmark; showing prow with iron bolts, iron 'mane' and anchor

(Text, p. 120)

XXI Section of cave deposits at Et-Tabun, Mount
Carmel, Palestine

B, Upper Levalloiso-Mousterian; *C* and *D*, Lower Levalloiso-
Mousterian; *E*, Micoquian; *F*, Upper Acheulian; *G*, Tayacian
(Text, p. 122)

XXII   Air-photograph of excavations at Ur
A, The Ziggurat; *B*, Cemetery site; *C*, Pit sunk to pre-flood level
(Text, pp. 108, 124)

XXIII   Excavations in the 'terp' at Ezinge, Holland

(Text, pp. 105, 126, 201)

Houses of phases V and VI, separated by a low turf mound; in background section through deposits of phases I–IV

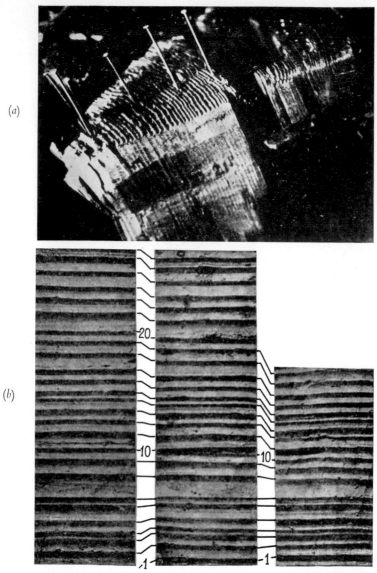

XXIV (a) 3,200-year-old tree growth-rings from *Sequoia* pine,
California

(Text, p. 159)

(b) Varved clay deposits at three Finnish sites

(Text, p. 157)

of the barrow would lead to the excavation of a new one and the covering of the old. This, together with old surface lines in the material of a barrow, will give the excavator a useful clue when it comes to trying to work out the sequence of burials. When a number of interments are found in the primary part of the barrow it is not always easy to demonstrate their relative ages. The Neolithic single-grave barrows of Central Jutland are exceptional in that burials were normally made one above the other. As a rule one has merely to work upon certain probabilities. For instance, burials on or below original ground surface are likely to be older than those higher up in the material of the mound, while, among the former, that at the centre is likely to be the oldest. Barrow-digging, like so many other things in life, was very much simpler for our forefathers than for us. For them it was a matter of a few hours' digging to penetrate to the heart of a barrow and extract its richest grave-goods. For us, the excavation of a large round barrow, removing its material down to bed-rock, may involve many weeks of hard work and careful surveying, and cost many hundreds of pounds. The 'loot' obtained by a modern excavator may not notably exceed that of his predecessors, but the success of an excavation should not be measured in terms of material things: scientific excavation is a road to knowledge.

Megalithic tombs. Megalithic tombs should be excavated in light of their use over long periods of time. Occasionally successive burials will be found stratified, sometimes divided into layers by stone paving, but more often many of the earlier ones have been thrown out of the tomb. When this has happened the tip, if located, may provide a useful sequence. Only too often, however, the excavator will find the most recent burial in good order, the rest in a confused mass; and even then he cannot be sure how many of the earliest generations have been swept clean away.

Cemeteries. Flat cemeteries of inhumation graves and cremation urn-fields pose much the same problem as do open settlement sites. Occasionally one grave will truncate another, but as a rule it is the horizontal spread of a cemetery that gives the best clues. Once the original core can be located by the occurrence of early grave-goods and the general line of its

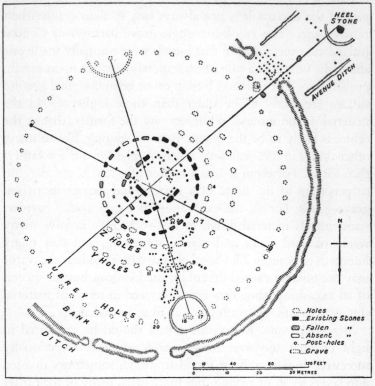

FIG. 16
Plan of Stonehenge

expansion established by similar means, it is possible to obtain a fair idea of the relative age of individual graves, even when provided with no closely datable grave-goods. But to do this it is necessary to excavate and to plan the entire cemetery.

'Henges'. Let me conclude by considering that best known of all English prehistoric monuments, Stonehenge.

The problem facing the excavators of Stonehenge has always been how to disentangle the sequence of events that brought the monument to its present form (fig. 16). This they have solved by studying its plan in conjunction with such stratigraphical evidence as they were able to recover. The results of their labours, together with the chief evidence on which their conclusions are based, have recently been summarized in a book[1] which gives an admirable insight into the process of modern archaeological detection.

By contrast with the immense antiquarian literature that has grown up round Stonehenge during recent centuries the pages which set out the conclusions of scientific research are few indeed. To read them is to appreciate the reality of the progress made in the investigation of the past by means of excavation and field observation.

[1] R. J. C. Atkinson, *Stonehenge*, London, 1956.

V

CHRONOLOGY

Since prehistory is a historical discipline in the sense that it deals with events and developments in time, it follows that an adequate system of chronology is a basic necessity. Until the material evidence has been tabulated it is quite impossible to deduce what it means in terms of prehistory. Indeed the much greater length of prehistory and the fact that it witnessed changes of far greater magnitude than those recorded by history only serves to emphasize the overriding need for an adequate chronology. Yet the mere fact of being prehistoric implies an absence of calendrical dates, which only literate societies are capable of bequeathing to posterity. One of our most urgent tasks is to find a substitute. As a beginning we may set out to establish a bare sequence of cultural assemblages in each particular area, dating each in relation to one another and to the environmental background, and then by means of synchronisms to extend the range of the relative chronology over more extensive territories. Yet our ultimate aim must always be an absolute chronology based on solar years, if only because this forms the readiest means of synchronizing events in far distant areas.

The extent to which the prehistorian depends on relative chronology has its drawbacks, though in practice these are not always so serious as might appear. We become so used in ordinary life to exact dates that there is some possibility of forgetting that the difference between relative and absolute dates is less one of kind than of degree, the degree of attainable precision. Obviously by using dates of years, months, and days it is possible to define events far more closely in time than when one has to rely upon the cruder scale afforded by changes in fashion or technology. But the fineness of the scale should have reference to what it is proposed to measure. A year, a month, a day, or even a few hours can make a world of difference to the interpretation placed on events of modern history, but they have no more relevance to the dating of a Lower Palaeolithic culture than a centimetre has to the measurement of Mount Everest. It may indeed be doubted whether even in the later prehistoric periods anything more is normally attainable or necessary than accuracy to within a human generation. One has after all to remember that we are not dealing with the particularities of history so much as with its regularities: we are concerned as prehistorians above all with communities rather than with individuals, and as a rule with processes and trends rather than events.

A further point that needs to be emphasized in relation to chronology is that in this, as in all aspects of his subject, the prehistorian is by no means limited to archaeological data. He disposes of two main sources of chronological information, those provided respectively by human activities and natural processes. Most of the former is archaeological in character, being based on the nature of artifacts and on the circumstances under which they are found, although in the case of secondary prehistoric groups living on the periphery of civilized communities historical sources can often be brought to bear on chronological problems. On the other hand, geochronology, the chronology based on the natural changes recorded in the geological sequence, depends upon many branches of natural science, notably geology, seismology, astronomy, physics, climatology, palaeontology, and palaeobotany. Thus, to obtain an adequate chronological framework for human prehistory involves co-operation between many distinct kinds of science and scholarship. In this sense the quest for prehistoric chronology is symptomatic of the whole adventure of prehistoric research.

(A) RELATIVE CHRONOLOGY

TYPOLOGY

The fact that industrial and art forms are subject to evolutionary processes is a great aid when it comes to arranging them in sequence. Sometimes, as for instance with the metal axe of the European Bronze Age, evolution is dictated mainly by

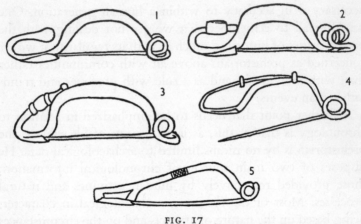

FIG. 17

The evolution of La Tène safety-pins

considerations of improved efficiency, both in production and in use, but even in this case there were alternative lines of development, and the choice of these was culturally determined. Thus, whereas flanged axes cast in bivalve moulds normally succeeded flat ones cast in open ones, the smiths then had a choice of methods of improving the hafting: they might by developing the stop-ridge and casting the lower portion of the implement solid produce the palstave; or by magnifying the middle portions of the flanges and wrapping them round the forked end of the haft form winged axes; or, again, by adopting core-casting, turn out socketed axes, so saving metal and making it possible to avoid forking the haft. In the case of objects of adornment, on the other hand, fashion divorced from functional efficiency might be the sole factor in typological evolution, though even here there is often an element of practical convenience, as for instance with the La Tène fibulae in which the foot, from standing clear of the bow and so affording a possible snag for catching material, joined and ultimately became an integral part of it (fig. 17).

FIG. 18
British coins: series showing derivation from Greek prototype

Very often typological development took the form of devolution or degeneration. One of the best instances of this is afforded by the earliest native coinage of Gaul and Britain. The derivation of a whole series of native coins from the *stater* of Philip II of Macedon was first advanced by Sir John Evans in his lecture on the 'Evolution of British Coins from Philippi' delivered to the Numismatic Society as long ago as 1849 and later elaborated in his standard work on *Ancient British Coins*. In the hands of artificers, to whom the naturalistic rendering of Philip's head had no particular significance other than as a mere mark of identification, the design rapidly disintegrated: certain elements, notably the garland and fringe of curls, were seized upon, but the actual face soon disappeared completely (fig. 18). Similarly, the charioteer on the reverse, originally shown with wings, was early reduced to a meaningless blob; his chariot survived as a wheel, at first spoked, but in time rendered by a single dot; and his steeds were soon reduced to a single creature, which in turn disintegrated into full elongated strokes and a number of irregular dots. By noting the progress of this degeneration, Evans was able to devise a chronological sequence. It is interesting to note that Evans was fully aware of its analogies in biology, as we see in the following quotation: 'I attempted to apply the principles of "evolution" and "natural selection" to numismatic inquiries; and, when, ten years afterwards, Darwin's great work on the origin of species was published, I found that I had been approaching the study of barbaric art on much the same lines.'

Again it was the degeneration of wavy-ledge handles on pottery buried with the dead, from functional elements into mere decorative squiggles, that suggested to Flinders Petrie the possibility of devising a system of Sequence Dates, by means of which he was able to arrange in chronological order the very large numbers of pre-dynastic graves that he excavated in Egypt and so build up the first framework for Egyptian prehistory.

It is not always easy when confronted with a typological series to determine the direction in which development has proceeded, to determine in other words whether one is dealing with progressive evolution or with a series of degeneration. Indeed some of the great archaeological controversies have hinged on this very point. One of the most important of these concerns the relative dating chamber tombs in western and south-western Europe. Because simple dolmenic structures had been shown to appear earlier in Denmark than the more elaborate passage-graves, it was assumed that a similar sequence obtained in Iberia: so the small closed chamber or dolmen was placed at the head of the series and from this more elaborate forms were derived, first chambers with incipient passages, then great passage-graves, and, finally, tombs constructed with corbelled vaults or cut out of the living rock. Advocates of this progressive elaboration in tomb-structure were also able to point to a parallel increase in the wealth of grave-goods. Both the tombs themselves and their contents seemed to speak of a progressive increase in wealth and elaboration. Yet modern opinion is almost unanimous in reversing this apparent sequence, which holds good only on the assumption that the development was indigenous. Once accept the notion that the whole phenomenon of chamber-tombs marks the impact of higher cultures from outside, and the whole sequence must be overturned: the elaborate tombs and the rich grave-goods representing exotic influence will be placed first in the sequence and the other simpler and poorer forms successively later. Incidentally, this provides an admirable example of the need to view local sequences in the light of considerations drawn from the broadest possible field. The danger of basing broad conclusions on local observations stands out again and again in the history of prehistoric research.

Associations. Typological development carries more weight when supported by the evidence of associated finds. When certain forms at analogous stages of evolution are consistently found together, and when more evolved stages of these forms are likewise found consistently in association, the reliability of any sequence based on a theoretical line of evolutionary development is sensibly increased, subject always to the broader considerations previously noted.

The chronology of the European Bronze Age has been built up almost entirely on a study of associated finds or hoards. Hoards of course differ greatly in their chronological value. Objects found in hoards which represent the equipment of an individual, whether buried for safety during his lifetime or placed with him as grave-goods for use in the next world, are likely to be in contemporaneous use, although allowance must be made for heirlooms. Merchants' hoards, the stock-in-trade of travelling salesmen, can certainly be taken as comprising

objects of the same age. Votive hoards vary in value: where
only a few objects, apparently deposited at the same time, are
in question, these can be regarded as contemporary with one
another, but temple offerings, for example, may represent
accumulations over several generations. Founders' hoards,
which are particularly common in the latter part of the period,
comprise essentially scrap-metal and are therefore likely to
include objects of varying dates. Before attempting to draw
chronological conclusions from a hoard, therefore, it is important to determine its character and the conditions under which
it was deposited in the soil.

GEOLOGICAL SEQUENCE[1]

The evolution of the geographical setting of prehistoric man
worked out by geologists provides important clues to relative
chronology, provided that archaeological objects can be found
in their true position in the stratigraphical sequence. The basic
concept of geological stratigraphy is sufficiently simple, but this
does not mean that it is easy to apply or that sections can be
interpreted from book knowledge or by rule of thumb. The
geologist himself, confronted by a purely natural succession,
interprets what he sees with caution, in the knowledge that the
various strata may not always occur in the order in which they
were originally laid down and that some of them may have
disappeared more or less completely. The prehistorian, being
concerned with the products of human societies, has to take
account of an additional complication in the behaviour of men.
The effect of this depends mainly on the economic effectiveness
of the societies in question, but even for the most primitive
communities it cannot be left entirely out of account.

Climatic fluctuations. Even the student of the Old Stone Age
needs to concern himself with the precise circumstances under
which artifacts have come to be incorporated in the deposits in

[1] For general reference see F. E. Zeuner, *Dating the Past*, 2nd edition,
London, 1950.

which he finds them. Broadly speaking, the chronological framework of the older periods of prehistory is provided by fluctuations of Pleistocene climate as these are reflected in the geological record, whether in the form of traces of former extensions or contractions of ice-sheets or of variations of rainfall of pluvial or interpluvial status, or of changes in the relative levels of land and sea, or of interlocked changes in plant and animal life. Although it is unlikely that any particular thread of inquiry will provide a complete answer it is often possible by combining several to build up a sequence of changes, which in so far as they relate to world-wide fluctuations of climate can be used to synchronize events in widely separated territories. Yet it is important to remember that these fluctuations are likely to produce widely varying results in different areas, so that the sequences established by Quaternary research are valid in detail only for the areas in which they have been worked out. Widespread synchronisms can only be effected by means of patient correlations between sequences established in intervening provinces. This makes it all the more necessary to obtain as fine a stratigraphy as possible in each region and at the same time to ensure that phases of human settlement are dovetailed as accurately as possible into the natural sequences.

The fact that neither of these conditions can easily be fulfilled for the very earliest periods of prehistory is not so serious as it might seem because cultural change proceeded at so slow a tempo. Even so, prehistorians have ceased to be content with locating a few individual specimens of flint- or stone-work in geological sections, specimens which may have been eroded from more than one deposit before being incorporated in the one in which ultimately found. The aim is now recognized to be the discovery of complete industries in their original position. This is likely to be extremely difficult in territories greatly disturbed by glaciation, and this is one reason why Africa has proved so important as a field of research on the earlier phases of the Old Stone Age. Examples of the kind of discovery on which progress depends are those made by the Cambridge prehistorians, Leakey, Caton-Thompson, and latterly Desmond Clark, on the shores of the old Pleistocene lake at Olorgesailie, Kenya, in the fossil springs in the Kharga Oasis, Egypt, and in the neighbourhood of the Kalambo Falls on the frontier of Northern Rhodesia and Tanganyika; at such sites we have the impression of making real contact with the makers of hand-axes and other early tools and definitely fixing their context in the geochronological sequence. In the glaciated areas of the north temperate zone the best hope is offered by discovering settlements by Interglacial lakes, such as that at Hoxne made famous by John Frere's discovery of Lower Palaeolithic hand-axes towards the close of the eighteenth century and lately re-explored by Dr Charles McBurney: the flints from the bed of this old lake, fresh and sharp and including waste material, can certainly be taken as marking a correct stratigraphical level, even though the actual settlement on the old lake margin has presumably been eroded.

Fluorine tests.[1] The problem of determining the true stratigraphical horizon of loose finds arises in a particularly acute form in the case of human skeletal remains found in quarrying deposits of high antiquity. Reliable traces of Lower Palaeolithic man are so rare that any new find is of commensurate value, but the chances are that such will be made by chance under circumstances that do not allow the overlying section to be studied. How then can it be decided for certain whether the fossil is really of the age its depth in the section would suggest, or whether it had been inserted, for instance, in the form of a burial? Once again science comes to the rescue, this time in the form of the fluorine test originally devised by a Frenchman, A. Carnot, in 1893, and recently perfected by Dr Kenneth Oakley. The method depends on the fact that the fluorine content of bones increases with their age, so that in any given

---

[1] K. P. Oakley, 'The fluorine-dating method', *Yearbook of Physical Anthropology*, v, 44–52, New York, 1951.

section the bones from upper levels ought to show less fluorine than those from lower levels. If therefore the bones in question are tested together with a series from successive levels in the parent section, it should be possible to determine from their fluorine content whether they were in fact in their correct stratigraphical position. Naturally this only holds good for a particular site, since the rate of fluorine formation varies in different localities. What matters is that examination of bones from any particular section should quickly reveal any discrepancy in the series, and allow one to determine the status of any particular specimen. Thus Dr Oakley was able to show that the Swanscombe skull really can be accepted as belonging to the Great Interglacial deposit in which it was supposedly found and as contemporary with hand-axes of Middle Acheulian type, whereas the skeleton found near by at Galley Hill showed so much less fluorine than bones included in the stratum from which it was supposed to come that it must be interpreted as a burial of younger age inserted from a higher level.

Changes of sea-level. The fact that land- and sea-levels have changed frequently and sometimes markedly during the Quaternary period offers another opportunity for dating human settlements. Some of the most important causes for these changes were the direct result of the spread and contraction of the Pleistocene ice-sheets, but the relationship between sea levels and glaciations is for various reasons complex. Two main factors were at work and these operated with varying intensities in different areas. Thus the eustatic factor, due to the alternate withdrawal and release of water as ice-sheets grew and melted, affected all the oceans and open seas of the world, whereas the isostatic fall and rise of the earth's crust under the weight of ice was restricted to territories subject to glaciation. The geographical outcome depended on the interaction of these two variables: in areas like the Mediterranean only the former operated, and in Central Scandinavia on the other hand only the latter, whereas in regions marginal to the Pleistocene

ice-sheets, such as South Scandinavia was in the final stages of
the Late Glacial period, the outcome might be a highly intricate
series of oscillations. Further, there are reasons to suppose that
the situation has been complicated locally by tectonic disturbances, which are reflected, for example, in distortions of the
ancient shore-lines of the Mediterranean. Even so, in areas free
from isostatic displacement there is an alluring prospect of
being able to effect correlations between traces of early man
and of his culture in widely separated parts of the world by
observing the relationship of ancient sites and sea-levels. In
areas subject to glaciation and by consequence to isostatic displacement the problem is more difficult, though the minor
oscillations found in some of these are capable, when they have
been worked out, of yielding a correspondingly fine chronological grid. In such regions it is of the utmost importance that
the altimetric levels of archaeological sites should be expressed
in terms of their relation to ancient strand-lines, since these will
be found to slope quite steeply towards the heart of the old
ice-sheet: consequently, prehistoric sites at the same height
above modern sea-level might differ widely in age, as shown
on our diagram illustrating the situation of sites of the Finnmarkian Stone Age culture in northern Norway (fig. 19). For
obvious reasons most of the evidence relates to periods when
sea-levels were higher than today, but excavations below sea-
level or finds dredged from the sea may yield occasional
evidence of high value.

In seeking to relate archaeological sites to ancient strand-lines
the main reliance has necessarily to be placed on situation and
stratigraphy, even though indications that sea-food was consumed on a large scale may often provide strong corroboration,
more especially when this takes the form of extensive shell-
mounds situated on obvious beaches. Where, as on the Litorina
coasts of Denmark, there were numerous oscillations of sea-
level, involving repeated minor transgressions of the sea, it is
important to obtain the most accurate correlations between

human settlement and the geological sequence. As in the case of bog stratigraphy the best results can be got from studying marginal scatter round a site, in this case noting the context of debris in sediments dating from the various transgressions. A classic demonstration of this method was given by Therkel Mathiassen at Dyrholmen in East Jutland, where he succeeded in attaching three phases in the development of the Ertebølle culture to their respective transgressions of the Litorina Sea. It

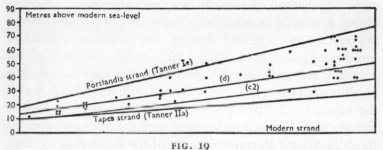

FIG. 19

Relation of Finnmarkian Stone Age sites to ancient strand-lines, North Norway

not infrequently happened that, as on the coast of Italy, caves eroded by the sea were occupied by early man as soon as they were available and in such cases their stratigraphy sometimes makes it possible to fix precisely the context of phases of human occupation in relation to changes of sea-level, and in consequence to Pleistocene chronology. Under favourable conditions, where the land gained progressively on the sea and sufficient sites attributable to coastal hunter-fishers are available, it has been possible for Swedish and Finnish prehistorians to distinguish fine subdivisions in the sphere of culture; for example, by analysing the altimetric values for the occurrences of different pottery styles, as Europaeus did for the Finnish dwelling-place culture.

Vegetation and pollen analysis.[1] Among the most sensitive

[1] K. Faegri and J. Iversen, *Text-book of Modern Pollen Analysis*, Copenhagen, 1950; H. Godwin, *The History of the British Flora*, Cambridge, 1956.

indicators of ecological change is vegetation, which depends directly on the climate and soil of the habitat and itself provides the essential organic basis for other forms of life, including man. By means of the technique of pollen analysis, first developed for forest trees by the Swedish scientist Lennart von Post in 1916, and since 1937 extended to the whole range of pollen-liberating vegetation, it is possible to recover a remarkably complete record of fluctuations in the composition of vegetation. The method rests on the fact that pollen has a surprising ability to survive in identifiable form once it has been incorporated in an unaerated deposit. By counting a standard number of grains from samples taken at intervals throughout a section and analysing the composition of each sample it is possible to obtain a clear picture of the changes through which the vegetation has passed while the deposit was in process of formation. Pollen analysis has been used to distinguish deposits from the various Interglacial phases of the Pleistocene Ice Age, but the most detailed results have so far been obtained from sediments in the beds of lakes formed by the melting of the Late Glacial ice-sheets. These sediments reflect the final fluctuations of Late Glacial climate, the progressive amelioration that marked the establishment of temperate conditions, and the deterioration that occurred during the final phases of the pre-historic period. By defining crucial stages in this progressive development palaeobotanists have succeeded in zoning the deposits of this final phase of the Quaternary period in such a way as to provide a chronological yardstick for students of human settlement. A generalized diagram illustrating the zonation of vegetational history worked out by Knud Jessen for Jutland is given by fig. 20, but it may be emphasized that it has generally been found possible locally to subdivide each major zone and so to obtain a correspondingly fine time-scale.

Although climatic change has determined the main changes in the composition of vegetation for the Pleistocene period as a whole, the effect of human activity must always be taken

account of locally, and with the introduction of farming this
ultimately became a major factor. The possibilities this affords
of reconstructing details of the economic life of prehistoric man
will be discussed in a later chapter (p. 177). The point to be
made here is that in so far as the effects of human activity are

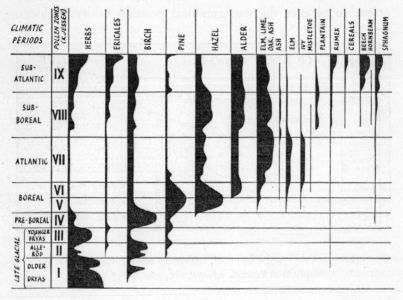

FIG. 20
Diagram showing development of vegetation in Jutland since the
retreating ice-sheet uncovered the land

registered directly in pollen diagrams they are automatically
keyed into the geochronological system, once the diagrams
have been adequately zoned. For example, the fact that the
Middle Acheulian flints from the Interglacial lake deposits at
Hoxne coincide stratigraphically with an abrupt decline in the
pollen of forest trees and a corresponding increase in that of
grasses and herbs, a change which points strongly to human
activity, gives convincing support to the view that these were
found in their primary geological context. Again, the fact that

the effects of farming are recognizable in the pollen diagrams
means that it is relatively simple to date the spread of the new
economy by reference to the pollen zonation.

Nevertheless, if full advantage is to be gained from this
zonation, it is necessary to key into it an adequate range of
archaeological material as accurately as possible. It is not sufficient to observe the stratigraphical position of living-floors,

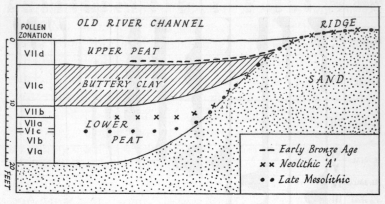

FIG. 21
Diagram showing relation of 'settlement scatter' to post-Glacial
deposits at Peacock's Farm, Shippea Hill, Cambs.

since the mere fact that a surface could be occupied implies a
certain break in the geological succession. What is needed is
archaeological material incorporated accidentally in geological
deposits accumulating at the time, and such evidence is most
likely to be obtained by investigating natural deposits in the
immediate neighbourhood of a settlement from which waste
materials like bones, flints, and sherds were discarded in
antiquity. The ideal is a site occupied more than once and in
immediate proximity to deposits that accumulated during the
period of occupation and have since remained unaerated. Such
a one was a sand ridge flanking one side of an ancient river
channel on Peacock's Farm, Shippea Hill, in the North

Cambridgeshire fens. Here indications of three phases of occupation were found on the surface of the crest of the ridge, and borings showed that some twenty feet of post-Glacial deposit had accumulated in the channel, and that the ridge shelved sufficiently rapidly to offer a good chance of finding occupational scatter in place. Excavation in due course revealed three levels of rubbish neatly stratified in polliniferous deposits (fig. 21). The correctness of our findings was checked by microscopic examination of samples from the section. It was found, for instance, that the levels at which Late Mesolithic and Early Neolithic material occurred coincided with thin sandy levels in the peat, caused by down-wash from the ridge, presumably associated with disturbance of the vegetation-cover during phases of human occupation, and that the Early Bronze Age level corresponded with a temporary dry phase when conditions for settlement were particularly favourable.

Bog stratigraphy, though it is capable of yielding results of the utmost value, is not without difficulties of interpretation. For instance, it has been demonstrated by an intensive study of the stratigraphy of the Danish bog of Aamosen that Stone Age hunters sometimes camped on what were in effect floating islands, great rafts of peat that became temporarily detached through a rise in the level of the lake: debris from their occupation would accumulate in the surrounding deposits, but some of it would find its way under the raft, only to become trapped when the 'island' sank with a lowering of lake-level. One has only to imagine a repetition of such a process to appreciate the dangers of accepting at their face-value stratigraphical successions obtained from borings, or from imperfectly studied sections. Again, the possibility that objects may have sunk from a higher level has to be reckoned with, but this can be avoided by concentrating on settlement scatter comprising objects of widely varying gravity as well as by minute study of the section itself. In the case of hoards, which can be assumed to have been buried, the problem is to decide the level from which this has been carried out: circumstances of discovery usually mean that the overlying section has already been removed, but it is occasionally possible by taking samples from sockets or cores and testing the age of these by pollen analysis to discover the true stratigraphical context of a hoard.

One of the most successful applications of pollen analysis has been the dating of numerous finds of wooden sledge-runners and skis from bogs of Finland and Sweden. Since they are relatively light and can be assumed to have been discarded or lost accidentally while traversing snow-covered marshes, these can safely be accepted as having been found in their true stratigraphical position. By fitting these into the pollen zonation it has been possible to trace the history of the evolution of snow transport and travel from the earliest times. Other features of interest for early transport to be dated by means of pollen analysis include stray canoes and paddles and timber causeways of the type well known from the Somerset levels and from many parts of central and northern Europe.

A recent development, pioneered by Waterbolk in Holland and tried out in England by Dimbleby,[1] is the application of pollen analysis directly to archaeological monuments on ordinary dry ground. This can only be done successfully where the soil is sufficiently acid for pollen grains to survive, and it is particularly unfortunate for British archaeologists that the method is useless for the limestone and chalk formations on which so much early settlement was concentrated. By analysing pollen samples taken from the old ground surface under barrows on the heathlands of the Netherlands, as well as from the original upper side of turves used in the construction of the mounds, Waterbolk has been able to fit the results obtained from individual structures into the sequence obtained from neighbouring bogs, and so to tie them into the local pollen

[1] H. T. Waterbolk, *De Praehistorische Mens en zijn Milieu*, Groningen, 1954; G. W. Dimbleby, 'Pollen analysis as an Aid to the Dating of Prehistoric Monuments', *Proc. Prehist. Soc.*, xx, 231–6.

zonation. Even where there is no bog sufficiently close for reliable connexions to be made, it has been found possible by comparing the proportion of non-tree to tree pollen to place barrows from any particular stretch of country in their correct chronological sequence, since the progress of deforestation, though uneven, has been continuous from the beginning of the Bronze Age down to modern times. When associated grave-goods or radiocarbon dates are available the reliability of such a sequence has been tested and proved, which suggests that with proper safeguards it can be made to yield valid results for monuments not datable by other means. Since many barrows, at any rate in their present state, are in this condition, the value of the method for topographical studies of the Bronze Age settlement of country-sides with acid soils needs no further emphasis.

Animal remains. Although not so sensitive as a rule to minor fluctuations of climate as plants, the larger mammals which provided early man with so much of his food were after all herbivorous, and therefore responsive to major changes in vegetation. The fact that Palaeolithic and Mesolithic man hunted such animals for food is an added reason for finding his settlements and examining his food refuse. Although it has always to be borne in mind that the animal bones from archaeological sites are the product of human selection, the choice of game was itself restricted to what was available, and fluctuations over a long period can be taken, by and large, to reflect ecological changes. With regard to the earliest periods the prehistorian may be aided by observing the progress of the evolution of species, as with the Pleistocene elephants. The unspecialized ancestor of the Pleistocene elephants of Europe, *Elephas meridionalis*, made its appearance in the Pliocene, but already in the course of the Early Pleistocene this had given rise to the modified form *E. meridionalis nesti* Pohlig, from which two ecologically and morphologically distinct species were to develop in the course of the Middle Pleistocene, namely the woodland *E. antiquus*, requiring a temperate to warm climate, and the mammoth (*E. primigenius*) of the steppe and tundra, specialized to cold climatic conditions: none of the intermediate forms survived into the Late Pleistocene, but the mammoth lived on until the end of the Ice Age. For the later stages of the

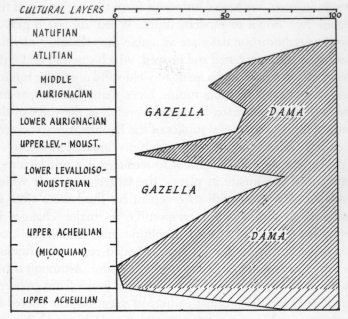

CULTURAL LAYERS

NATUFIAN
ATLITIAN
MIDDLE AURIGNACIAN
LOWER AURIGNACIAN
UPPER LEV.- MOUST.
LOWER LEVALLOISO- MOUSTERIAN
UPPER ACHEULIAN (MICOQUIAN)
UPPER ACHEULIAN

GAZELLA   *DAMA*

GAZELLA

DAMA

FIG. 22

Diagram showing fluctuations in the proportion of grassland *Gazella* and the woodland *Dama* in successive levels of the Wady el-Mughara deposits, Mount Carmel, Palestine

Quaternary period, on the other hand, it is fluctuations in the relative importance of ecologically specialized species that are of most chronological assistance: for instance, in territories periodically affected by glaciation characteristic faunal groups have been equated with stages in the tundra–loess–forest–loess–tundra cycle; and, again, in lands like Palestine, subject to periodic pluvial and interpluvial conditions, one finds evidence for fluctuations in the successive levels of caves inhabited by Palaeolithic man of such diagnostic species as the woodland *Dama* and the grassland *Gazella* (fig. 22).

Critical evidence is often provided by such minor elements in the vertebrate fauna as lemmings, marmots, and jerboa rats, and birds like ptarmigan and arctic grouse may be decisive indicators. The chronological possibilities of molluscs are considerable because many species are adapted to a comparatively restricted environment. The sensitivity of certain marine shell-fish to changes of temperature has rendered them of special value as chronological indicators in the Mediterranean and Baltic areas. Land molluscs are even more relevant since they not only occur in geological deposits containing artifacts, but actually in and under archaeological monuments. Provided account is taken of the artificial conditions at such sites, a critical analysis of the proportions and individual development of different species of snail may throw invaluable light on minor changes of climate, vegetation, and land-utilization and so help to link archaeological monuments to minor stages in the local system of geochronology.

ARCHAEOLOGICAL STRATIGRAPHY[1]

No hard and fast line can of course be drawn between geological and archaeological stratigraphy, since on the one hand every section containing artifacts, however rude, has to some extent been affected by man, even if this is imperceptible or can only be measured by microscopic examination, and on the other every archaeological section, however sophisticated the cultures involved, will enshrine the result of such natural processes as erosion and the accumulation of sediments. All one can say is that in archaeological stratigraphy the human element is stronger, where it is not positively predominant.

With caves it is a nice question under which head these should be placed. To interpret their stratigraphy correctly it is

[1] Sir Mortimer Wheeler, *Archaeology from the Earth*, Chap. IV, London, 1954.

important to know as much as possible about how they were formed and under precisely what natural conditions their fillings accumulated. On the other hand, the prehistorian has to reckon on the human factor: in particular he will want to know why a cave was inhabited when it was, precisely where in the cave or cave-mouth successive groups chose to live, and how far they disturbed traces of their predecessors by inserting burials, making fire-places, or evening out the floor. Much the same problems, though at a higher level, face the explorer of stratified tells: the more advanced their technology, the more likely and the more capable people are to raze, excavate, and in all manner of ways interfere with the stratigraphy of their predecessors. Thus, in interpreting archaeological sections the prehistorian has to take progressively greater account of the activities of prehistoric people, the more advanced these are economically. The mechanical levelling of finds, or even the recording of strata without understanding how the section was formed, is never of much value, but in the case of sites occupied by settled communities it is worse than useless as a source of chronology: thus, to record the sequence of rubbish shot into a disused store-pit within a few minutes is a pointless exercise; but to treat material thrown out of collective tombs or representing the clearance of buildings or the recutting of ditches as though it represents a progressive sequence is likely to lead to 'results' the very opposite of the historical truth.

Further, it has to be remembered that even a sound stratigraphical sequence does no more than provide proof of succession at a particular site. The significance of such can only be assessed when the geographical extent of the culture involved has been ascertained and the succession verified at a number of well-chosen points. One may think of the cultures prevailing over a tract of country at any particular moment as a series of irregular lenses with frilled and undulating edges, so that neighbouring ones might be expected to overlap one another in different order at separate points along their frontiers: until the precise outlines and contours of the lenses have been ascertained one must be cautious of drawing far-ranging conclusions from limited observations. The moral of this is that stratigraphy must consistently be interpreted in relation to geographical distribution, if it is not to give rise to erroneous conclusions. In the case of Neolithic and later cultures, their comparatively limited distribution has made this fairly evident, but from a broad enough perspective it is no less true of the cultures of the Old Stone Age.

GEOGRAPHICAL DISTRIBUTION

In the first flush of evolutionary zeal some of the earlier prehistorians were so preoccupied with establishing sequences, that they did not always concern themselves with the geographical extent of the cultures which they found in stratigraphical succession, each in his own area: indeed, some of them seemed to imagine that they were revealing stages in the general progress of humanity rather than local sequences of cultures which occupied varying geographical areas. It was because of this that archaeological mapping made little headway until well into the twentieth century. It is true that J. Y. Akerman had published a map of inscribed British coins as early as 1849, but the first maps to show other kinds of artifact were not published until the last decade of the nineteenth century, and it is significant that maps made for the Swiss cantons by Heierli and Oechsli, and in the first decade of the twentieth century for the *Victoria County History of England*, were designed to record antiquities by period rather than by culture; it was not until 1912 that Crawford first used distribution maps to argue questions of cultural history. Yet for the past thirty or forty years archaeological distribution maps have been one of the main weapons in the armoury of the prehistorian.

In discussing the chronological possibilities of such maps one has to distinguish between those which indicate the extent of cultural assemblages and those which show individual traits. In the former more or less complementary distributions, like those of the younger Cortaillod and Michelsberg Neolithic cultures of Switzerland, argue for a substantial degree of synchronism, whereas distributions which coincide or strongly overlap suggest that the cultures are successive. On the other hand, where individual traits have closely similar distributions, this may clinch an argument for contemporaneity, and cultural identity based on it may be on one or two associations in burials or hoards. Sometimes it is useful to take account of more than two traits, more especially if the third is diagnostic of culture. For instance, it was found that when the distributions of two types of personal ornament, known to have been in use comparatively early in the British Bronze Age, were plotted on the map they were found to be mutually complementary, but taken together to agree closely with that of 'food-vessel' pottery: from this it was deduced that the gold lunulae and the crescentic plate necklaces of jet were not merely contemporary but in fact variants of the same basic ornament worn by members of the same prehistoric group, a conclusion independently suggested by a formal analysis of the decoration found incised on the lunulae themselves.

(B) ABSOLUTE CHRONOLOGY

For a strictly limited sphere of secondary prehistory some assistance in the task of establishing exact dates can be gained by seeking to extend 'historical' dates to barbarian peoples by means of synchronisms with civilized communities. On the other hand, the only methods which hold out any prospect of a world-wide chronology extending back into primary prehistory are those contributed by the natural scientists, and it is with these that we shall begin our review.

ASTRONOMICAL

An ambitious attempt to establish a geochronological system for the whole Pleistocene epoch has been made by collating the curves for major fluctuations of solar radiation calculated by Milanković, and by him equated with absolute dates in solar years, with the glacial phases worked out by the geologist Soergel. According to Koppen and Zeuner it is no accident that glacial maxima should coincide with radiation minima, since glacial episodes are held to be the product of declines in solar radiation and vice versa. Soergel has shown that the first three glaciations in reality comprised pairs of glaciations with interstadials and the fourth and last three glacial episodes, and further that the interglacial separating the second from the third cycle of glaciation, the so-called Great Interglacial, was much the longest. This has been claimed to match the minima of solar radiation during the Pleistocene so well that Milanković's dates could safely be transferred to deposits—and to any archaeological objects which they contain or which can be correlated with them—referable to any particular phase of the Pleistocene. It need hardly be emphasized that such dates depend on a hypothesis which is by no means generally accepted. If radio-carbon dates for the final glacial phases and for a number of Upper Palaeolithic sites are anything to go by, the Zeuner-Milanković dates seem to be substantially too high, at least for the episodes as yet within the range of the new technique.

GEOLOGICAL

Rate of sedimentation. Attempts have frequently been made to obtain absolute dates by measuring the amount of accumulation of a deposit between known dates and then by measuring the total thickness to arrive at a total age. As an example one might quote the several efforts to estimate from the thickness of river deltas the time elapsed since the ice withdrew from lakes on the northern edge of the Swiss Alps. The weakness of all such estimates is that the rate of growth cannot justifiably be assumed to have remained even approximately constant. Yet the method is not without its uses in archaeology, more particularly where, as in the case of the Minoan sequence, fixed dates are available for certain stages: in such cases the thickness of deposits can be used as a hypothetical guide to the relative duration of periods or sub-periods, especially when verified at more than one site.

Varve analysis. Accurate time-scales can only be obtained from sediments when these are composed of a complete series of well-defined varves, such as those deposited in the melt-waters of the Scandinavian ice-sheet, always assuming that each varve represents a year's sediment. The varves in the series studied by Baron de Geer consist of two parts, one thick, pale-coloured and coarse-grained, considered to represent the rapid silt of the summer melting-season; the other thin and dark, representing the slow sedimentation of fine grains that settled during the winter. This made it comparatively easy to measure the thickness of individual varves and to express graphically annual variations in sedimentation. Since the ice-sheet withdrew fairly rapidly across a considerable tract of country, one cannot expect to find more than a comparatively short series of varves stratified at any one point: it is rather as though a pack of cards had been thrown on a table and slithered forward, so that, although the whole was still in order, not more than a few cards overlay each other at any one point. One of de Geer's first problems was to discover by trial and error at what intervals to cut his sections so as to get the overlaps necessary to ensure that he obtained a complete series. He took as his base-line the moment when the ice-sheet split in two, an event which released a great quantity of melt-water and resulted in the deposition of a varve of exceptional thickness. By counting varves formed since then along the Ångerman River he was able to assign a date of *c.* 6800 B.C. to the point of bi-partition of the inland ice. The Fenno-Scandian moraine, generally taken to mark the final phase of the Ice Age, goes back to *c.* 8200 B.C., and around 12000 B.C. the ice-sheet was somewhere in the extreme south of Sweden.

The variations in annual sedimentation implied by the wide range in the thickness of varves (0·2–3·0 cm.) were ascribed by de Geer to minor fluctuations in solar radiation. That some more than local cause was at work is supported by the fact that the sequence of variations seems to have been remarkably constant over the whole territory of the Scandinavian ice-sheet wherever it has been tested. M. Sauramo's researches in Finland confirm in signal fashion the results obtained by de Geer in Sweden. Attempts to extend the sequence across the Baltic have not met with general acceptance, any more than have the still more ambitious 'teleconnexions' between the Swedish varve-sequence and those in North and South America. If at any time in the future such teleconnexions should be success-fully established, they would of course be of enormous value in building up a system of absolute chronology applicable to the whole world (pl. xxiv*b*).

At present, however, the varve chronology can be applied only in northern Europe, and there only to such events as can be brought into relation to the old ice-margin or to actual varve sediments. The absolute dates assigned to the various phases of the Baltic are all based on de Geer's system. For instance, the transition from the Baltic ice-dammed lake to the Yoldia Sea, being defined by the movement of the ice-margin past the Fenno-Scandian moraine, can be dated to 8200 B.C. From this it follows that within broad limits absolute dates can be assigned to anything datable in relation to the Baltic phases, such as human settlements on old strand-lines, the sequence of old sea-levels on the oceanic coasts of Scandinavia, the geogra-phical evolution of the North Sea area, and the major phases in the forest history of the Baltic area.

BIOLOGICAL

Tree-ring chronology (Dendrochronology). The method of exact dating most easily and directly applied to archaeology is that which depends upon variations in the annual growth-rings of trees. Dendrochronology, as it is sometimes called, is a biological counterpart of varve-chronology, and, like this, is thought by its discoverer to record minor changes in solar radiation. It was, indeed, discovered between 1901 and 1913 during an investigation of the incidence of minor solar variations by Dr A. E. Douglass, Director of the Arizona University Observatory. He was led to study trees because meteorological records were too short to afford evidence of climatic fluctuations by which he hoped to reconstruct the course of minor solar variations over a period of centuries.

In his researches he concentrated mainly on the yellow western pine (*Pinus ponderosa*) and the Scotch pine (*P. sylvestris*) as possessing well-defined growth-rings. Marginal forests in North Arizona and New Mexico he found to be especially favourable, because dry conditions made the trees peculiarly sensitive to minor climatic changes. As a basis he studied living trees, cross-dating many of the same age to make sure of eliminating individual or purely topographical variations. By these means he obtained a sequence of some 500 years. His next step was to extend by using the 'bridge-method'. This involved first of all finding dead timber incorporated in ancient structures, which nevertheless overlapped the lower end of the living sequence, and then tying on timbers from successively older ones. In this way he succeeded in prolonging his sequence back to the beginning of the first century A.D. When a building contains substantial timbers within the span of the continuous sequence established for the same area, it is often possible to determine the date when these were felled, and so to obtain an idea both of the period of initial construction and of structural alterations. For instance, the well-known ruin of Pueblo Bonito has been shown to date from around A.D. 919 and to have received additions in 1060–70 and again in 1090. Traces of an intense drought revealed in stunted growth-rings for the period 1276–99 provide a motive and probable date for the abandonment of the settlement.

As in the case of varves, attempts have been made to connect sequences of tree-growth-rings in different parts of the world. A well-known instance is that of a wooden fortress built in Lake Tingstade Trask, Gotland, Sweden, timbers of which were measured and claimed to fit into the sequence of 3,200 growth-rings given by the *Sequoia* pines of California (pl. xxiv*a*) so as to indicate a date somewhere in the middle of the fifth century A.D. for its construction. In the existing state of knowledge, however, such teleconnexions are at best premature and even tend to bring discredit on the whole method. Dendrochronology worked well in the rather special conditions obtaining in the area for which it was first devised, but until local sequences have been built up it is useless to try and date timbers in other regions; indeed, it needs first to be discovered whether the method can be applied at all in the area in question. Meanwhile the first measurements of tree-growth-rings from an ancient structure in Great Britain and Ireland were taken in 1934, when timbers from the Ballinderry crannog in County Westmeath were examined; some day perhaps these and other measurements made in Britain may be fitted into local sequences and the structures to which they belong dated accurately in terms of absolute chronology.

PHYSICAL

Radiocarbon dating.[1] The most promising method of obtaining absolute dates for prehistory provided by natural science is that based on measurement of the residual radioactivity remaining in the organic substances found on archaeological sites and in geological sections. The chronological range of the radiocarbon method is already four times that of de Geer's varves (and ten times that of the longest 'historical' dates); it is world-wide in its range; and it can be applied directly to any archaeological layer containing the requisite materials, among which the most suitable are the charcoal and charred bones normally associated

[1] W. F. Libby, *Radiocarbon dating*, 2nd edition, Chicago, 1955.

AGE, YEARS	PERIOD	POLLEN ZONE	SITE	MATERIAL	ESTIMATE OF AGE	C$_{14}$ ASSAY	CULTURE
—1,000	SUB-ATLANTIC	VIII					
—2,000			Shapwick, Somerset	Sphagnum-Calluna peat	1,600 to 2,200	3,100 ± 200	Roman to mid-Iron age
—3,000	SUB-BOREAL	VIIb					
—4,000			Stonehenge	Charcoal	3,800	3,798 ± 275	Late Neolithic
			Ehenside, Cumberland	Wood	4,500	4,964 ± 300	Neolithic 'A'
			Shapwick, Somerset	Sphagnum-Calluna peat	c. 5,000	6,044 ± 380	
—5,000							
—6,000	ATLANTIC	VIIa					
—7,000			Clonsast Bog, Ireland	Peat	c. 7,000	5,824 ± 300	
—8,000	BOREAL	VI					
		V					
	PRE-BOREAL		Star Carr, Yorks	Birchwood	c. 9,000	9,488 ± 350	Mesolithic
—9,000		IV					
—10,000			Lagore, Ireland	Lake-mud	9,500	11,787 ± 700	
			Hawks Tor, Cornwall	Peat	10,000	8,275 ± 400	
	LATE-GLACIAL	III					
—11,000			Hockham Mere, Norfolk	Lake-mud	11,000	6,555 ± 280	
		II	Hawks Tor, Cornwall	Mud+peat		9,861 ± 500	
			Neasham, Co. Durham	Lake-mud	} 11,500	10,851 ± 370	
—12,000			Knocknacran, Ireland	Lake-mud		11,310 ± 720	
		I					
FULL-GLACIAL			Nazeing, 'Arctic Bed'	Plant tissue		>20,000	
INTER GLACIAL			Histon Road, Cambridge	Oak wood		>20,000	

FIG. 23

Table of British radiocarbon assays

with hearths. Although so recent in conception and still in process of refinement, the method already holds out the prospect of an agreed chronology for the last 50,000 years of human history. Our diagram (fig. 23) illustrates the first results obtained for the British Isles by Libby, and shows neatly how this method of absolute dating lends precision to the relative chronology established by pollen zonation.

We owe this in the first instance to the preoccupation of an American physicist, Willard F. Libby, with 'what the neutrons known to be produced by the cosmic rays might be expected to do to the earth's atmosphere'. Libby supposed that the neutrons produce in the atmosphere a small amount of carbon of the atomic weight 14; some of this C^{14} is taken up by living organic matter; and, when this dies, half the residual radioactivity disintegrates each $5,568 \pm 30$ years, the half-life of C^{14}. Thus, by measuring the amount of C^{14} remaining in a sample of organic matter, it should be possible to calculate within certain limits of probability the number of years since it died and so dropped out of the cycle of interchange. Conversely, it should be possible to check the validity of the theory by obtaining C^{14} readings for samples of known antiquity. It was the value for this physical experiment of archaeological objects made from organic materials that gave the original stimulus to and provided the means for a project which now engages the attention of laboratories all over the world.

There are still many difficulties in the application of the method, and it is indeed due to these in large measure that we owe the continued interest of scientists in a field of research which promises so much to prehistory. As regards the collection of samples, research is going forward with methods of concentrating minute particles of charcoal by means of floatation from strata deficient in pieces of organic material of adequate size, and again the properties and suitability of different materials are the subject of continued tests. Of more fundamental importance is the continued effort to recognize and remedy sources of error and contamination in the collection and preparation of samples: in particular a watch has to be kept to prevent samples being rejuvenated by enrichment with C^{14}; and equally a watch has to be kept on possible ways in which the age may be exaggerated, whether by the inclusion of older charcoal derived from earlier periods of occupation or through the introduction of inactive charcoal, such as one is likely to get from lake marls or calcareous *gyttja* deposits that contain bicarbonate derived from ancient limestones and brought into the lake and fixed in organic compounds or precipitated through biological activities. Finally, several different ways of processing samples are being tried out: originally the carbon was treated solid, but this proved wasteful of the material, and the trend is now to convert it into gas (carbon dioxide, acetylene, or methane) for which the samples needed are smaller; in addition, the search for greater precision has led to the development in several American centres of the liquid scintillation method. The amount of research devoted to perfecting the radiocarbon method of dating is encouraging, as is also the degree of international co-operation, extending to the sharing of samples for processing by alternative methods.

In view of the amount of expensive and exacting work expended on the method, prehistorians might well take to heart the considered verdict of a leading authority that 'the very large majority of the errors are traceable to the process of selection and collection of samples'. Successful realization of the full potentialities of the method, on which the possibility of being able to recover an intelligible record of human prehistory depends, hangs on interdisciplinary co-operation, not merely between the physicists, chemists, and biologists concerned in the immediate process, but between these and the geologists and archaeologists on whom they depend for a critical selection of samples.

HISTORICAL

Range of historical dates. In relation to the immense span of prehistory the few thousand years, for which even approximate historical dates are available, are proportionately brief. Exact dates for Egyptian history began with the Persian conquest of

525 B.C., but the fact that the Sothic date[1] for the beginning of the eighteenth dynasty (1580–1576 B.C.) agrees with that obtained by direct reckoning (1577 B.C.) suggests that the Sothic date for the beginning of the twelfth dynasty (2000–1996 B.C.) is also likely to be correct. Exact dates are first available for various parts of western Asia from the eighth and ninth centuries B.C., but the accession of Hammurabi, the last king of the third dynasty of Ur, is reasonably well fixed at the middle of the twentieth century B.C. Dates for earlier periods in each area are less certain, though there is some consensus of opinion that the dynastic period began within a century or two of the close of the fourth millennium, both in Egypt and Mesopotamia. In the Far East exact dates extend back to the ninth century B.C. in China, and the earliest records of the oldest or Shang dynasty are not earlier than the fourteenth century B.C.

Synchronisms. It has further to be remembered that historical dates can only be extended to secondary prehistoric cultures, and among these only to those within reach of civilized communities. Fortunately the more powerful and richer economic units of the ancient world exercised a widespread peripheral influence on the outlying poorer ones. Culture tended to expand outwards, so that, for instance, metallurgy spread from the East Mediterranean over temperate Europe, and in so doing projected a chronological base-line. On the other hand, this does not of itself provide a basis for exact chronology, since it leaves open the question of the rate at which diffusion proceeded. Much more to the point is evidence for trade relations, more particularly where trade flowed in both directions and

[1] The ancient Egyptians based their calendar on the heliacal rising of Sirius (Sothis); that is, its latest visible rising before sunset. By this means they arrived at a year of 365 days, but they failed to intercalate one day each four years, and so their calendar passed through a complete cycle every 1,460 (4×365) years. Since it is known that one such began in A.D. 139–43, it is possible to arrive at exact dates for events designated by reference to the preceding Sothic cycles.

where as a result sound synchronisms can be effected between the prehistoric sequence and the historical dates of the civilized community concerned. It goes without saying that the possibility of extending historical dates effectively depends on prior establishment in the prehistoric zone of a fine periodization, such as Evans and his successors established for the Aegean area. With such a system, and taking account of the different duration of individual phases as measured by the thickness of deposits and other criteria, it has been possible to devise a system of absolute dates that is probably accurate to within a generation, even though only a few of the indigenous stages have been linked with Egyptian dynastic history.

Mycenaean stages	Dates B.C.	Egyptian synchronisms	Minoan stages
III C 2	1125–1100		Sub-Minoan
III C 1 (late)	1200–1125		
III C 1 (early)	1230–1200	Seti I	LM III B, 2
III B	1300–1230	Ramses II	LM III B, 1
III A 2 (late)	1375–1300	Tell el Amarna	
III A 2 (early)	1400–1375		LM III A, 2
III A 1	1425–1400		LM III A, 1
II B	1450–1425		LM II B
II A	1500–1450	Thothmes III	LM I B/II A
I	1550–1500		LM I A

Chronological table for the Late Bronze Age
in the Aegean (based on Furumark)

Unhappily a two-way trade in manufactured objects is restricted in the main to peoples more or less on the same economic level: as a rule when civilized people traded with barbarians they did so in order to obtain scarce raw materials, so that finished objects generally passed in one direction only. Although such trade-goods may have travelled great distances and so hold out the prospect of a wide extension of historic dates, it is rare to obtain a check in the form of reciprocal changes. As a rule objects originating from historic milieus, but found in prehistoric contexts, can only be used to provide a *terminus post quem*, and in this connexion it must be remembered that exotic trinkets in particular are only too likely to be handed down as heirlooms. Nevertheless objects which can be shown to have been manufactured in historical contexts during only a brief period and to have been extensively traded are likely to be a promising medium for attaching absolute dates to archaeological periods. A first-rate example is offered by certain types of bead made of faience, known to have been manufactured in the East Mediterranean area and to have been diffused widely over prehistoric Europe, Africa, and India.[1] Faience, which has been described as 'man's first conscious essay in the production of a synthetic material', comprises a core of finely powdered angular quartz grains cemented together by fusion with small amounts of alkali or lime or both and an outer glaze of isotopic soda-lime-quartz glass, commonly tinted green or blue by the addition of copper compounds. It is a substance beyond the technical reach and capacity of barbarian peoples, who were only able to obtain supplies of faience beads by means of trade directly or indirectly with the East Mediterranean. Now, although the manufacture of faience goes back to a remote period, for example, in Egypt, it is known that a particular type of segmented bead was traded with special vigour during the period 1600–1300 B.C. For instance, beads closely resembling those from the Temple Repositories at Cnossos and dating from *c.* 1600 B.C. were found in a late context (period V) at Harappa, which agrees with the fact that seals of Indus Valley style from Ur, Kish, Tell Asmar, and other sites fall within the range 2500–1500 B.C. in terms of Mesopotamian dates. In parenthesis it is amusing

[1] See H. C. Beck and J. F. S. Stone, 'Faience Beads of the British Bronze Age', *Archaeologia*, LXXXV, 203–52; also Stone, *Proc. Prehist. Soc.*, XXII, 37 f.

that faience beads of cylindrical form closely comparable with
those of Mycenaean age in Greece were found with a burial
at Nakuru in Kenya associated with the so-called Gumban A
culture of sub-Neolithic type, combining hand-made pottery

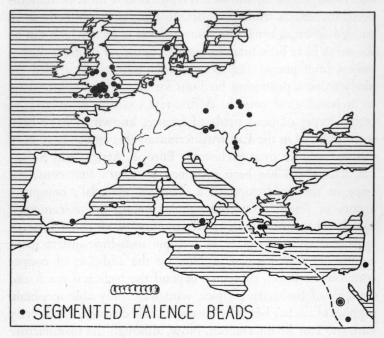

FIG. 24

Map of segmented faience beads in the Mediterranean area and in temperate Europe. The broken line defines the contemporary frontier of
literate societies

with a microlithic industry in obsidian. It was the Mycenaeans
almost certainly who were responsible for the diffusion of segmented beads into Central Europe and by way of the Mediterranean to the West during the century following the fall of
Cnossos around 1400 B.C. By noting the associations of these
beads it has been possible therefore to trace a chronological
datum line across much of prehistoric Europe (fig. 24). For

instance, it is because these beads have been found in about thirty graves of the Wessex Bronze Age people, associated with the construction of the trilithons of Stonehenge,[1] that we are able among other things to suggest a date for this phase of the monument—and it is not without significance that a dagger of supposed Mycenaean type has been found engraved on an upright of one of the trilithons together with representations of numerous flanged axes of native type.

Similarly, it was the extension of literate civilization to the western Mediterranean in the seventh and sixth centuries B.C. and the establishment of trade relations between Greek colonists and Etruscans on one hand and Celts on the other that makes it possible to assign dates to the various phases of the Iron Age Hallstatt and La Tène cultures. In particular it was the acquisition by the Celtic leaders of a taste for wine that led to the importation of the drink itself, and what from our point of view was even more important, of the bronze and pottery vessels needed for its proper service. Since the Celtic leaders were commonly buried in their finery, wearing the jewellery on which the archaeological periodization of the Early Iron Age mainly depends and accompanied by their cups and flagons, these exotic accessories of wine-drinking form most acceptable media for extending historic dates to the subdivisions of the Early Iron Age in the Celtic areas of temperate Europe. Farther north the Teutonic peoples of Denmark and Scandinavia, living far beyond the Roman frontier, can be brought within the range of Roman chronology because they were accustomed to import metal objects of Roman manufacture or at least of Roman inspiration almost as far north as the Arctic Circle. By the same token the native inhabitants of Scotland north of the Roman frontier, by acquiring Roman artifacts, ensured a firm basis for the chronology of the final stages of their own prehistory.

A much more recent example may be quoted from North

[1] R. J. C. Atkinson, *Stonehenge*, London, 1956.

America. When archaeologists of the University of California[1] excavated sites in an area due to be flooded in connexion with the Shasta Dam on the Sacramento River in the interior of North California they were faced with the problem of trying to tie in what they had found in this remote region to the framework of history. They were able to do so because some of the burials were accompanied by beads, which were known to have been traded during a period within the extreme range of 1840–1910, and one of them was associated with 517 china buttons of a type which could be shown to have been invented in France around the middle of the nineteenth century.

The whole possibility of extending historical dates to pre-historic communities was, as we have seen, due to the economic predominance of the contemporary civilized peoples. This superior power found its ultimate expression in the conquest or absorption of ever-widening territories and in the progressive termination of prehistory. The most securely fixed absolute dates for prehistoric communities are those which marked their introduction, often forcible, to the stage of history.

[1] Clarence E. Smith and W. D. Weymouth, 'Archaeology of the Shasta Dam Area, California', *Rep. Univ. of California Archaeological Soc.*, no. 18, 1952.

VI

RECONSTRUCTION:
Economic Life

GENERAL

The object of all the activities described in this book may be simply stated as the reconstruction as far as may be of the course of human prehistory. As we have earlier emphasized, the prehistorian works at a higher level of abstraction than the historian proper, who is able to take account of individuals as well as of groups. Indeed one of the prehistorian's first tasks is to define the social units of his study. In practice his concern will chiefly lie in distinguishing the main groups through and by which culture is shared and transmitted from one generation to another. It is not merely that such groups have been the most influential: they provide a frame of reference by which other categories and classes can be detected; and they form units by comparing which prehistorians are able to detect the major changes of cultural history. The criteria for defining prehistoric cultures vary in particular cases, but the most reliable ones are those expressive of choice or style, rather than those controlled by ecological or even by economic factors, and it goes without saying that the more numerous the elements or traits, the more valid the cultural entity defined. A main test and one of the most important tools used in defining such entities is the distribution map, showing the occurrence of diagnostic traits and making clear the spatial limits of individual cultures at any particular period.

It is only when he has defined his cultures that the prehistorian is ready to interpret his data in terms of social history, and he can only hope to do this with any success if he has a clear idea of how communities function. An understanding of the framework and dynamics of social life is important enough to the historian equipped with the direct insights that only written records can give: to the prehistorian, whose data are as a rule so much more vestigial, it is even more vital. He is somewhat in the position of a palaeontologist trying to reconstruct the life of an intricate organism from a few surviving fossils: his only hope is to understand the principles by which organisms live and by which their members are shaped. That his task is even more difficult one can see by comparing the organization of the most complex animal with that of the most primitive society of human beings; but fundamentally it is analogous. How far, then, is the prehistorian justified in following the palaeontologist's practice of interpreting fossil by living forms?

The old evolutionists had no doubts on this matter. As Sven Nilsson of Lund wrote in the introduction to his *The Primitive Inhabitants of the Scandinavian North* (1843, but quoted from the English edition of 1868):

'If natural philosophy has been able to seek out in the earth and to discover the fragments of an animal kingdom, which perished long before man's appearance in the world, and, by comparing the same with existing organisms, to place them before us almost in a living state, then also ought this science to be able, by availing itself of the same comparative method, to collect the remains of human races long since passed away, and of the works which they left behind, to draw a parallel between them and similar ones, which still exist on earth, and thus cut a way to the knowledge of circumstances which *have been*, by comparing them with those which still exist.'

From this it followed, in the words of Sir John Lubbock, that:

'If we wish clearly to understand the antiquities of Europe, we must compare them with the rude implements and weapons still, or until lately, used by savage races in other parts of the world. In fact the Van Demaner and South American are to the antiquary, what the opossum and the sloth are to the geologist.'

The very title of his book, *Prehistoric Times, as illustrated by Ancient Remains, and the Manners and Customs of Modern Savages* (1865, p. 336), implies that the prehistorian not only could but should interpret the dead by the living. The doctrine was set out in its most extreme form by General Pitt-Rivers, who as late as 1906 went so far as to claim that:

'The existing races, in their respective stages of progression, may be taken as the bona fide representatives of the races of antiquity. . . . They thus afford us living illustrations of the social customs, forms of government, laws, and warlike practices, which belong to the ancient races from whom they remotely sprang, whose implements, resembling, with but little difference, their own, are now found low down in the soil. . . .'[1]

From this distance of time it is easy to see that the evolutionists made a grave error in treating human prehistory on the same level as the prehistory of animal species. They were misled into applying purely naturalistic criteria to human affairs by their conviction that mankind had emerged by imperceptible stages from the animal world. Yet the cardinal fact is after all that he has emerged and that having emerged he needs to be studied by historical as well as by merely biological criteria. Whereas the palaeontologist is justified in using living forms as exemplars of fossil ones, subject only to the processes of biological evolution, the prehistorian has also to take account of the processes of history. We must admit that modern savages have a history precisely as long as that of the most civilized peoples, even if it does not happen to have been written down. It is inconceivable that even the remotest and apparently most primitive communities can have preserved their culture intact since an early period of the Stone Age: they must have been

[1] J. L. Myres (Ed.), *The Evolution of Culture and Other Essays*, Oxford, 1906, p. 53.

influenced by adaptation to environmental change, and above all been enriched by contact with groups emerging at progressively higher levels of cultural evolution; on the other hand, some must have been driven into less desirable habitats and sustained cultural impoverishment. Primitive man in the literal sense lived in the remote past and is properly within the province of prehistorians concerned with the beginnings of the Old Stone Age. Existing peoples can only be used as sources for reconstructing the lives of prehistoric peoples with extreme caution and within well-defined limits, since one is otherwise in danger of assuming what one is after all trying to discover.

This is very far from denying that prehistorians have nothing to gain from the study of existing peoples: on the contrary, prehistory can only make its fullest contribution in partnership with the social sciences and in particular with Ethnography and Social Anthropology. From the former the prehistorian learns how particular peoples adapt themselves to their environments, and shape their resources to the ways of life demanded by their own cultures: he thus gains a knowledge of alternative methods of solving problems and often of alternative ways of explaining artifacts resembling those he recovers from antiquity. Study of ethnography will not as a rule, *pace* Lubbock and Pitt-Rivers, give him straight answers to his queries. What it will do is to provide him with hypotheses in the light of which he can resume his attack on the raw materials of his study. In fact, the great value of ethnography to the prehistorian is that it will often suggest to him what to look for. To take a simple example, he may find that a certain type of implement is used in any one of four or five different ways among the various groups described in the ethnographic literature: these uses may involve differences in hafting or mounting and will often result in characteristic kinds of wear or fracture; by a more intensive examination of prehistoric specimens it may be possible to decide from these criteria which of the alternative hypotheses presented by the ethnographic parallels to adopt. Nor is this by any means confined to artifacts. It applies to all kinds of traces of human activity, including, for instance, methods of clearing forests, growing crops, or disposing of the dead. By constant reference to the culture of living or recently living societies, the prehistorian should be able to enrich and fortify his interpretation of the past, as well as to bring into the open problems calling for further research.

The value of ethnography is by no means confined to the lead it gives in interpreting traces of any particular community at one period of time. It is also capable of helping us to interpret the dynamic aspect of prehistory, the story of change, which after all constitutes the subject. Although comparative ethnography cannot be held any longer to give an infallible key to cultural history in the way envisaged by those who believed in the unilineal progress of culture, it nevertheless gave rise to a fruitful concept of levels or stages of cultural development. The more weight one attaches to historical factors in the building of individual cultures, the more significant become the broad fields of agreement between such widely separated social groups such as the Bushmen, Vedda, Andamanese, and Tasmanians: such groups are limited by what Thurnwald termed a common 'cultural horizon' in the degree of control they were able to exercise over external nature and by consequence in the social superstructure they were able to build on this basis. If we can no longer follow the Victorian ethnologists in the stages they deduced from comparative ethnography, at least we may agree that in attempting to reconstruct those of prehistoric times from the contemporary evidence provided by archaeology we should do so with the insights to be gained from a study of living peoples at a broadly analogous stage of development. It needs a sustained effort of the imagination to reconstruct traces of societies remote, not merely in time, but also in their very categories of thought and modes of social organization, and we need all the help we can get from the study of modes of life and thought quite different from our own and much more nearly n the same level as those of prehistoric peoples subject in some cases to similar limitations.

If descriptive ethnography will often suggest fruitful parallels, define problems for research, and assist the prehistorian to approach his data freed from the limitations of his own experience in a mid-twentieth-century urban community, it is social anthropology that demonstrates how societies function and provides him with a theoretical model on which to base his reconstructions. Analyses of the workings of individual societies based on intimate field studies, like those carried out by Radcliffe Brown, Malinowski, and their pupils and followers among the Andamanese, Trobriand Islanders, and many other groups, have shown first and foremost that they are integrated wholes; that the various elements in their cultures are interrelated; and that, indeed, they acquire their meaning for the societies concerned by the way in which they are organized. This is full of promise to the prehistorian whose evidence is necessarily vestigial: it suggests that if only he consents to approach it in the spirit of a social scientist he may well be able to infer something from what has perished; or at least that by viewing the archaeological material and related evidences as traces of societies that once functioned as entities he may hope to understand it more fully.

In interpreting the evidence surviving from prehistoric societies it is useful to construct a model of the various aspects of social life, show how these are interrelated, and consider how a study of each may contribute to an understanding of the whole. This is illustrated, albeit inadequately, by a flattened two-dimensional diagram, by fig. 25, and it is around this that the rest of this chapter will be written.

ECOLOGICAL SETTING[1]

The fact that culture is artificial—that it is the distinctive contribution of man—does not mean that it can exist outside

[1] See Grahame Clark, *The Economic Approach to Prehistory*; Albert Reckitt Archaeological Lecture, British Academy, 1953.

nature. It is not merely that man, the creator and bearer of culture, is a natural organism and one that has emerged from those which conform to merely instinctive patterns of be-

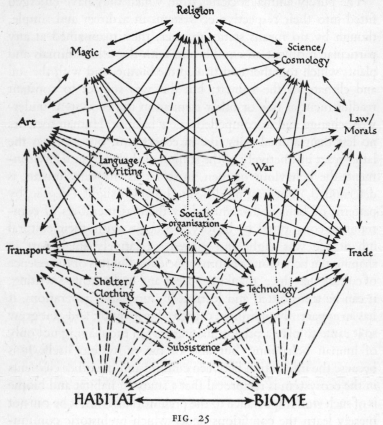

FIG. 25

Diagram illustrating interrelations of different aspects of culture

haviour, but that culture itself is essentially no more than a traditional medium for harmonizing social needs and aspirations with the realities of the physical world, that is with the soil and climate of the habitat and with all the forms of life, including man himself, that together constitute the biome. Soil, climate, vegetation, and fauna are no mere background to human cultures, but the very seed-bed in which they grow and which in turn they have helped to form.

The purely animal societies from which they have emerged fitted into their respective ecosystems in a direct and simple, though by no means static, manner: they maintained at any particular moment an equilibrium with the other animals and plants which together constituted the biome, and with the soil and climate of the habitat; but this was subject to constant readjustment as one or other element in the ecosystem underwent change and so compelled a new balance. Human societies no less than animal ones live in ecosystems, but whereas the latter react instinctively to the stimuli of their physical environment, the behaviour of men, in so far as they are human, is determined, or at least modified to however slight a degree, by patterns of behaviour acquired by them as members of communities constituted by history. To begin with, their cultural inheritance was slight and played a relatively small part in shaping the behaviour of human societies, but it is of the essence of culture that since, thanks to speech and in due course writing, it can be transmitted and learned by successive generations, it has an apparently unlimited capacity for growth; and as it grew so it came to play a predominating part in the shaping not only of human behaviour, but also of the ecosystem itself. It is because the interaction between cultures and the other elements in the ecosystem is reciprocal that a study of habitat and biome is of such vital importance to the prehistorian: from it he can not merely learn the conditions under which prehistoric communities developed their culture, but quite often by noting the impact of culture on vegetation, for example, he can gain direct information about land-utilization that would otherwise elude him.

Thus the pioneers of farming in temperate Europe, like their successors, the white colonists of North America, were confronted by forests, which with few exceptions covered the entire landscape up to the limits of tree-growth. They could only plant their crops by clearing the natural vegetation, and it was on such that their livestock mainly fed. The broad effect of this on the pollen-rain, and hence on the record obtained by pollen analysis, was to reduce the contribution of forest trees and correspondingly magnify that of grasses and herbs so markedly that the near presence of prehistoric farmers can be detected from pollen diagrams even though no archaeological material whatever is available. But palynological research is able to tell us far more than this: whether, for example, a clearance was temporary, pointing to shifting agriculture, and at what stage it became permanent; or, again, how far cattle were allowed to browse at will in the forest, whether particular kinds of tree were lopped for fodder, to what extent cereals were grown and whether meadows were maintained.

SUBSISTENCE[1]

The most vital aspect of the life of prehistoric, or indeed of any communities is subsistence. It is not merely that human beings depend for their survival on food, but that the methods used to obtain this depend upon and influence every aspect of the life of the community. Again, it is through food that prehistoric peoples are most intimately linked with their habitats, since under the economic conditions of prehistoric times food was caught, gathered, or raised locally. Yet it would be quite wrong to suppose that their mode of subsistence was determined by geographical circumstances. Soil and climate set well-defined limits to the plants and animals available to any particular community, but within this range of possibilities there was still ample scope for choice and above all for progress in the understanding and utilization of natural conditions: indeed, if this were not so, one would have to suppose that changes in the habitat were of themselves responsible for the immense strides in human progress recorded in prehistory.

[1] For general reference see J. G. D. Clark, *Prehistoric Europe, the Economic Basis*, Chaps. II–V, London, 1952.

Something will be said in a later section of this book (p. 246f) about the dynamism that led from ape-like prototypes to the creative genius in civilized society. Here it need only be emphasized that the rate and scope of social evolution have to a large extent been conditioned by the development of more effective means of obtaining food and most notably by its production through control of animal and plant breeding. More food led to growth in the density of population, the creation of a surplus over and above what was needed to live, and to successive refinements in the subdivision of labour; and these in turn made possible the technical advances needed to produce ever greater quantities of food for the same labour.

In seeking to reconstruct the economic life of any prehistoric community, one of the first questions to be asked is how far it depended on hunting, fishing, and gathering, and how far on farming. In the former case one wants to know which of the three activities was mainly stressed; how far attention was concentrated on particular species; whether economic activities were focused entirely or mainly on the interior or the coast; what evidence there was for variation with the seasons, and precisely what methods were employed. Again, with farmers, one is concerned to discover to what extent the old catching activities continued to supplement the food-supply; whether farming was primarily pastoral or agricultural; how far settlement was fixed or shifting; what species of animals and plants were domesticated and to what degree their breeding was controlled; how the soil was cultivated, whether manure was used and what régime was followed; whether the cattle were stalled for the whole or part of the year, and how they were fed in the winter; to what extent the land was fenced off; and what arrangements were made for drying and storing crops, and so on.

Hunter-fishers. As regards hunting, fishing, and gathering activities the most reliable source of evidence is of course that provided by actual remains of the animals and plants concerned.

In the case of plants the record is likely to be defective, more particularly for the remotest periods during which gathering activities can be expected to have played their most significant role, and in the rare instances where abundant traces of wild plants are available from prehistoric deposits, as in the Swiss lakeside settlements, it is often difficult to be certain whether they were in fact gathered, and if so for what purpose. On the other hand, the shells of mollusca commonly survive, and in the case of edible species occurring in large quantities there can be no reasonable doubt that they were in fact gathered for food. Fish bones, though less likely to survive than the bones of the larger mammals, do manage to persist, notably in limestone caves and acidic lake deposits, usually in the form of jaw-bones and vertebrae, the latter of which were sometimes treasured for beads; and even scales survive more frequently than might be supposed. Although bird bones are fragile, they may be expected under most conditions under which skeletal material survives in its primary position, at any rate sufficiently to show whether any particular kind of fowling was indulged in, and it is worth noting that fragments of egg-shell may be very persistent. Inevitably the main weight of evidence will be remains of the larger mammals: even these may disappear completely on adverse soils, like sand, but in most territories the right conditions exist somewhere and skeletal material can be obtained if sought for. It cannot be stressed too strongly that bones of animals are just as worthy of the prehistorian's attention as the artifacts employed to kill them, prepare their skins, or shape their antlers and bones into tools or weapons, and that it is just as important to keep the faunal as the archaeological remains from each layer distinct. In analysing the fauna associated with any community of hunter-fishers the first point to establish is the relative importance of the various species. The value of such information, which is better based on identification of the number of individuals represented rather than on the mere number of bones of each species, may be illustrated by comparing data from Upper Palaeolithic stations in the north and south of Germany. In both the range of species is limited by the glacial climate, and forest forms are almost entirely lacking. Reindeer was important to both groups, but

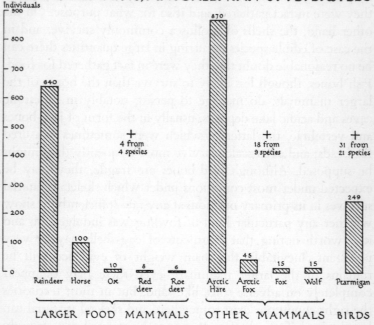

FAUNAL REMAINS, MAGDALENIAN OF PETERSFELS

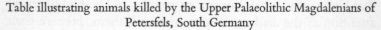

FIG. 26

Table illustrating animals killed by the Upper Palaeolithic Magdalenians of Petersfels, South Germany

whereas the Magdalenians of the south (fig. 26) hunted a considerable number of horses and also trapped arctic hares and partridges on a big scale, the Hamburgians and Ahrensburgians in the north (fig. 27) depended so exclusively on this one animal that they must have attached themselves to individual herds and followed them during their seasonal migrations. By contrast the fauna from the Early Mesolithic site of Star Carr,

Yorkshire,[1] reflects a forest environment. The way in which the long bones of the herbivorous mammals have been broken open for their marrow shows that they were eaten, and this justifies us in assessing their relative importance more accurately in terms of the meat they would have yielded (fig. 28).

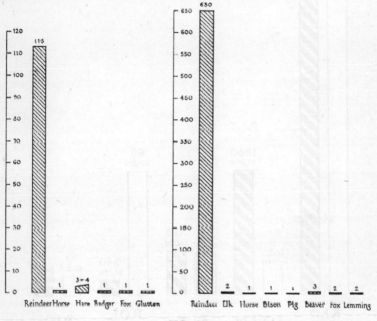

FIG. 27

Table of animals represented on sites of the Upper Palaeolithic Hamburgian and Ahrensburgian reindeer-hunters, North Germany

The primary evidence for the methods used in hunting and catching comprises archaeological traces of the actual gear used. Where, as so often happens, only the flint or stone heads or barbs of missile or thrusting weapons survive, it is common to identify these in conventional terms, as say spear-heads or

[1] J. G. D. Clark, *Excavations at Star Carr on Early Mesolithic Site at Seamer, near Scarborough, Yorkshire*, Cambridge, 1954.

arrow-heads, conventions which depend ultimately on analogies with the weapons of modern 'primitive' peoples; yet one has only to observe the immense range of variation in the mounting of closely similar forms and, on the other hand, in

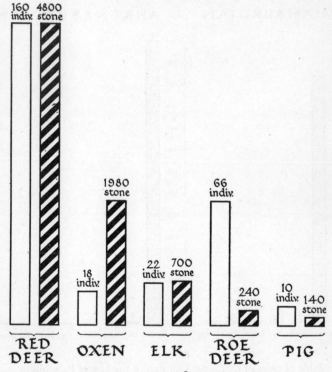

FIG. 28

Table showing proportions in which food-animals were killed by the Mesolithic hunters of Star Carr, Yorkshire

the types of head used for the same purpose to appreciate the dangers of this procedure. Much more promising is the quest for traces of actual haftings on sites where natural conditions have made possible the survival of organic materials. Sites of this character are also liable to yield a wide range of weapons of bone and antler, as well as in exceptional cases portions of netting and even more or less complete traps and weels, like those recently investigated by Danish archaeologists and dated to the Stone Age.

The mere coincidence of specific types of weapon and animal

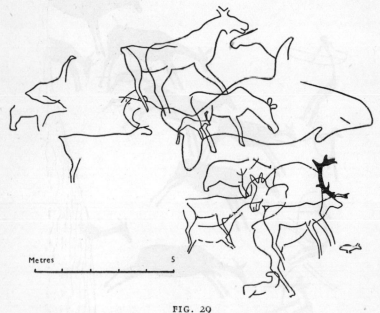

Metres   5

FIG. 29
Rock-engravings of the Arctic culture, Leiknes, Norway, depicting land and sea mammals and water-birds

on the same site may in itself be suggestive if sufficiently frequent, but much more decisive is the discovery of the heads of weapons embedded in the skeletons of victims which somehow escaped the hunter only to sink into the bed of sea, lake, or swamp: finds of this sort are by no means rare in northern Europe, and indeed our knowledge of the methods used in the chase by the Stone Age hunter-fishers of this region is largely based on their study; even commoner are traces of wounds, sometimes with portions of flint-heads still in position, among

FIG. 30
Wall-painting of the Eastern Spanish style, Cueva de los Caballos,
nr. Albocacer

the bones discarded from settlements such as Meiendorf and
Stellmoor.

Another source of information is representational art, since
this commonly depicts the animals in which the hunters were
most concerned (fig. 29) and which formed the basis of their
supply of food and raw materials; and even more important, it

sometimes gives information about the methods used in catching and hunting which could hardly otherwise be available. For instance, the rock-paintings of eastern Spain depict bows and feathered arrows and show that game was driven into lines

FIG. 31
Woman gathering wild honey, wall-painting, Alpera, eastern Spain

of bowmen, a manœuvre which clearly involved co-operation between a considerable number of people bearing witness to a highly organized system of hunting (fig. 30). Another scene from the same art provides evidence for gathering activities in the shape of a woman collecting wild honey in some kind of bag (fig. 31). Again, the association in middens on the coast of Bohuslän in western Sweden of the bones of bottom-feeders like cod, ling, and haddock with bone fish-hooks of the appropriate sizes suggests that the off-shore line fishery still practised on this coast was already established during the Stone Age: the discovery of a rock-engraving in the same area depicting just such a fishing scene (fig. 32) proves that it was certainly going on by the end of the local Bronze Age.

In prehistory, as in other fields, the best-founded conclusions

FIG. 32
Rock-engraving, Kville, South Sweden, showing men fishing from boat

are those based on the convergence of different kinds of evidence. For instance, any attempt to reconstruct the seal-hunting practised with special vigour during the Stone Age in the Baltic area must be based on knowledge of the habitat of the various kinds of seal that frequented these waters during the period in question, and of the methods used to take them at the earliest periods of which we have written records. In the light of this, one can interpret the remains of large numbers of young grey and ringed seals from the Stone Age middens as the result of clubbing on the breeding-grounds. On the other hand, the frequent association on the Norwegian rock-engravings of seals and what appear to be skin-boats argues that adult seals were hunted from boats, and the recovery of at least three skeletons from old marine deposits with bone or antler harpoon heads strongly suggests that harpooning was among the methods used on such occasions. Or one might consider the heavy

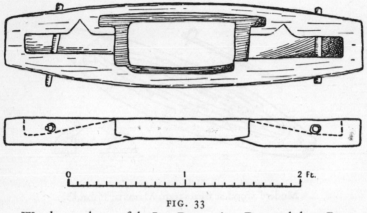

FIG. 33
Wooden tread-trap of the Late Bronze Age, Drumacaladerry Bog,
Co. Donegal, Ireland

wooden objects with oblong apertures closed by valves held in place by wooden springs (fig. 33) found, sometimes in groups, in bogs from different parts of temperate Europe; for years their use was disputed, alternatives including musical instruments, devices for catching pike, traps for otters or beavers, models of boats, and machines for making peat-bricks, all but the first depending to some degree on the nature of the finding-places. It was not until someone noticed that a deer on an early tenth-century carved stone from Clonmacnoise in Ireland appeared to have one foot caught in a heavy oblong trap that their true interpretation as tread-traps was guessed. Then, some years later, it was found that traps of almost precisely similar type (fig. 34) were used down to modern times in parts of Poland for catching deer and bear—and the fact that these were set in groups in marshes close to drinking-places parallels exactly the circumstances of the prehistoric finds, and also explains why so many have survived.

Farmers. In the case of farmers it is again the biological material that yields the richest quota of information: the new economy was after all based fundamentally on the breeding of

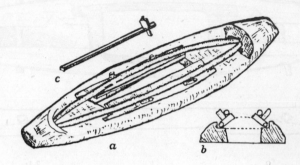

FIG. 34
Modern wooden tread-trap, Masovia, Poland

animals and plants, and the whole superstructure of the early peasant societies rested, as that of all such societies must always rest, squarely on their herds and crops. Moreover, the relationship between farmers and animals was more dynamic, and analysis of faunal remains can therefore yield evidence of more direct historic interest. Thus, the proportions between domesticated and wild animal remains throws light on the economic and cultural status of communities, and major changes in these proportions over a period of time may suggest historical conclusions of real significance; for example, on the whole process whereby the new economy spread and established itself in temperate Europe. The evidence at present available from Denmark suggests that there the story may have been more complicated than was formerly supposed: it looks as though in this marginal territory the Ertebølle people, who maintained a vigorous hunter-fisher culture on the coasts, managed to absorb certain elements of Neolithic culture from the peasant communities flourishing in Central Europe; but that a fully formed Neolithic culture was later introduced from outside and had to live alongside communities of basically hunter-fisher type, in themselves already modified in part by Neolithic concepts, before finally absorbing or converting these, and so providing the basis for the rise of a native Bronze Age. The rich material from the lakeside settlements of Switzerland shows clearly enough that the spread of stock-raising depressed the role of hunting and fishing, but that after the first impact these recovered and continued to play an important part throughout Neolithic times. Analysis of the bare proportions of domestic and wild animal bones leaves no doubt that in temperate Europe at least the new economy had to make way in the face of an established one based on the old hunter-fisher way of life. This impression has been confirmed by the detailed study of pig remains from a settlement of the Baltic pit-ware people of sub-Neolithic type at Stora Förvar on Stora Karlsö, off the island of Gotland, on the northern fringe of the prehistoric farming zone: the fact that no clear division could be drawn between wild forms and those showing varying degrees of domestication argues, not merely that hunting was carried on alongside pig-keeping, but that no close control was exercised over breeding.

Again, analysis of the changing proportions in which different species of domesticated animals were kept by farmers at different periods may help to confirm the conclusions reached by palynology about the history of land utilization. As we have already seen, the broad picture in temperate Europe since the introduction of farming up to quite recent times has been one of deforestation and clearance. One might expect to find some reflection of this in the composition of the flocks and herds kept at successive periods, and in fact there is evidence, in regions which underwent this change, for some shift in emphasis from swine-keeping in Neolithic times to the maintenance of sheep and horses which normally graze on open vegetation. Again, differences in the composition of their flocks and herds may prove a valuable criterion for distinguishing contemporary cultural groups, particularly where these coincide, for example, with differences in the style and decoration of pottery. To take

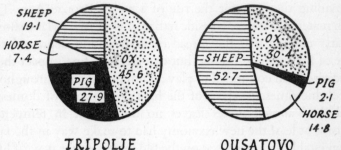

SHEEP
19·1

HORSE
7·4

OX
45·6

PIG
27·9

TRIPOLJE

OX
30·4

SHEEP
52·7

PIG
2·1

HORSE
14·8

OUSATOVO

FIG. 35

Proportions of domestic animals from sites of the Tripolje and Ousatovo cultures, South Russia

an instance from South Russia, significant differences have been noted between the composition of animal remains from sites of the Tripolje culture marked by painted and grooved pottery and from those of the neighbouring Ousatovo culture, the pottery of which is predominantly, though not entirely, of corded ware type; these differences, though at bottom ecological in character, reflecting two distinct habitats, those of the Black Earth and the Steppe, have important implications in the sphere of culture, and make it plain that two distinct groups are in question. In both (fig. 35) the proportion of cattle is high, though noticeably more so in the former, but the most striking differences lie in the respective roles of swine and of the open forms, sheep and horse: whereas the Tripolje people kept 27·9 per cent of pigs against only 2·1 per cent, the

Ousatovo group maintained 67·5 per cent of sheep and horses as against only 26·5 per cent.[1]

Archaeological evidence for the management of livestock is less abundant, but traces of enclosures and boundaries too slight to be of defensive value have been considered in relation to cattle. In the excavation of settlements the question of stables and stalls is always to the fore, and the occurrence of deposits of excrement may throw light on the extent to which different kinds of domestic animal were kept under shelter. In connexion with winter-feed, we have already seen that palynological studies may indicate tree-lopping, and in such cases knives suitable for this purpose may be sought in the archaeological material; no evidence for mowing hay by means of iron scythes is, on the other hand, available in Europe until the Roman Iron Age. In connexion with livestock, also, account should be taken of the needs of plough traction and wheeled transport, not to mention industries based on the use of animal hair. Moreover, it must never be forgotten that, except among pastoral societies adapted to well-defined steppe or desert habitats, stock-raising was carried on in intimate association with agriculture in a variety of mixed-farming régimes, the livestock feeding on the pastures, helped out by the woodlands, and in some cases on a portion of the cereal crop, and contributing manure and traction for ploughs and wagons. As to the relative importance of stock-raising and agriculture in the economies of particular groups, it must be admitted that no ready means of measuring this exists, even if by subjective means it is usually possible to decide whether one or the other activity was markedly predominant.

As we have already seen, some idea of the intensity with which agriculture was practised can be gained from its impact on the pattern of vegetation, but the extent to which it was settled or shifting in character can also be estimated from the evidence of the actual settlements, which may show signs of

[1] See Hančar, *33rd Ber. Röm.–Germ. Komm.*, 1943–50, pp. 40–1.

continuous or markedly interrupted occupation. Evidence for
tillage includes traces of cultivation plots in the form of low
banks or ditches, as the case may be, and occasionally of actual
furrows traceable in the old ground surface underlying barrows
or houses, as well as of the implements employed or representations of such. Down to near the close of prehistoric times
ploughs and spades were made entirely of wood, and even
when iron came into common use it was only such parts as

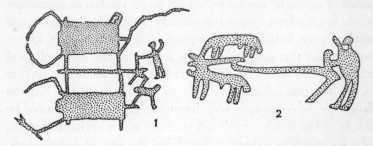

FIG. 36
Engravings of ards (light scratch-ploughs), Alpes Maritimes and
South Sweden

shares, coulters, and the cutting-edges of spades that were made
of metal, which means that traces of the main framework are
only likely to survive where they were discarded in swamps
that have since remained waterlogged. In most areas we have
to depend on representations in the form of rock-engravings
(fig. 36) or models of fired clay or metal, but in interpreting
these one has to remember that they were presumably executed
in relation to some cult activity, often in conformity with
artistic conventions and not necessarily with any idea of
accurate representation, and further that with primitive tools
it would not in any case have been possible for the artist to
engrave all the details he might have wished. Nevertheless,
although there may be grounds for argument in interpreting
details, there can be no doubt of the value of models and
engravings in providing information about plough-teams and

their attendants hardly to be obtained from any other prehistoric source. Provided one remembers the difference in
historic context, useful hints can sometimes be gained from the
more naturalistic and skilful representations found on the
tombs, vases, and manuscripts of early literate societies. Moreover, down to quite modern times, it was still possible to
witness the soil being cultivated by implements differing hardly
at all in form and construction from those used in prehistoric
times. This has often been noticed by archaeologists working
in the Mediterranean and not least by Schliemann, who wrote
in his description of his work at Troy:[1]

'On the way to the mountains I saw the villagers ploughing
with oxen; some of the ploughs were entirely of wood, and
had no iron at all; others had a point of iron only about two
inches long. Agriculture indeed is here still in the same condition in which it was 3000 years ago.'

Abundant evidence is available for the cereal crops on which
arable farming depended in the shape of carbonized material,
mostly charred accidentally in the process of parching or roast-
ing the grain, and in impressions on pottery and other clay
fictiles. All early assessments were based on the former, which
has the advantage that it sometimes includes complete spikes
or heads and allows study of parts (pl. IVa) not accessible in
impressions. On the other hand, it suffers from two major
disadvantages: the grains are sometimes so distorted as to lead
to incorrect identifications—early investigators frequently mis-
took naked barley for naked wheat for this reason; and the
finds, ranging from stray grains to large caches resulting from
unfortunate incidents, are difficult to evaluate quantitatively.
Imprints are only available on hand-made pottery (pl. IIIb),
and more particularly that manufactured under domestic conditions, in which it would commonly come into contact with
cereal grains before firing, but they have the great advantage

[1] *Troja*, London, 1884, p. 332.

that they record the natural size and shape of the grain and above all that they lend themselves to statistical treatment. As random samples, automatically assignable to their proper cultural milieu, they provide, when an adequate number of identifications has been made, an unrivalled source of information about the crops grown by specific communities and above

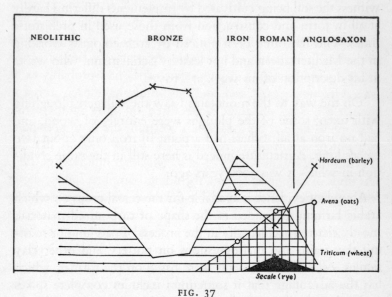

FIG. 37

Diagram illustrating fluctuations in the main cereals grown in early Britain, as recorded by impressions on pottery

all about changes in the composition of crops in different regions. Such changes (fig. 37) may reflect broad fluctuations of climate or hint at changes in the agricultural régime—the swing-over from barley to wheat at the close of the British Bronze Age, for instance, has been connected with the beginning of a shift from spring- to winter-sown crops. In a broader context the study of prehistoric grains may throw light on the domestication of cereals and the diffusing of farming, as well as locally on the movements of peoples. In addition to cereals, pulse, and beans, early farmers cultivated a number of plants with oil-bearing seeds, including flax, which was also important as a source of fibre and the basis of a linen textile industry.

Equipment used for reaping is relatively well represented in the archaeological material. The flint blades of the earliest reaping-knives and sickles can be identified, even when their bone or wooden handles have disappeared, from the presence of diffuse lustre caused by friction with the silica in corn stalks, and the metal forms which succeeded them are so like ones still in use as to be easily recognizable. A relatively large fraction of the grain harvested in prehistoric times had probably to be saved for next year's seed, and this would have been stored in granaries: as a rule these were lifted on piles in temperate Europe to keep it out of reach of vermin, the deep post-holes of which would alone remain; but in dry regions like the Fayûm they might consist of basketed-lined hollows (pl. IVb). As finds of carbonized grain, including complete spikes, show, the remainder was commonly parched or roasted before being threshed and in due course ground. Because of the materials of which they were made, querns and millstones normally survive, even if in fragments, and the history of their development is tolerably clear.

Food and drink. As regards food itself information can be gained from the treatment of animal bones and from the residues of food inside pots and other containers. The discovery of fire, making it possible to cook, was a major event of prehistory, and it can be assumed that flesh would have been roasted from early times. To judge from residues from the bottoms of pots, cereals were apparently taken boiled as a kind of porridge; it is probably for this reason that pottery and some form of ladle is found among all but the earliest agriculturalists; and, conversely, why it is correspondingly scarce among, say, the Iron Age pastoralists of Ireland and Wales, who used containers of wood for dairying and bronze cauldrons for boiling when they could afford them. A remarkable chance of checking the diet of a peasant of the Roman Iron Age of Denmark was provided by the examination of food-residues from the intestines of a well-preserved bog-corpse from Tollund in Jutland, and it is satisfactory that this corresponded closely with what had been deduced by normal methods, showing that flax and cameline seeds and a variety of herbs were consumed as well as cereals, probably to give flavour to the gruel. No doubt it was the supplementation and probably to a great extent the replacement of meat by cereals that led to the importance of salt as a commodity among peasant peoples; although the salt itself has disappeared, abundant traces remain of its mining and evaporation, as the case may be, and there is plenty of indirect evidence for its trading. Examination of residues is also capable of giving information about drink: for instance, we know that cranberry wine was taken during the Bronze Age in Denmark, and the pitch from amphorae found in Celtic territories shows that Mediterranean wine was imported for the use of the upper classes, who were often accompanied to the grave by flagons and drinking-cups associated with wine-drinking.

SHELTER AND CLOTHING

Next to food, shelter from the elements is one of the basic requirements of man and one which he shares with many other animals. The way in which this need was satisfied depended partly on the habitat, notably on the climate, and on the availability of natural shelter or of raw materials for artificial ones, but to a very significant extent on the kind of society in which he lived: the type of settlement and the nature of the buildings[1] which composed it depended upon, and consequently throws light upon, the mode of subsistence, the type of social organization, and the technology of the people responsible for them; and since buildings were erected for religious and military, as well as for economic and domestic purposes, and might also be

[1] See *Prehistoric Europe*, Chap. VI.

designed on aesthetic principles, they may also be expected to give some information on religion, art, and relations with other societies.

Settlements. A prime essential in investigating settlements is to establish their dimensions, since before the days of modern

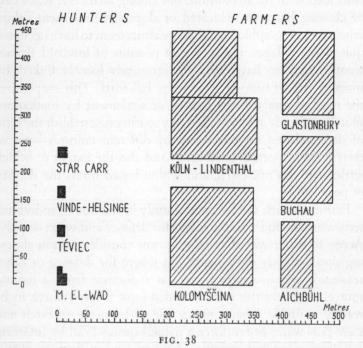

FIG. 38

Diagram illustrating sizes of settlements of prehistoric hunter-fishers and farmers in prehistoric Europe

transport and communications there was a direct connexion between their maximum size and the economy of the people occupying them. This is brought out by our diagram (fig. 38), which, though based on only a few sites, shows that even in temperate Europe prehistoric farmers were capable of living in larger groups than hunter-fishers—as, by the same token, contemporary town-dwellers in the Near East were able to maintain concentrations of population far exceeding what was possible among prehistoric peasants. On the other hand, it by no means follows that people necessarily lived in the maximum concentrations of which their economy was capable: it is true that in the case of hunter-fishers the normal unit of settlement coincided with the maximum; but among farmers it was a case of chosing between nucleated or dispersed settlement—thus, whereas the Neolithic Danubian peasants seem to have occupied quite large villages, the Iron Age peasants of lowland Britain seem mainly to have lived in farmsteads loosely linked by markets and in time of trouble by hill-forts. This emphasizes the need to establish the pattern of settlement by meticulous plotting of finds in key areas. Only so can one establish the kind of site preferred for settlement by different cultures—one of their most important attributes—and also the extent to which settlement was nucleated, and within broad limits the density of population.

Features which call for special study in the case of individual settlements include arrangements for defence and water-supply. Access to water was obviously a prime consideration in choosing sites for early settlements, but where for defence or other reasons it was necessary to live at a distance from a natural source, or where this source needed some improvement to be readily available, arrangements had to be made to catch and store rain-water or reinforce a natural spring-head by inserting a hollow tree-trunk or some kind of timber framing. Deep wells with brick or stone lining, on the other hand, first appeared among urban communities needing to tap subterranean supplies, often through an accumulation of settlement debris. The actual plans of settlements, the disposition of buildings, roads, and tracks, is again something which needs to be established and can only be achieved by means of extensive, if not of complete, excavation. Finally, there is the important matter of the duration of settlements, and the extent to which they underwent reconstruction on the same site, though on a different centre, or alternatively suffered breaks in occupation, questions which need careful interpretation of sections as well as of plans.

Buildings. The first thing to establish about buildings is their function, that is, their meaning in terms of the societies which created them. It is important among other things to discover how far the various activities of social life were housed in separate buildings and how far under the domestic roof, since among other things this has a direct bearing on the extent of and manner in which labour was subdivided—for instance, one wants to know whether such crafts as weaving, potting, and smithing were domestic activities or in the hands of craftsmen occupying separate buildings. Again, it is important in connexion with farming to know whether cattle were kept in stalls, either in separate stables or at one end of dwellings, and again what arrangements were made for storing agricultural produce. Then, it is of interest to know how far cults were domestic in character, and how far they required a special public building or temple. Finally, it has to be remembered that buildings formed, as it were, the outer shell of the social structure, and ought to be studied as a source of information about the organization of the societies responsible for them: for instance, it should be possible to determine how far buildings were those of social equals and how far they showed gradations, and, again, whether individual dwellings housed single primary families or great families comprising several hearths.

The character of their dwellings depends more than anything upon whether people are living a settled or nomadic life, and this in turn is closely linked with their mode of subsistence. By and large, hunter-fishers require extensive territories over which they have to move in pursuit of food, often following a well-worn round with the seasons. Under such conditions natural shelters are obvious choices where these are available, but in territories from which they are lacking, such as South Russia or the North European Plain, it was necessary to employ structures such as tents which could easily be dismantled and moved. Traces of such are most likely to be found by stripping the surface of areas known, through the discovery of characteristic flints, to have been settled by hunter-fisher people. In cases where the floor was lowered below the contemporary surface, traces may even be found sectioned in the course of quarrying and are easily recognizable when found. In other instances the outlines of tents can sometimes be picked up, as they have been for various groups of Late Glacial hunters in Schleswig-Holstein, by recognizing the rings of stones and boulders used to weight down the skin covering. Where conditions for catching wild animals were especially favourable, as they often were on the sea-coast, hunter-fishers were able to live permanently on the same site, or at least to maintain a permanent home to which they could return after expeditions, as did the arctic hunter-fishers of North Norway: such people were able to build substantial oblong dwellings, semi-subterranean and provided with thick turf walls faced on either side by dry-stone construction, like those explored by Gutorm Gjessing in the far north of Scandinavia.

Farmers, on the other hand, were obliged to settle the soil, even if they had in the initial phases to shift their areas of cultivation, and so they built real houses as a matter of course. The methods of construction were limited by the technology of the builders, and in all but the most sacred structures by whatever materials were locally available. Although stone could be dressed by the primitive method of pounding by mauls, this was usually reserved among prehistoric communities to sacred or funerary edifices; as a rule stone was built up in dry-stone technique and often as a facing to an earth or turf core (pl. XI). Timber was frequently used in conjunction with earth and stone to provide roofing, but in forested areas it commonly formed the main if not the sole building material. In this case the house might be built on the frame principle, by which rigidity was supplied by upright posts bedded in post-holes cut into the subsoil (pls. XVIII, XXIII) or set in sleeper-beams, or alternatively by interlocking the horizontal wall-timbers themselves, but this blockhouse technique did not come into use until metal tools had become relatively cheap in the last phase of the Bronze Age, and even then was only adopted in Central and Eastern Europe.

In exploring timber houses it need hardly be added that, except on waterlogged sites, examples destroyed by fire in antiquity are those most likely to provide detailed information, since organic building materials are only likely to survive under normal conditions when carbonized. A principal aim in investigating house remains must always be to recover the principles on which they were erected, principles which apply in all essentials whether the round or oblong plan was adopted. First and foremost one needs to establish how the roof was supported, since on this the character of the walls largely depend: either the walls had to carry the weight themselves, or this would be borne on rows of posts dividing the house into aisles, or, simplest of all, the thrust of the roof-beams would be taken directly by the soil so that the house would have the form of a cone or wedge as the case may be. The arrangement of posts and the nature of the wall make it an easy matter to decide as between the first and second alternatives, but the third, dispensing with side walls, is not always easy to check and has frequently given rise to controversy: huts based on conical arrangements of pine stems, like the recent *kota*, were almost certainly occupied by the dwelling-place people of Finland already during the Stone Age, and clay models from Bulgaria (fig. 39) show that in Neolithic times oblong houses were made both with the roof reaching down to the ground and with vertical side walls. Pitched roofs are demanded by all but the most arid climates and, provided the material used for covering can be established, as it can be, notably when the roof has been fired and collapsed on the floor, it should be possible to estimate the angle by reference to local practice. The position of the entrance is commonly marked by a break in the wall, but sills, paving of pebbles or stones—or alternatively hollows worn in the subsoil—and occasionally socket-stones for doors, provide additional clues, where indeed, as often happens with round houses, this is not clearly indicated by a porch. Details to observe in the interior are clues to internal divisions given by traces of posts, beams, or walls, by changes in the nature of the flooring, by the location of hearths or by the distribution of

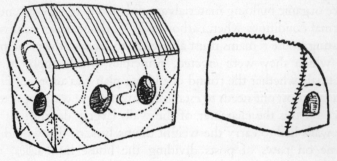

FIG. 39

Fired clay models of Neolithic huts, Kodža Dermen, Bulgaria

rubbish: from such indications it is often possible to determine where people slept, cooked, ground their grain, wove textiles, stored produce, and kept livestock. Where fissile stone was used, the general furnishing of the interior is particularly plain, as with the beds, fire-places, and elaborate dressers found in the Skara Brae huts (pl. XI). Invaluable information can sometimes be obtained by pottery models, such as that from Popudnia in the Ukraine (fig. 40), attributable to the Neolithic Tripolje culture, which shows a row of storage pots on a low bench along the wall, a great clay oven, and, in the daylight close to the entrance, the housewife grinding her flour at the quern. Indications that the floors even of Neolithic houses might be covered with plaited mats is suggested by traces from sites in Switzerland and elsewhere and also by the fact that hand-made

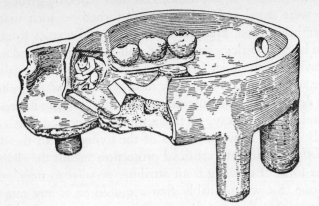

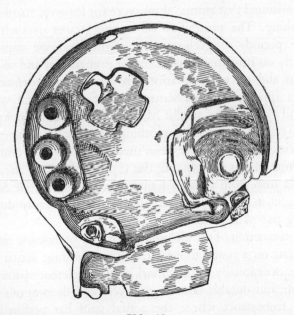

FIG. 40

Model of Tripolje house, showing oven, woman using saddle-quern and
stone jars, Popudnia, Ukraine

pots sometimes bear impressions on their bases, suggesting that they were stood and possibly hand-turned on such matting before being fired. Elaborately embroidered textiles from the Swiss lakeside settlements suggest wall-hangings, and indeed an engraving on the inner face of the slab of a megalithic gallery-grave at Göhlitzsch in Germany shows the inner wall of a house with decorated textiles suspended from the eaves, an interesting reminder, by the way, of the intimate connexion that commonly existed between houses of the living and of the dead.

Clothing. Individual artificial protection against the elements in the form of clothing is an attribute peculiar to man, and it was one that was probably first acquired or at any rate first became necessary when he spread from the tropical and sub-tropical zones into the realms of winter-frost. Since weaving was first introduced among communities based on farming, it can be assumed that animal skins were for long the main source of clothing. The possibility of finding traces of such from remote periods of prehistory is slight, and we must rely primarily on implements used in the preparation and working of skins and on representations in art. Of the former, flint scrapers appeared in the Mousterian of Europe and western Asia and eyed needles in the Magdalenian of western Europe, but one can hardly infer skin clothing from such evidence alone, since skins could well have been used exclusively for tents. It is this which makes so valuable the representation of the upper part of a man from a Magdalenian level at the cave of Angles-sur-Anglin in the department of Vienne, apparently depicted wearing two skin garments.

Reconstruction of the garments worn by prehistoric peasants often rests on a much more satisfactory footing: actual traces survive, occasionally with remarkable completeness; the more elaborate and durable fastening devices and decorations allow one to reconstruct where the actual stuff has perished; and representations are more plentiful and more revealing. By the same token the more advanced the society, the more one can as a rule expect to learn from a study of its dress, which reflects the economic and social differentiation which grew with each advance towards civilization, and more accurately than almost any other element of material culture betrays the organization of society.

The most prolific sources of information are burials, and this applies especially where, as in the Bronze Age oak-coffin burials of Denmark, the bog-corpses of that country and of Schleswig-Holstein, or, again, the desiccated burials of Egypt or Arizona or the frozen ones of the Far North, certain organic materials, particularly leather and wool, happen to survive with exceptional completeness: here we may find everything from woollen garments (pl. VII), some with tartan patterns, hairdressing styles (fig. 5), hair-nets (fig. 8), head-gear (frontispiece), leather capes, and plaited (pl. VI) or leather footgear (pl. Xa). Even where all traces of actual garments have perished it is often possible to obtain clues about the dress worn by the dead man by observing the precise disposition in relation to the skeleton of fastenings and furnishings of garments. For instance, fringes of perforated seal-teeth found lying in arcs across the thighs of burials in a cemetery of Neolithic hunter-fishers at Västerbjers on Gotland (fig. 41) argue that leather (sealskin?) upper garments were worn with a convex or pendant lower edge. Quite apart from any hints that may be given about the kind of garment worn, such features may be important in their own right for differentiating cultural groupings: for instance, during the Bronze Age buttons held perfect sway over Mediterranean and western Europe, whereas in Central and northern Europe pins and later brooches were the fashion. It was not until the Early Iron Age that the safety-pin or fibula (fig. 17) was spread far and wide over the Continent by the movements and influence of the Celtic and Teutonic peoples. The ornaments used to secure and decorate garments are also of importance in relation to art and trade, as well as adding occasionally to our knowledge of cults, magic, and social gradation.

Representations may confirm what is known directly, as certain little bronze figures do the peculiar string skirts worn by women in the Danish Bronze Age, or like the representations of Celtic people on the Gundestrup bowl (pl. VIII)

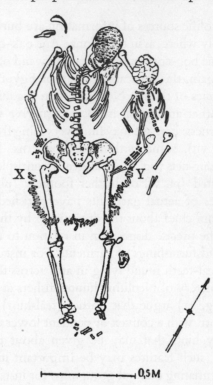

0,5 M

FIG. 41
Burial of woman and child, showing seal-tooth fringe of garment (X-Y),
Västerbjers, Gotland, Sweden

they may reveal new features such as the combination-like garments. Some of the most valuable information of this kind comes from representations of contemporary barbarians by craftsmen working in civilized society, as for instance those of European Scyths depicted by Greek vase-painters and

metal-smiths (fig. 42) and of Asiatic nomads by the carvers of
Persian bas-reliefs. Sometimes the information comes from
representations of cult significance: to take foot-gear as an
instance, the use of esparto-grass sandals by the inhabitants of
South Iberia, depends partly on the find of actual specimens in
the cave of Murciélagos, but partly on the occurrence of ivory
and stone models in chamber tombs; again, though it is known
from one of the Danish oak-coffin burials that leather shoes

FIG. 42
Scythic costume as shown on electrum vase from Kul Oba, Kerch,
South Russia

were worn in the Northern Bronze Age, it is reassuring to find
that despite the fact that the majority of the human feet depicted
end on in the south Swedish rock-engravings are shown naked,
a substantial number are shown wearing foot-gear.

TECHNOLOGY[1]

The importance of technology as the means whereby human
societies not merely utilized the resources of their environment,
but to a growing extent modified this to meet their needs,
hardly requires stressing, and, since every archaeological object
is a product of technology, the evidence for reconstructing
prehistoric technology can be almost embarrassingly abundant.
It is thus no accident that the first objective classification of

[1] See *Prehistoric Europe*, Chaps. VII–VIII; also Singer, Holmyard and Hall,
A History of Technology, vol. 1. Oxford, 1954.

archaeological material was based on the minerals used for the dominant types of implement and weapon, or that this should have persisted in a qualified manner down to the present day.

Although it was possible during the Stone Age to transform the whole future of the human race by the discovery of domestication and the beginning of food production, it is significant that in all but the very earliest centres of farming the adoption of the new economy was rapidly followed in the Old World by the invention of metallurgy and the advance towards literate civilization; and, conversely, that the progress of communities whose technology was based on the use of flint and stone was slow and restricted. The art of metal-working was indeed the key to material progress, but it was one that was only gradually mastered. One of the most important things to establish about any culture is the mode in which metal was used: whether metal objects were made locally or imported; if the former, whether the metal was worked cold or whether true metallurgy was practised; and again, for what purposes metal was used—was it treated as a precious substance for ornaments or weapons, or was it cheap enough to use for commonplace tools, displacing inferior materials, and even to give rise to new types based on exploitation of its own peculiar properties? The most obvious way of answering such questions is to examine the metal objects themselves, taking account of their range of forms and of the weight of metal employed, but important clues may often be gained from traces of their use on objects of antler, bone, wood, and similar organic materials, particularly when such were for whatever reason left unfinished.

A problem of the first importance is how the materials for implements were obtained. The use of exotic substances will be considered under the heading of trade. In the present context what need to be discovered are the methods by which prehistoric communities extracted or diverted raw materials for use directly as implements or weapons or as a medium for trade. How far, for instance, was flint or metal ore mined, grubbed from outcrops, or merely gathered from the surface? If mined, what were the mines like? Above all, was the raw material won as a full-time occupation by specialists for a wide market or was it a part-time activity aimed to satisfy local needs? Among obvious clues are the scale of the works, the nature of the occupation in their proximity, evidence for large-scale knapping or smelting activities and, above all, the distances to which the products were traded.

Of the organic materials which played a leading part in the lives of prehistoric peoples, the most important were by-products of the food-quest, or at least were associated with this. For example, with hunters it was the skins, sinews, antlers, bones, and teeth of their victims that provided many of their most useful raw materials; the same applies to stock-raisers, for whom wool and hair were also important for textile and felt industries; and for agriculturalists one should include straw and flax, not to mention the timber won from forest-clearance. Conversely, the introduction and above all the cheapening of metal, once iron-working had been established, aided clearance, improved the effectiveness of implements of tillage, and so made it possible to produce food more easily and provide the basis for further technological advance.

So long as prehistorians were content to treat finished objects as mere types for defining archaeological periods or cultures, there was no need to bother with the waste products of manu-facture or with traces of their use. Today, when the accent is much more on the social function of artifacts and on the arti-facts themselves as the product of socially learnt techniques, prehistorians are concerned less with selected specimens than with the total output. For instance, in studying flints the modern prehistorian wants to know how they were made, and this he can only do by patient analysis of waste material and of specimens broken in the making. Again, even the classification of metal forms, let alone their understanding in relation to prehistoric society, requires a knowledge of their mode of production, such as can only be won by a study of defective castings, moulds, anvils, hammers, and, if possible, smiths' working-places. Pottery needs to be assessed in relation to non-ceramic prototypes and alternatives: then, as regards the pots themselves, broken sherds can usually give more information about their shaping than complete vessels; impressed decoration can only be finally assessed when the tools employed have been identified; and, on matters of firing, kilns may have the decisive word. As regards textiles, even fragments can be made to yield the nature of their weave by mounting them between glass plates, tugging individual threads, and observing their precise relations with the rest, a method which made it possible to recognize eleven distinct weaves in the linen textiles of Neo-lithic Switzerland; and further light can of course be thrown on the industry by seeking traces of the apparatus used in spinning and weaving, not forgetting in the latter instance the information to be got from contemporary representations (fig. 43). In the case of wood-working, it is particularly impor-tant to study unfinished objects, on which traces of actual tool-marks still remain; by testing against such the metal tools available to the culture in question it is often possible to gain precise information, both as to how the wood was shaped and how specific metal tools were used.

To what extent the preliterate peoples of prehistory general-ized about the mechanical or scientific properties of matter as distinct from applying an empirical knowledge to the solution of day-to-day problems is another question. Something will be said of science in a later section. As regards mechanics, one takes leave to doubt whether the savages or barbarians with whom we are concerned formulated principles or were even aware of such a concept as rotary motion: were it otherwise it would be difficult to explain why the principle should have been applied so much earlier to the wheel for transport in prehistoric Europe than to potting or milling; indeed, it may be questioned whether civilized peoples were any more advanced in this respect until the classical Greeks showed the way. Be that as it may, the discovery of the extent of early man's empirical knowledge of these matters should be a major aim of the prehistorian when studying artifacts, because it was ultimately due to this 'know-how', combined with the power of their

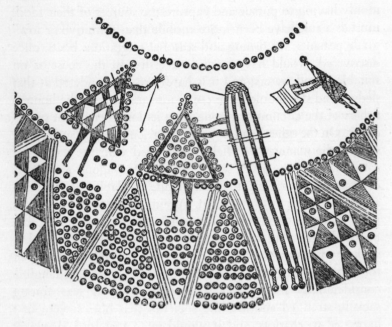

FIG. 43
Women spinning and weaving, depicted on Hallstatt urn, Ödenburg, Hungary

social organization, that prehistoric communities were able to shape their environment, satisfy their traditional requirements, and even make new advances in material well-being.

TRANSPORT[1]

Since the purpose of transport is to traverse land and water, the means employed must always have borne a direct relation

[1] See *Prehistoric Europe*, Chap. X.

to the habitat, and the more primitive the means the closer this must have been. Yet here again the dynamic factor must always have been the requirements of human communities, and these varied first and foremost according to their mode of subsistence. Hunter-fishers, occupying more extensive territories and commonly having to pursue and capture the sources of their food, must as a rule have been more mobile than primitive or low-grade peasants: for fishing and seasonal migrations boats, once discovered, would have been a necessity on the coast or on suitable inland waters; and it is hardly to be wondered at that sledges and skis should have come into use among the hunter-fishers of the circumpolar zone with its long periods of snow-cover. On the other hand, so soon as agriculture was sufficiently settled, the manuring of fields, associated with the stalling of cattle, would have given scope for carts or wagons, and it was of course stock-raising that first made available the draught-animals needed to draw them. Again, technology played its part: flint and stone tools were sufficient for dug-out or skin boats, sledges, skis, and vehicles with solid disk wheels; but spoked wheels and sawn plank boats, for example, had to wait for copper or bronze, and riveted boats for iron. Less tangible considerations also played their part. Thus it was among socially stratified and warlike societies that horses were first harnessed to chariots, and it would seem that spoked wheels first spread over temperate Europe, at least in any numbers, attached to the undercarriage of cult objects.

Evidence for early types of transport has only survived in tangible form under rather special circumstances and in a highly selective manner. Thus under temperate conditions skin boats have disappeared more or less completely and carts, wagons, and sledges are as a rule represented only by the odd wheels or runners that happen to have been discarded in wet places; whereas dug-out canoes, because substantial in themselves and commonly abandoned in rivers and lakes, are over-represented in the archaeological record, more especially those made of the more resistant oak. On the other hand, parade wagons and chariots, which served as hearses or as part of the personal grave-goods of dead leaders, have quite often survived remarkably intact, because buried with their lords or deposited in some bog as votive offerings, as was also the case with the elaborate war or pleasure boats of the later Iron Age in northern and north-western Europe (pls. XIX, XX).

FIG. 44
Bowman on skis pursuing elk, rock-engraving, Zalavrouga, Carelia,
North-west Russia

Representations in art, not infrequently with magico-religious associations, are a particularly important source in this field. This applies to peoples as widely separated in civilization as the hunter-fishers of northern Norway or the Minoan traders of Crete, our knowledge of whose boats, skin-covered umiaks and oar-propelled sailing ships respectively, is based on rock-engravings and gem-cuttings, together with a few crude models. Again, one might instance the elk hunter on skis represented in the arctic art of North-west Russia (fig. 44) or the four-wheeled hearse depicted on a Hallstatt urn from Hungary (fig. 45).

Sometimes one can infer the use of particular forms of transport, even where no tangible traces or representations survive. For instance, wheel-tracks may not only indicate the use of wheeled vehicles, but even give their span. Similarly, timber tracks of the kind preserved in bogs, and therefore as a rule datable in terms of pollen analysis, may, when of the requisite width and strength, suggest the use of carts or wagons, as well as point to the location of settlements. Again, the use of the

FIG. 45
Horse-drawn hearse, depicted on Hallstatt urn, Ödenburg, Hungary

travois has been inferred for prehistoric Malta on the basis of tracks worn in the rock-surfaces: from their nature these tracks could hardly have been caused by wheeled vehicles, but could on the other hand have been worn by the trailing lower ends of the side members of sliding vehicles, and indeed no obvious alternative suggests itself. Less conclusive attempts have been to infer horse-riding for peoples without spurs or stirrups, and of whom no representations are available, on general economic grounds: for instance, the battle-axe peoples of Central Europe are sometimes credited with this on the score that they spread rapidly over considerable distances, were predominantly pastoral in their mode of life and maintained horses. On the other hand, evidence for overseas migration or trade, like the primary Neolithic colonization of Britain or the secondary Neolithic stone-axe trade between the north of Ireland, Scotland, and

England, points unambiguously to some form of overseas transport. It is above all by collating hints of this kind with representations and tangible remains, together with references in ancient
authors like Caesar's famous description of the ships of the
Veneti, and clues from recently existing folk usage, that one is
most likely to gain an insight into this as in most other aspects of
prehistoric life.

TRADE[1]

The object of trade is to enable communities to live more
abundantly than they could do on their own resources of raw
materials and skill. Whereas a pure subsistence economy re-
stricts a community to whatever minerals or animal or plant
materials happen to be available within its own territories, it
is possible by means of trade to supplement these by importing
substances found only in neighbouring or more or less distant
habitats. Thus from one point of view trade is a means of
surmounting ecological limitations, and its range and extent is
a measure of the degree to which communities have emanci-
pated themselves from these. But equally it is a way of breaking
out of cultural limitations, of supplementing the skills available
in one's own community by those of others more advanced in
culture or in some other way more favourably placed for the
practice and development of a particular craft. Although these
two aspects of trade can be distinguished in theory, in practice
it is often difficult to separate them: for instance, stone or
copper axes may have been traded as tools, and amber beads
or necklace-plates as ornaments, yet owe their principal
attraction to the nature of the raw materials of which they
were made.

From a practical point of view the prehistorian needs to begin
with precise identifications of the materials of which objects
were made: for instance, distinctive combinations of impurities,
such as may be detected by chemical or physical means, often

[1] See *Prehistoric Europe*, Chap. IX.

make it possible for scientists to assign metals to their correct sources in nature, and a simple measure of the succinic content of amber enables them to distinguish Baltic or North Sea from Mediterranean amber. This need for expert determination of materials extends also to manufactured objects, including those made of an artificial substance like faience (fig. 24). For all such determinations the archaeologist must rely on his scientific colleagues and it cannot be emphasized too strongly that he ought in his own interests to provide them with the fullest information about the circumstances of the find, and about the possible significance of their determinations.

Another obvious requirement for studying prehistoric trade is a knowledge of the natural occurrence of the critical raw materials, and above all the extent to which they were exploited in prehistoric times. This is not always easy. There is every chance of finding deep mines, like the copper mines of the Tyrol, but many of the outcrop and alluvial workings, which must have played a leading part in the initial phases of metal-winning in any region, have perished in modern times, if not indeed earlier, and one cannot even be sure that areas now lacking in a scarce metal like tin were equally deficient in prehistoric times. Again, some of the substances most widely traded in prehistory, such as amber and shells, had merely to be gathered. This means that we are often left to infer the original sources of many of the materials traded in the remote past by observing concentrations of trade objects within or in a significant relation to the places where they occur in nature.

Yet in dealing with artifacts it is above all with details of technique—on which, by the way, physical methods like X-ray and micro-photography are having an increasing amount to tell us—and with questions of style that the prehistorian is primarily concerned: it is by fine details of craftsmanship and aesthetic feeling that he is able to distinguish exotic from native work, and to assign foreign objects to their probable place of manufacture. The subjective element in such attributions can sometimes be checked by reference to the sources of the materials used, but even so it is easy to be misled. In particular the greatest reserve is needed when dealing with material, which like the great bulk of museum specimens has often been in the collections for a long time, subject to all the vicissitudes of labelling, and is in any case in the nature of a stray find or at least of a find not made under conditions of which a scientific record exists. The great quantities of ancient objects brought into a country like England, not merely in modern but also during Roman times, is alone sufficient to cast doubt on finds not strictly associated in the soil with indigenous antiquities.

Trade is particularly important to the prehistorian because it touched so many aspects of social life. The conduct of trade was intimately bound up with means of communication: in the case of islands, indeed, the whole possibility of trade depended on sea-going craft; and the course of inland trade was strongly influenced by natural routes and by the availability of such amenities as wheeled vehicles and, particularly in areas with prolonged snow-cover, sliding devices. Then, again, the motives of trade, though primarily economic, may also be non-material in character: indeed, some of the earliest evidence for trade is provided by substances of supposed magical or religious efficacy. Trade was also closely linked with social structure: where the subdivision of labour was sufficiently advanced, one finds evidence of the emergence of a trading class, a class which in some Bronze Age societies seems to have combined commerce with smithing; then, trade may be associated with private ownership evinced by seals engraved with the names of merchants; moreover, in stratified societies, the demand for exotic commodities or manufactures was normally centred on the ruling class, which found in foreign imports scope for the conspicuous consumption intended to emphasize their superior status; and finally, when coinage (fig. 18) came into use, as it did only in the concluding phase of prehistory, it may throw important light on political units. Similarly, the weights and measures associated with trade in precious commodities may give valuable information about the mathematical knowledge of early peoples. Again, trade has often been associated with, and indeed is not always easy to separate from, aggression and war.

VII

RECONSTRUCTION:
Social, Intellectual, and Spiritual Life

SOCIAL ORGANIZATION

The astonishing progress to which prehistory bears witness can most easily be measured in terms of the increased knowledge of and control over the physical environment in subsistence, shelter, technology, transport, trade, and the like, but it is essential to remember that all these achievements were carried through by men living in communities and it was the social organization of these which made them effective, both in enhancing their standards of living and in perpetuating their kind. Prehistorians may well envy their anthropological colleagues their ability to study directly the social organization of the living 'primitive' peoples with whom they are concerned, but they need not despair of recovering at least some information on this crucial matter.

Something can be inferred of the size of individual communities, provided only that settlements are completely excavated or at least that their dimensions are determined. By and large, the maximum size of settlements attainable by any particular people is limited by the nature of their food-supply, but their actual size depends on social choice, and this is one of the most important things to determine about them. The best evidence for deciding the units of which such communities are composed is to be gained from the number of hearths in contemporary use in each house, since by this means it is possible to determine whether the occupants belonged to a primary biological family or to some form of enlarged family comprising a number of pairs with their children. Then it should be possible to decide whether a community was composed of social equals or whether and to what extent of stratified classes by comparing the size and character of a cross-section of the houses and graves and assessing the status of their grave-goods: marked differences of social status might be expected to show in dwellings, tombs, and perhaps most clearly in dress, ornaments, and accoutrements, particularly in weapons. It is difficult to see how the keeping of a few domestic slaves could be proved for a prehistoric society: barracks would only be needed for the extensive estates of the upper classes of a civilized society; and of course the slave chains, known, for instance, from Belgic times in Britain, relate not to domestic slavery but to a trade in slaves, prisoners in all probability and destined for export to the Roman world. By far the safest clues to social grades in the final phases of prehistory are to be gained from the reports of ancient authors, like those given for the Germans by Tacitus.

A question vital to the understanding of prehistoric societies is the degree to which their economic and other activities were subdivided. So far as basic subsistence is concerned, comparative ethnography shows that among hunter-fishers the only generally recognized subdivision is that between the sexes: thus, hunting is essentially a male and gathering a female activity, whereas fishing might be shared or carried on by men or women, particularly old ones. Direct evidence for the hunter-fishers of prehistory can sometimes be gained from an analysis of the grave-goods buried with the two sexes and with different age groups within each; for instance, it is significant that at the Stone Age cemetery of Västerbjers on the Baltic island of Gotland sealing harpoons were invariably found with men, whereas fish-hooks were buried with old women. Representations in art provide another source, as witness the exclusively male character of the hunters depicted in the French Upper Palaeolithic cave art and on the rock-paintings of eastern Spain (fig. 30), and, conversely, by the woman shown on one of the latter gathering honey (fig. 31).

Among farmers the important things to establish are how far raw materials were won for local use or were extracted and processed by professionals for export, and how far crafts were carried on domestically by members of ordinary households or by craftsmen provided with food partly or wholly in exchange for their products. As we have seen (p. 209), the former can only be decided by taking account of the scale of the mines, quarries, and workshops and of the extent to which the products were traded. In deciding whether pottery and implements of different kinds and materials were made professionally, the most direct evidence is that to be gained from the identification of actual workshops as a result of the total, or at least by the extensive, excavation of settlements, but as a rule one has to depend on clues: for instance, the use of the fast-spinning wheel on pottery is a fair indication that potting had ceased to be a domestic craft, and the existence of a well-developed metallurgical industry can be taken to imply smiths, though here again the extent to which products were traded gives an added indication of the way in which production was organized.

The principle of the subdivision of labour, or at least of functions, goes far beyond the economic basis of society and in more advanced communities includes callings which in some cases carry with them a markedly superior status. Indeed, it would be safe to say that the emergence of class society was not merely a consequence, but also in large measure a cause of the emergence of man from the brutish communism of primitive bands of root-grubbing, flint-bashing precursors of Homo sapiens or even of the higher hunters responsible for the cave art of the Dordogne. Among the callings to free themselves from the basic but limiting drudgery of food-winning, as prehistoric societies advanced towards civilization, may be numbered artists, bards—and ultimately scribes—magicians, astrologists, scientists, priests, warriors, and rulers. Of these it would seem that the priests, who acted as full-time intermediaries between human societies and the powers of the unseen, and the warriors and rulers, who by their armour and the superior mobility conferred by chariots or cavalry undertook to lead and protect them from their earthly foes, were the classes of most significance in prehistoric societies, as it is certain that they enjoyed the highest status. How far these were whole-time specialists, who avoided physical labour and partly for this reason enjoyed a superior status—and one which in the case of warriors and chieftains might well be hereditary—can only be judged from a study of the archaeological evidence resulting from or reflecting their several activities.

LANGUAGE AND WRITING

Speech, making possible the transmission and storing of social tradition and lore from one generation to another and facilitating the formation of ideas, must have played an outstanding role in the evolution of culture. Lack of the power of speech alone, quite apart from their physical handicaps, would prevent chimpanzees, for example, from entering on a course of cultural development and, conversely, it was by learning how to speak that our primitive forebears were able to start on the long road that ultimately led to literate civilization. Further, as anthropologists well recognize, a knowledge of their language gives a greater insight into a people's culture than any other of their attributes, since it betrays not merely their knowledge of the external world, but also their social organization and underlying concepts and beliefs.

This only makes it the more regrettable that no way exists of recovering the speech of prehistoric peoples other than from the records of early explorers, missionaries, or administrators, unless by the dangerous route of philological reconstruction. Nineteenth-century philologists were impressed with the possibility, not merely of recovering the prototype of the Aryan language by a comparative study of existing Aryan tongues, but also by the same methods of reconstructing and so localizing the original habitat of Aryan-speaking peoples and similarly of discovering their material culture, habits, and personal appearance. This held out the further possibility of equating the early Aryans with an archaeological culture or cultures occupying the same habitat and with the appropriate material culture at the right period, and so in effect recapturing the speech of prehistoric groups. Similar attempts have been made in connexion with individual Aryan tongues, such as Greek or Celtic, to identify their actual bearers in antiquity. The dangers of identifying cultural and linguistic groups in the more or less remote past need hardly be emphasized, more particularly when either or both of these are themselves linked with racial characters, but the possibilities of the philological approach when made critically and in conjunction with the findings of modern archaeology ought not to be overlooked as we have recently been reminded through the decipherment of the Mycenaean script.

Among primitive societies with a relatively simple material culture and social structure oral communication must have been adequate for social needs. It was only with the emergence of societies at a more advanced stage of development that writing became necessary as a means of transmitting social tradition—for codifying laws, inscribing dynastic records and liturgies, and for carrying out the contracts and obligations of a more complex and impersonal type of economic life. Yet, although people ceased to be prehistoric when they became literate, this was in itself a gradual process, and in fact, in cases where prehistoric peoples impressed their scripts on clay tablets, painted it on pots or engraved it on stone, the archaeological record may be able to throw a unique light on the process of learning. Although study of pictographic writing, which can profitably be extended to include some of the schematic signs of Upper Palaeolithic and Mesolithic art, ought properly to be conducted by literary scholars, it still falls to some degree within the context of prehistory and above all of protohistory. Moreover, it should never be forgotten that the genesis of much of the world's earliest literature, particularly in the spheres of epic poetry and religious writings, was prehistoric in the sense that it was originally composed during the pre-literate period and transmitted by word of mouth. By the same token this early literature—the Homeric poems are a case in point—can sometimes be made to throw light on the mentality and customs of prehistoric peoples that could hardly be obtained from any other source.

ART

Although art is an expression of feeling, it is by no means spontaneous: on the contrary, the essence of art is style, and the style which endows any particular art with its distinctive character is one which the artist shares by belonging to a specific group. It is this social character of art, a character which it loses only during periods of social disintegration, that, together with its almost infinite range of expression, makes its products so uniquely valuable for defining cultures and histori-cal phases. But art is equally significant both for the insight it gives into the aesthetic values of prehistoric peoples and for the way in which it mirrors and to some extent even embodies other aspects of social life, not forgetting even their physical environment.

It must be recognized that only limited aspects of the total field of art have come down to us from prehistoric times sufficiently completely to give us any real insight into its nature. Thus music, drama, and poetry survive only in the form in which they were first enshrined in the literature of civilized peoples, though some idea of the general character and limita-tions of the first-mentioned can often be gained from a study of surviving traces of musical instruments supplemented in some cases by representations of these (fig. 46). Although foot-prints and representations in the cave-art show that dancing was already practised as far back as Upper Paleolithic times, here again we have to make do with no more than a few hints. Architecture, on the other hand, although commonly represented in the archaeological record of civilized communities, can hardly be recognized in any strict sense in that of prehistoric

FIG. 46
Musicians depicted on Iberian vase, San Miguel de Lina, Spain

communities: one finds abundant traces of buildings, but these should be regarded as prototypes rather than as productions of architecture as a fine art.

Only the graphic and plastic arts are at all adequately represented from prehistoric times. It is true enough that drawing, painting, and sculpture do not appear in the archaeological record until the Late Glacial period, but their absence from earlier periods is in itself a fact of outstanding historical importance. When they do appear they do so in each of their main guises and exhibit a quality which challenges comparison with anything achieved since. Indeed, it seems to be a characteristic of art-history that there is no such thing as progress, only the unfolding of successive styles in different territories. The materials in which the prehistoric artists worked were limited in part by their physical but in large measure by their technical environment, and this latter was the main determinant in the techniques employed: the art of the Franco-Cantabrian caves shows what Stone Age hunters were capable of achieving, but bronze casting and gem-cutting, for example, depended on a relatively advanced technology and subdivision of labour. The physical environment influenced even the content of representational art, more particularly when magical control over game was a principal motive in its production: yet even if hunter-fishers frequently depicted the game on which they depended, game which varied according to the climate and geography of the territory, the style in which they did so varied greatly from one group to another, as a comparison between productions of the Franco-Cantabric (fig. 47), East Spanish (fig. 30), and Arctic Stone Age (fig. 29) art groups will immediately confirm. Moreover, not all hunter-fishers practised a naturalistic art—as witness the patterns of the Central and Eastern European Upper Palaeolithic art, as abstract as anything produced by Neolithic peasantries. The fact that, as we have already seen, representational art is one of the principal sources for our knowledge of methods of hunting and ploughing, is sufficient indication of the influence of the basis of subsistence on the content of prehistoric art. Decorative art, more particularly as applied to metal-work, is further important as a clue to social standing, because most schools were supported by a small minority representing the ruling group. Again, art was a vehicle both for magic and religion, and indeed is a main source of information about both these fields of activity. Finally, it is through art that we get some of the subtlest indications of the effect of contact between different cultures and of the genesis of new ones.

MAGIC

Before man began to discern the processes of cause and effect operating in their natural surroundings and in their dealings with one another, they sought to obtain their ends by magical means. Often this magic must have been verbally invoked through spells and incantations that must for ever elude us. Another means was the enactment by mime and dance of what it was desired to achieve, the only indications of which likely

FIG. 47
Bison with arrows and wounds, rock-painting, Niaux, Ariège, France

to survive are in representations. A method, to which archaeological evidence can sometimes testify abundantly, consists in the delineation of the wish in paint, engraving, sculpture, or modelling. The interpretation of examples of prehistoric art in terms of magic must depend on an assessment of all the circumstances: for example, representations of game animals on the walls and ceilings of caves and rock-shelters occupied by prehistoric hunters could hardly in all cases have been merely decorative, because they commonly overlie previous ones and may be situated far from the light of day in narrow galleries; others, again, may provide more positive indications of magic in the form of arrows or wounds (fig. 47), showing that the artists were primarily interested in the animals as sources of food. Finally, there are a number of prophylactic or talismanic usages, which betray themselves in material objects or other visible indications, such as the wearing of amulets or ornaments of substances with peculiar attributes to avert the evil eye, ward off evil influences, or endow the wearer with vigour or, again, the burying of axes in house foundations or the wearing of axe-amulets as safeguards against lightning.

Many of the aims of magic are basic to the condition of man, and concern such elemental emotions as fear of illness, barrenness, lightning, or famine. It is only in their idiom that they reflect the economic background of the people concerned. Thus, hunters and fishers are likely to be concerned with magic designed to secure luck in pursuit of game, whereas farmers are above all interested in the fertility of the crops and herds. In dealing with primitive peoples it is hardly possible to insist too vigorously on the distinction between magic and religion, as we see, for instance, in such a vital matter as fertility rites, or again, between magic and science. A matter of some importance so far as magic, religion, and science are concerned is how far their practice was concentrated in the hands of specialists; in the case of magic there are hints in representations like that of the Sorcerer of Trois Frères (fig. 48) that already in Upper Palaeolithic times some individuals were particularly gifted in this respect, as is commonly the case among modern 'primitives'.

SCIENCE AND COSMOLOGY

It could hardly be claimed that prehistoric peoples had any science or cosmology in the sense of an ordered system of natural laws, by which the behaviour of natural phenomena could be explained in abstract terms. On the other hand, there can be no doubt that they possessed a detailed knowledge of their natural surroundings in all matters relevant to their way of life, and that it was from the body of such empirical knowledge accumulated in prehistoric times that the Greeks and other civilized peoples were able ultimately to formulate general laws. Indeed it was precisely the ability to accumulate such knowledge and gradually to discern causal relations between

FIG. 48
The Sorcerer of Trois Frères, rock-engraving and painting, Ariège, France

phenomena that gave man the power, not merely to exist in his environment like other animals, but constantly to improve his own position in relation to it: he achieved power over his surroundings by means of knowledge, and this knowledge was

)ased on the storing and classification of observations made over countless thousands of generations of men. This knowledge was shared by individuals by virtue of belonging to the social groups which stored and transmitted it to succeeding generations and, conversely, such new discoveries or observations made by individuals as commended themselves to the group were absorbed by it and incorporated in the social tradition.

All this knowledge, on which subsistence, technology, and the whole superstructure of social life ultimately depended, was transmitted by means of language. The prehistorian is denied this approach, but this is not to say that he need give up hope of reconstructing what the preliterate peoples of antiquity knew of their environment. His most valuable documents are the materials he excavates from early sites: to begin with, by piecing together what he finds from many sites he is able to discover precisely what materials from among those available were utilized by any particular community (fig. 49); by examining the remains of domesticated animals and plants he can form some conclusions about prehistoric man's understanding of breeding; from artifacts he is able to deduce his empirical knowledge of the physical sciences, such as chemistry, physics, and metallurgy; and his knowledge of mathematics can sometimes be deduced from weights and measures, as well as from the geometry of his buildings. Again, it is safe to infer that early man was keenly interested in the behaviour of the heavenly bodies, so far as these could be observed by the naked eye, at least since he took to farming, since accurate knowledge of times and seasons was essential to success in this calling: the evidence for solar cults alone is sufficient indication of this; and we know that the astronomical lore of the earliest civilized peoples of Egypt and Mesopotamia were based on prehistoric beginnings. There seems no reason to doubt, moreover, that the orientation of such a monument as Stonehenge was related to midsummer sunrise. A word of caution may yet be in place against reading advanced astronomical knowledge into random positionings of boulders in barrows, cup-marks on rocks, and the like. It is legitimate and indeed necessary to keep in mind

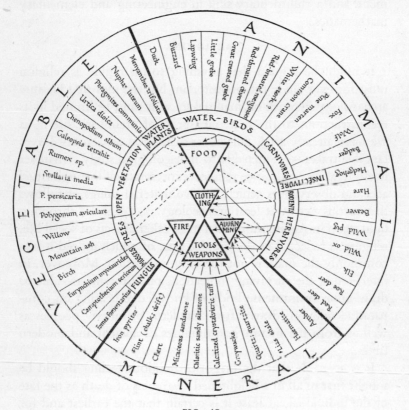

FIG. 49

Diagram illustrating utilization of environment by the Mesolithic hunters of Star Carr, Yorkshire

that prehistoric man must always have been interested in the stars, if only for guiding him in the dark, but it would be quite as wrong to attribute to him a conception of the world or of its relation to the universe as it would be to imagine that he had reduced the physical world to a system of scientific laws because he displayed a comprehensive acquaintance with natural history, a working knowledge of the properties of many of the raw materials he encountered in his environment, and a rudimentary skill in engineering and elementary mathematics.

RELIGION

It might be argued that anything so intangible as religion must for ever elude the prehistorian, but the idea that because archaeology depends on material traces it must be limited in its reconstructions to the material aspects of prehistoric life is, as we have already seen, fallacious: so long as an activity leaves tangible traces it is amenable to archaeological study, whatever its motivation; and, since religion expresses itself through ritual acts and observances which involve material things, it follows that to this extent at least archaeology is capable of throwing light upon it. Again, more than most other aspects of social life, religion is reflected in the graphic arts, of which indeed it was commonly the main if not the only inspiration. Moreover, in interpreting the surviving indications prehistorians are able to draw upon an immense body of knowledge bearing on comparative religion, drawn from modern 'primitive' peoples as well as from the literate communities of ancient and modern times.

It is arguable that the origin of religious feeling should be sought first of all in a heightened awareness of death as the fate of the individual: at least it is certain that the earliest and for the whole of prehistoric times the most abundant evidence for a religious view of life is that afforded by burial ritual (fig. 50). Whatever motive be ascribed to the construction of tombs on a scale that might, as in the case of the megalithic chamber-tombs of Atlantic Europe, represent a major charge on society or to the provision of more or less elaborate grave-goods, ritual burial presupposes some recognition of the spiritual nature of man, of the existence of a soul capable of living on after death.

Yet it would be a mistake to try and draw general conclusions about religious belief from archaeological traces of burial: even the most drastic changes in burial practice, such as that from inhumation to cremation or vice versa, need not imply, even though they sometimes accompany, significant alterations in religion. Funerary practices—tombs, rite, attitude of the dead,

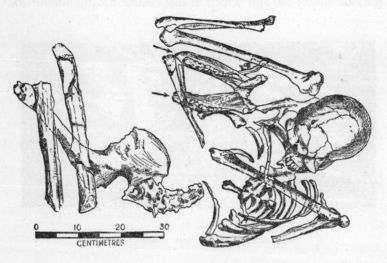

FIG. 50
Burial of Neanderthal Man accompanied by jaws of giant boar, Mugharet es-skuhl, Mount Carmel, Palestine

grave-goods, and so on—are worthy of study both in themselves and for the information they can give about such things as methods of building construction, art, subdivision of labour and social status, clothing and technology. Other practices, besides burial, which appear to indicate an interest in soul as distinct from mere body, include head-hunting and cannibalism, practices which had the object of acquiring soul-stuff and which frequently leave behind them traces in the form of human skeletal material treated in an unmistakable fashion (fig. 51).

The essence of religion is the worship of powers transcending human life, and the study of prehistoric religion is concerned first and foremost with the forms taken by this worship. Among prehistoric peoples these would have been natural forces, powers of the earth and sky, vegetation, springs, sun, moon, and thunder, powers to be encouraged or propitiated as the case might be, and which in due course became identified

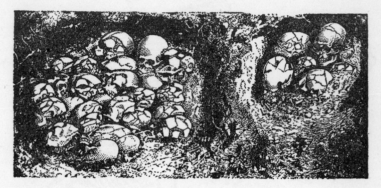

FIG. 51
Nests of Mesolithic skulls, Ofnet, Bavaria

with anthropomorphic deities and mother-goddesses, thunder-gods, and the like. Such powers and deities were symbolized by things like plastic models, paintings or engravings of trees, mother-goddesses, bulls or bulls' horns, male figures, phalli, axes and the like, and it is these symbols which provide the bulk of the archaeological evidence for prehistoric cults. Other sources include such things as rich treasures deposited in bogs or springs, which from their nature and location suggest the character of votive offerings, as well as finds which suggest the sacrifice of animals or even of human beings. Then again, there are the actual locations or even the shrines and temples at which cults were performed or the gods worshipped. Where definite temples, as distinct from domestic shrines, appear, as in a rudimentary fashion they do in Britain towards the end of Neo-lithic times and at the beginning of the Bronze Age (fig. 16), the question arises whether and in what sense a priesthood had arisen. Direct evidence for this and for much else concerned with religion is only available from the closing phases of pre-history, from which references are known in the writings of contemporary civilizations—as witness the description of Druids in Tacitus—but traces are sometimes forthcoming in the shape of priestly regalia or of the burials or representations of what appear to be priestly individuals.

WAR

If the basic function of culture is to ensure the survival of society, it follows that the methods and organization adopted for self-defence and for the acquisition of social objectives by force is a particularly vital aspect of culture. In some aspects it is indeed the most vital one, since the cultures which have survived have done so in the main at the expense of other militarily less effective ones; moreover, it is in their preparations for and conduct of war that communities exert the greatest strain upon, and deploy most fully their economic, social, and often their moral and even religious resources. Indeed warfare seems to have played a part in prehistory that grew in importance with every advance of culture. From this it follows that traces of warlike activity ought to be capable of throwing light on most other aspects of culture, as well as in itself providing material for a study of the very highest interest.

Evidence for warlike activities is particularly well represented in the archaeological record. Weapons were not only made from the mineral materials most likely to survive, but as the most precious possessions of their owners were among those most frequently hidden in the soil for security, deposited as votive offerings or buried as grave-goods to accompany the departed. Again, down to modern times the most effective means of defence has consisted of earthworks (pl. II), which are more enduring than most structures even of masonry. Human skeletal remains, which are also well represented in the tangible evidence of prehistory, may also throw light on the methods used in combat. Furthermore, the social importance of warfare and the fact that its conduct was commonly associated with the leading figures of society means that it features in the graphic arts (pl. VIII). Finally, since it was through warfare, which was not always clearly defined from trade, that barbarian peoples were chiefly brought into contact with their civilized contemporaries, either as adversaries or as mercenaries, it is not surprising that ancient literature forms an important source of information about the tactics and warlike equipment of the later prehistoric inhabitants of many regions.

The capacity to wage war is one of the most convenient yardsticks for measuring the cultural attainment of human societies. In the first place it is directly limited by the basis of subsistence, since the conduct of any sustained conflict presupposes a surplus of food and man-power: groups of hunter-fishers might nourish quarrels over the boundaries of hunting territories over long periods of time, but could hardly sustain anything beyond brief encounters; farmers, even more deeply involved in regular work, were, to begin with, in little better shape; and it was not until they had reached the threshold of civilization that human societies were well equipped to wage anything like prolonged campaigns. Equally, the efficiency of weapons was closely linked with the progress of technology and transport; not merely did the bringing into use and cheapening of more effective materials such as bronze and iron make possible the production of more effective weapons as means of defence, but the exigencies of war were in themselves a formidable spur towards technological advance; similarly, improved means of transport, like horse-riding or charioteering, were often adopted in the first instance because of their value in waging war.

Detailed study of the armament of prehistoric peoples is primarily of value for the light it throws on the methods used in fighting, but it is also capable of yielding exceptionally important information on the craft of metal-working, since for obvious reasons the most advanced techniques were used in fabricating weapons and defensive armour. Further, it reflects the degree to which society was stratified, since in barbarian communities weapons were one of the principal badges of rank, as well as, incidentally, being a main vehicle of decorative art. Defensive works, which, it need hardly be emphasized, ought to be studied in conjunction with the offensive weapons of potential enemies, are again of importance both as military works and as products of human labour: estimates of the man-power involved in their construction may throw light on the population and economic power of the societies concerned, as well as on the power and authority responsible for concentrating this on a single task; and, indeed, in the final resort, hill-forts and linear defences stand as monuments to the directing power of leaders.

LAW AND MORALS

Although law could hardly be codified in any modern sense before it could be written down, this is by no means to say that prehistoric societies made do without it. Indeed, the fact that one of the first uses to which writing was put was precisely to codify laws shows that there must have been an impressive body of orally transmitted law only waiting to be written down, a body of law that must have been basically prehistoric in origin. It was by means of such customary law that the rights of property and the relations between individuals and groups were regulated. Both these are matters of crucial importance to prehistoric as to any other communities. The question remains, what if any information can be gained about their operation in prehistoric societies? Quite clearly very little in relation to what can be learned about economic or even about some other non-material aspects of life. Yet something can still be gained, provided the question is kept in mind.

In the matter of property, it may be accepted that in the earliest human societies the means of subsistence, the territories within which gathering and hunting activities were carried on, were owned, in so far as they were owned at all, by social groups. To begin with, when humans were still rare animals, it is conceivable and even probable that no precise limits were set to the territories of different groups, and it may well be that this definition came at a relatively late stage and may even have spread to retarded hunter-fishers from communities based on farming, so that the whole concept of property may have been restricted to the very limited range of personal chattels that existed among primitive hunter-fishers, such as clothing, ornaments, tools, and weapons. In this connexion one might well expect to find marks of ownership on surviving artifacts of antler, bone, and similar materials and such have indeed been claimed.

It is hardly too much to say that the economic progress of human society has consisted in an emergence from the basic primitive communism, which, appropriate though it may have been to squalid flint-using savages, was wholly inadequate for civilized man, or even for the barbarian societies from which civilization sprang. Just as economic advance was reflected in a subdivision of labour, which in turn gave rise to the appearance of class-society and literacy, so also were the growth in wealth and productivity associated with an ever stricter and more meticulous definition of the rights of ownership. Since there was more property, there was necessarily more to own. The only problem to decide is who did the owning. In the case of farmers something can be learnt from the nature of settlements and above all from the boundaries of land-divisions. It seems probable from the large size of the settlements of the pioneers of the new economy that the Neolithic farmers of prehistoric Europe, though occupying their own substantial houses, carried on the task of clearing the land and raising crops on a basis which involved at the least a considerable element of communal enterprise. By the Early Iron Age, on the other hand, from which we first have any clear picture of land-holdings in the shape of plans of the so-called Celtic fields, it would seem, to judge from the way in which individual fields were subdivided, as if land was subject to private inheritance. By contrast, we know from historical sources that the agricul-tural system of the Anglo-Saxons was organized on a more collective basis, in which individual members of the village community held strips scattered among the open fields of the village and contributed oxen to the communal plough, a system associated with the clearance and pioneering of the heavier clay soils of the secondary phase of settlement, soils that neces-sitated the use of true ploughs drawn by up to eight or more oxen.

As regards relations between individuals and questions of private morality, very little can be learnt, unless literary sources are available. Yet occasionally archaeological finds do some-thing to suggest or confirm how severe the sanctions might be against those who transgressed. One might take as an example the corpses of Iron Age date, whose preservation in the bogs of North Germany and Denmark has already been described (pl. xiva). A striking fact about many of these is that they had evidently been malefactors, choked by a rope or withy round the neck, cast into the bog and sometimes pinned down by branches as though to prevent their spirits from returning to plague the living. As it happens, Tacitus has described the treat-ment of persons taken in adultery, and there can be little doubt that we owe these useful documents of archaeology to the severity with which transgressors against marital morality were treated among the Teutonic peoples of the Iron Age.

THE BEARERS OF CULTURE

It has always to be remembered that the bearers of the cul-tures, the members of the communities studied by prehistorians, were themselves biological organisms; as such they merit the closest study both on their own account and for what they have to tell of social life in the prehistoric past. Indeed for the earliest periods they have probably more to contribute to our understanding of prehistory than the archaeological traces of their activities: after all, it is on human skeletal remains that we depend for knowledge of the evolution of the physical attributes, such as fully stereoscopic vision, upright posture, enlarged brain, and specialization of the forelimbs as hands, that made possible, not merely tool-making, but the whole apparatus of culture; then, again, study of the human physical types associated with the various traditions of flaking flint and stone current during Lower and Middle Pleistocene times promises to throw light on such a fundamental question as the centre or centres from which early man dispersed; and, further, it would seem important to decide how far the pronounced advance in culture marked by the first appearance of specialized missile weapons, made in antler and bone as well as flint, and of aesthetic sensibility as expressed in graphic art, was associated with the emergence, or at least the predominance, of *Homo sapiens* in his modern form, and how far with some such unverifiable factor as a trick or refinement in the power of speech.

The great expansion in human settlement that marked the Late Pleistocene and post-Glacial periods involved the occupation of environments with widely differing climates, and doubtless this had much to do with the shaping of the various races into which the species *Homo sapiens* divided. Since these races apparently retained the character they had originally assumed in response to specific environments, their range at different periods of prehistory promises among other things useful clues to movements of peoples. Further, though one must constantly be on guard against identifying race and culture, still more either or both of these with language, it may happen, particularly in the case of an island, that one may be able to determine the extent to which cultural changes were due to diffusion or migration of peoples by comparing the physical remains of the population immediately before and after. Again, by comparing burials with outstandingly rich grave-goods with poorer ones it may be possible to establish whether the racial composition of rulers and ruled was homogeneous or not—and if not whether the former were conquerors from outside. Unfortunately the evidence needed for such determinations is by no means all that could be desired: to begin with, many of the criteria used to distinguish living races, such as pigmentation, hair form, and blood-groups, are either completely lacking for the prehistoric period or available only in the most exceptional cases, so that the prehistorian is forced to rely on features which survive in the skeletal remains; then, it must be remembered that where cremation, tree-burial, or exposure was practised not even this evidence survives. Even so, provided sufficiently large numbers of inhumation burials are available, modern methods of statistical analysis should make it possible at any rate to obtain answers to the kind of questions the prehistorian most needs answering.

Human skeletal material, including in this case also cremated bones, can also be made to yield highly significant information about economic life. Analysis of the numbers buried in cemeteries, taken in conjunction with settlements, is capable, for instance, of throwing light on the highly important matter of the density of population at different periods, but to obtain reliable results from this direct method presupposes a completeness of documentation far beyond what is normally available from prehistoric times, and as a rule one is thrown back on estimates based on comparisons with known figures for recent populations at a similar level of culture occupying analogous environments. For instance, one can gain a fair notion of the population of the periglacial territories of Europe under an advanced hunter-fisher economy by reference to the sub-arctic regions of North America. Admittedly population densities in the extreme north of the New World varied locally in recent times within fairly wide limits, from around one person per thirty square miles in Alaska (1867) to one per two hundred square miles in the North-West Territories (1911)[1]—but the important fact is that they were in any case extremely low: one is reminded of what a late eighteenth-century author wrote of another part of North America: 'there are very few Californians, and in proportion to the extent of the country, almost as few as if there were none at all. . . . A person may travel in different parts four or more days without seeing a single human being.'[2] If we were to apply the figures for Alaska and the North-West Territories to England and Wales, we would get a population of 2,000 or 250 as the case may be, and this probably gives a good idea of the order of magnitude of the population during Upper Palaeolithic times. On the lower figure this would mean about ten small bands, and the poverty of the remains found in our caves may suggest that even this is too generous, even if we allow for open stations few of which have yet been identified. Conditions during the early post-Glacial period might on the other hand have approximated to that obtaining in Tasmania at the time of the discovery. Here, again, there is a wide range of doubt as to the correct figure, though the best estimates allow for between 2,000 and 5,000 aboriginals,[3] giving a population density of from thirteen to five square miles for each inhabitant. On the basis of the smaller density one arrives at a population of the order of 4,500 for Great Britain in Mesolithic times.

It is fair to assume that the introduction of farming made possible some increase in population, even though during almost the whole of prehistoric times occupation was confined to the lighter, well-drained soils of the area of primary settlement.

[1] Based on statistics in the *Encyclopaedia Britannica*, 14th edition, I, 501, and IV, 694.

[2] Quoted from L. Krzywicki, *Primitive Society and its Vital Statistics*, London, 1934, vol. II.

[3] Quoted from *Chambers's Encyclopaedia*, 1950, XIII, 473.

Yet, although mixed farming was practised from Neolithic times, the emphasis seems to have been on stock-raising until the close of the Bronze Age, and it seems unlikely that the population was capable of any very rapid expansion until the introduction of fixed fields, which themselves were confined in prehistoric times to the south of England. No valid analogies with existing primitive peoples are forthcoming for the farming stage of British or European prehistory, because no cereal-growing peoples any longer exist outside the pale of civilization. Estimates based on the archaeological and osteological evidence, on the other hand, require far more information than is ordinarily available: for accurate results one needs to know how many houses were occupied at any particular time, and how long cemeteries were in use, what areas they served, and what proportion of the population was ordinarily buried in them. Nevertheless it is instructive that in Caithness, an area in which megalithic chamber-tombs may be expected to have survived exceptionally well and which was, relatively speaking, well settled at the time, V. G. Childe has estimated the Neolithic population at between 300 and 400.[1] No less telling is his suggestion that the population of the mainland of Scotland during the Early Bronze Age may have averaged around 2,500. On the whole it seems doubtful whether there were more than 20,000 people in Neolithic Britain at any one time, or whether this number was more than doubled in the course of the second millennium B.C. It might be objected that structures like megalithic tombs, earthen long barrows, cursus monuments, and henges involve concentrations of labour that might suggest a denser population, but it must be remembered that societies depending largely on pastoral activities can dispose of considerable leisure, and that this could be harnessed more easily to religious needs than to any other, save only military ones, which at this time were far less pressing than during the Early Iron Age.

[1] *Prehistory of Scotland*, pp. 55–6 and 122.

Some check on the peak population of any region in pre-historic times should be forthcoming from the early historical period. Yet it must be understood that no reliable figures are available before the institution of official censuses early in the nineteenth century. Even so, it is possible from documentary sources to make estimates much more reliable than those at present available for the prehistoric period, and the figure of 1,500,000 for the population of England and Wales at the time of the Domesday Survey is probably not too wide of the mark. In view of the fact that tillage of the heavier clay lands, the secondary area of settlement, was first taken seriously in hand during the later Saxon period, it would seem that the figure for Roman Britain must, *pace* Wheeler, be substantially less: much more likely is Collingwood's estimate of 500,000.[1] Now, although it is true that the Roman province depended mainly for its grain supplies on the Celtic field system of 'scratch agriculture', it has to be allowed that a heavier type of plough was beginning to be brought into use to cultivate heavier soils, probably in connexion with the villa system, and that since the prehistoric Iron Age the Celtic field system had been extended to extensive areas, notably the rich silt regions of the Fenland, that had not previously been under cultivation. On the other side of the medal we know that the Roman province had to feed a substantial number of troops and administrators and to support in its southern parts a number of urban concentrations, all of which implies a considerable increase in food production over and above what had been attained even in the last hundred years of the prehistoric Iron Age. All this suggests that the population of the country at the time of the Claudian invasion was substantially less than it was after Roman rule had been firmly established.

The question of the density of population at different periods has been stressed because of its immense importance as a measure of economic progress, and though the difficulties in

[1] *Antiquity*, 1929, pp. 261–76; cf. 1930, pp. 91 ff.

the way of reaching even approximately accurate answers are formidable it is certain that we cannot afford to let slip any opportunity of gaining information on this point.

Another way in which population must have varied is in its age composition. In early times the expectation of life was short, marriage took place at an early age, and the generations followed one another rapidly. By studying skeletal remains, concentrating in the case of adolescents on the stage reached in the eruption of the teeth and the degree of fusion attained by the epiphyses of the long bones, and in that of adults on the sutures of the skull, it is not difficult to establish within limits the ages at which individuals died. An idea of the kind of results obtained for various groups of Europeans is given in the following table based on the work of Professor H. V. Vallois:

	0–14 years	15–20 years	21–40 years	41–60 years	Over 60 years
Neanderthal man (20)	40	15	40	5	—
Upper Palaeolithic man (102)	24·5	9·8	53·9	11·8	—
Mesolithic man (65)	30·8	6·2	58·5	3	1·5
Early Bronze Age cemetery, Austria (273)	7·9	17·2	39·9	28·6	7·3
Lower Austria in 1829	50·7	3·3	12·1	12·8	21
Austria in 1927	15·4	2·7	11·9	22·6	47·4

N.B.—For the prehistoric groups the numbers of subjects are shown in parentheses. Results are expressed as percentages.

The effect of settled life is brought out by comparing the figures for Early Bronze Age Austria with those for the three groups of European food-gatherers. The rapid improvement during the last hundred years reflects the unprecedented progress of medical science. It will be observed that, whereas the proportion of people surviving to the age of sixty or more has increased a hundredfold since the food-gathering stage, the increase between the Early Bronze Age and modern times has only been sevenfold, and half this has occurred during the last hundred years.

Much can be gathered about conditions of living, nutrition, disease, and surgery, as well as about methods of fighting and modes of cranial deformation, through careful study of individual skeletons conducted in the spirit of forensic medicine. Among leading clues one might list indications of the incidence of arthritis, dental decay, and lesions; evidence for a squatting posture, for occupational deformations, for the practice of trepanation, and for the precise methods used and their effectiveness judged by the survival of the patient; the presence of the heads or of fragments of the heads of missile weapons embedded in the spinal column or in other parts of the skeleton (fig. 52), or alternatively of sword-cuts on the skull; and the appearance of mutilations of the fingers, dislodgements of certain teeth, and flattening of the skull.

CONTACT AND CHANGE

For convenience of exposition we have chosen so far to adopt as a model a single culture functioning in its ecosystem at one moment of time, even if hints have occasionally been dropped of the process of growth and change. In reality no culture can long remain static: on the contrary, change is a very law of life, and it is the sum of a constant process of change that constitutes prehistory. Prehistory is substantially a record of the changes which have brought mankind from an animal state of existence to the threshold of civilization and literacy, and much of its interest rests precisely in the scale of the changes which it records. If the primary task of the prehistorian is to discover what happened in prehistory, his ultimate problem is to decide precisely how and why these changes occurred or, to put it another way, why prehistory—and for that matter history —exists at all.

The interdependence of the various aspects of culture stressed in the main part of this chapter is of key importance in this matter of change, since it implies that changes in one are liable to influence the whole. Thus, alterations in the method of food production will affect relations with the natural environment and may set up a complex chain reaction between economy

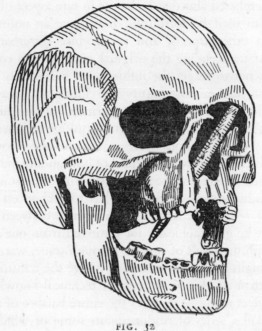

FIG. 32

Skull of Neolithic man with bone arrowhead in position, Porsmose, Naestved, Denmark

and ecosystem, as well as social organization, density of population, and often even religious belief. Equally, changes in the natural environment, such as fluctuations of temperature or rainfall or a deflection in the movements of shoals of fish, by upsetting the equilibrium between economy and environment may bring about quite unexpected alterations in apparently remote aspects of culture, as well as exercising direct influence in an obvious manner on the basis of subsistence. Conversely, changes in beliefs or value-systems, for which no rational explanation can be forthcoming, may affect the entire equilibrium of a culture. In seeking explanations for cultural change it is always important to bear in mind the potential importance of non-rational, even random or accidental causes, and it has to be remembered also that a change in one aspect of culture, that may in itself be fortuitous, may have an unforeseeable impact on other aspects, and so produce disturbances and changes far transcending the original cause. In this connexion one ought not to forget the influence of individuals: the fact that prehistorians cannot identify individuals is no reason why they should ignore their existence, particularly in this matter of change; no doubt it is true that in primitive societies custom was king, but innovations were made, and these commonly took the form of following the lead of outstanding individuals, a lead which might have been the outcome of personal whim or even indisposition. Lastly, one has to reckon on the unpredictable results that flowed from contact between cultures that might be geographically far removed from one another: even though the result of contact through trade, war, or even accident might in the first instance involve the transmission of no more than an idea or an item of technical knowledge, its ultimate effect might be to upset the entire balance of a culture and to entail a series of readjustments some of which might prove to be of profound importance.

Whatever their cause, the effect of such changes, so far as mankind as a whole is concerned, has been to enlarge the range and effectiveness of culture. Two distinct processes can be detected. To begin with, as the archaeological record shows, cultural change has led to a progressive evolution of more effective procedures and modes of life. Given the fact of change and the existence of competing societies, technical progress and the enlargement of opportunity which this brings, were only to be expected, since changes which impaired efficiency were in the long run eliminated in favour of those which improved it: this may have involved the temporary discomfiture or even the elimination of individuals, classes, or communities, but the overall picture was one of progress. In this sense progress was an inevitable result of the fact of culture, even if at first it was bound to be extremely slow: this initial slowness, eloquently reflected in the archaeological record by the progressive refinement over tens and even hundreds of thousands of years of the flint and stone tools of the Lower and Middle Pleistocene, was due to the small number of individuals forming social groups, the scanty possibility of subdivision of labour beyond that proper to the sexes, the comparative rarity of cultural contact, and the relative fewness of traits in each culture. Conversely, it was above all the increase in the size of social units and in the possibility for the subdivision of labour that accompanied the discovery and prosecution of farming, and in addition the intensification of regional variations in culture that followed the adoption of a more settled mode of life, and the consequent greater possibility of stimulating contacts, that speeded up the process of change and progress.

It was the emergence of farmers from a world of hunters, fishers, and gatherers, and above all of civilized peoples from farmers that intensified the other main process in the building of cultures, namely diffusion or devolution, whereby relatively backward peoples were enabled to share in the achievements of more advanced ones. At the same time the emergence of stratified classes that accompanied progress towards civilization created conditions for cultural devolution within individual societies. Indeed, when two societies came into contact diffusion most commonly proceeded from the more to the less advanced by way of the latter's leading class and only reached the ordinary members of the receiving group in a devolved form. Among the secondary prehistoric societies, like those of the European Bronze or Iron Ages, which existed in an era when the initiative had already passed to historical and literate civilizations, these processes of diffusion and devolution were the principal agents of cultural change: in studying such even more attention might be paid to points of contact with more advanced societies. Yet in concentrating on the prehistoric cultures themselves, prehistorians show a sound instinct. The secondary prehistoric cultures, though influenced by contemporary civilizations, were very far from being mere provincial or impoverished reflections of these: those that survived the impact did so because of their own native genius, which enabled them to react in a creative manner to stimuli from higher cultures and in many cases to develop original civilizations of their own. Outstanding exponents of this were the Celtic and Teutonic peoples of temperate Europe, who received successive impulses from the ancient civilizations of the Near East and of the Mediterranean, absorbing those that seemed appropriate to their genius, only to emerge after a long period of barbarism to create modern civilization and extend its dominance over the habitable world.

VIII

PREHISTORY AND TODAY

A s anyone who has read through this book so far will agree, the attempt to unravel man's prehistory is beset with difficulties and makes heavy demands. It calls on a multitude of disciplines and makes liberal draughts alike on the technical skill and imaginative insight of natural scientists and on the human understanding and intuitive sense of style of humanist scholars. Over and above all this it is extremely costly, and the expense is continually mounting, not merely because of the progressive inflation in the cost of labour and materials, but still more on account of the great expansion in the field of inquiry and of the ever more exacting standards of research. For technical no less than for financial reasons we must expect to rely more and more for advances in our knowledge of prehistory on professionals, and above all on institutions under professional leadership, even if the part-time worker and amateur can still render aid of the highest value. All this means in effect that prehistoric research requires ever larger sums of money, and this must come, under present social conditions, either from public funds or directly from large numbers of individual members of the public subscribing to particular projects.

However distasteful the question may be to those engaged in prehistoric research and to their immediate followers, the question has to be faced whether the study of prehistory has any relevance to modern society, or, more specifically, whether it is sufficiently relevant to warrant the diversion of funds and of potentially productive men, skill, materials, and land. Does prehistory really mean enough to us today to support such large claims on social resources?

The question has purposely been framed in a social context, because it is from society at large that today, as never before, the resources for any costly and unremunerative enterprise must come. This is not to imply that the individual can be left out of account: on the contrary, in a free society it is only possible to secure social action by appealing to a sufficiently large number of articulate individuals, and it is worth remembering that under whatever form of government they are at present ruled all men are potentially such.

So far as individuals are concerned it is evident that a keen appetite exists for archaeology, not merely among readers and listeners, but also, and from some points of view most notably, among the devotees of television. One can say, indeed, without serious fear of contradiction that archaeology—and more particularly prehistoric archaeology, which makes no demands on literary scholarship—has established itself as one of the few forms of entertainment at once harmless and equally acceptable to all grades of society: no doubt the more cultivated and intelligent derive a keener and more discriminating pleasure, but since archaeology appeals directly to interests and concerns basic to human beings, it can entertain almost anyone at whatever level they may be capable of responding. Since in an age of mass leisure the problem of filling time has become a matter of grave social concern, this ability to provide innocuous entertainment must be accounted one of archaeology's chief claims on our resources.

Yet entertainment in the merely negative sense of relieving the tedium of leisure, meritorious though this has become, is only the beginning. By its power to engage attention archaeology has also the opportunity to educate and to educate in the true sense of drawing out latent interests, enhancing a sense of awareness and stimulating the joy in living that many occupations of modern life have done so much to atrophy. Let us now consider very briefly wherein the special qualifications of archaeology as a medium for education consist.

To begin with, archaeology is a historical discipline: as such it helps to lift people out of the limitations of their own time and place and to make them free of the whole experience of mankind. By helping to develop the historical imagination, the power to stand aside from one's own, and to inherit the life of past ages, archaeology nourishes one of the few faculties peculiar to man, and for this reason alone is worthy of our special regard. It might be objected that in the case of prehistoric archaeology the demands made on the imagination are excessive in the sense that the societies of prehistory were too far removed from our own in time and character, and that their remains, while arousing curiosity and even wonder, are incapable of generating anything more productive of future growth. Yet the fact remains that public interest is sustained. Indeed, it would seem that prehistoric archaeology is able to make a more direct appeal than that devoted to civilizations, since these involve a knowledge of the relevant literature possessed by very few; moreover, literate civilizations reflect divergent traditions, whereas prehistory—at least primary prehistory—is relevant to the experience of all human beings in whatever civilization they may happen to have been bred. Even so, prehistory makes calls enough on the imagination, and it is this which helps to make it so valuable educationally.

Archaeology appeals to the imagination very specifically, in that its object is to help in recreating prehistory and fill some of the gaps in recorded history. In a vulgar sense the possibility of rich and startling new finds, often as not made by chance, can be said to fire the imagination, but what one is more concerned with in the context of education is the way in which archaeology brings us up against the frontiers of knowledge, bids us look into the void of the unknown, and shows how, by deploying the resources of modern science, technology, and scholarship, progressively larger areas can be brought within the sphere of exact knowledge.

Thirdly, archaeology stimulates an interest in geography in

the fullest sense of that term, developing an awareness of place and of everything that living in a defined area implies. It is not merely that archaeological material relates to specific places, but that the cultures whose history it illuminates occupied definite territories and indeed represent specific adjustments between traditional social requirements and particular habitats and biomes. The study of prehistory involves a close investigation both of existing and of former conditions of climate, topography, soil, vegetation, and animal life, as these can be reconstructed by geological and kindred sciences; but further than that, it calls for an understanding of the intricate relations between human societies and their physical environments, an understanding which despite the triumphs of modern technology remains and must always remain of the utmost value for contemporary living.

Fourthly, the dependence of archaeology primarily on artifacts and the fact that considerations of style enter so largely into the classification of cultures and of phases in their development both imply a strong element of aesthetic appreciation. Most of the material objects disposed of by archaeology, even when beautiful in the sense of being well designed for their purpose and utilizing to the full the inherent properties of the materials of which they were made, were objects of ordinary use. On the other hand, productions of fine art, engravings, paintings, and sculptures contribute much to archaeology, both for the light they throw on other aspects of culture and for the information they give about the aesthetic notions of their creators. In an age when objects of daily use are impersonal, standardized products, the pots and pans, and other hand-made things of prehistoric peoples are attractive in themselves simply as artifacts. Again, in the case of the fine arts, it must be remarked that the modern dethronement of academic representational art, stemming ultimately from Classical sources, as the sole canon of excellence has certainly made easier the appreciation both of prehistoric and of modern 'primitive' art, which is in many ways more in tune with modern living than most western art of the nineteenth century.

No doubt other ways could be found of illustrating the value of archaeology to the individual, but it now remains to consider its specifically social value. Anything that entertains individuals and at the same time increases their sense of being alive must be accounted a benefit to society at large, but what I am thinking of now is something more specific, the contribution archaeology can make to social solidarity and integration.

Archaeology is able to make this social contribution as a historical discipline and as one which, thanks to the nature of its material, is able to make history actual in a way that the written page can seldom do. In its broadest connotation history is a basic need, a very condition, of human societies, which are distinguished from others precisely in that they are constituted by historical rather than merely by innate, biological inheritance. Indeed, without the solidarity based on sharing common traditions, by an awareness of common histories, it is difficult to see how human societies could ever have developed their culture through long ages up to the point at which they could not only read and record their own history, but conceivably terminate it finally and irretrievably. Human societies exist in the last resort because their members are aware of belonging to them, and a major factor in this is a consciousness of sharing a common past.

In preliterate societies this is kept alive and made vivid by myths and ritual, by stories of ancestors mumbled round the camp-fire by tribal elders and by a whole series of traditional explanations for features of the natural environment, social usages, and so on. Historical awareness was no doubt restricted among prehistoric peoples to the hunting bands or settled clans, as the case might be, in which they were organized and to which they were conscious of belonging: indeed, it may be accepted as a general proposition that there is a direct relation between the unit of history and the unit of social organization.

As social integration proceeded, so it may be supposed must the maximum area of history of which men would have been aware have been enlarged, though it ought at the same time to be appreciated that parallel with this there has been a layering of historical consciousness corresponding to the stages passed through in the process: thus individuals belonging to a highly integrated society might be expected to be conscious of loyalties at several distinct levels and to cherish the history of many social units subsidiary to the dominant one.

Conversely, in so far as the enlargement and consolidation of social groups has been consciously pursued as an act of policy, attempts have usually been made to stimulate historical awareness of the maximum grouping, which during recent centuries has been the nation state and its empire: archaeology by recovering material, visible memorials of this history from the very soil of the homeland provides just the kind of evidence needed to reinforce the sense of belonging. That those concerned with building nations should have cherished archaeology —and the antiquarianism which was one of its main roots—is entirely in accordance with this. Although in Britain we can point to nothing equivalent to the office of King's Antiquary, instituted by Gustavus Adolphus of Sweden (1594–1632) and still functioning today as head of the Antiquities Service, it is significant that Henry VIII, having despoiled the monasteries, should have patronized John Leland in his endeavours to salvage their antiquities and that the first Elizabethan age should have produced a vigorous school of antiquaries, not least among them William Camden, author of *Britannia* (1586), concerned above all to recapture and celebrate the ancient glories of Britain as if in answer to the illustrious achievements of their own age.

The revival of national sentiment in recent times has been richly nourished by and has also favoured the prosecution of archaeology. It is no chance that a chair of Irish Archaeology was founded at the Catholic University of Ireland in 1854, and actually held for eight years by Eugene O'Curry, and it is significant that the Irish University Act of 1908 provided for a chair at Cork as well as at Dublin, leaving only that at Galway to be set up by the republican régime. Incidentally the fact that the period of intense archaeological activity that followed the establishment of the Republic has not been sustained at quite the same tempo only helps to show that some of the initial enthusiasm was political and has not entirely survived the attainment of political objectives.

Again, the peoples liberated by the destruction in the First World War of the Austro-Hungarian, German, and Ottoman Empires and by the temporary retreat of Soviet Russia, in achieving national independence, hastened to explore the archaeological riches of their respective homelands. The contributions made between the wars to prehistoric archaeology by such peoples as the Czechs, Hungarians, Poles, Yugoslavs, Esthonians, and Finns were among the finest as well as among the most voluminous in Europe, and their national collections, nourished by excavation, were turned into veritable shrines, store-houses of the tangible relics of their early histories. It is pleasant to be able to record that in the case of those able to preserve their national identity the work so well begun has recovered from the often grievous losses of the Second World War and gone forward with undiminished vigour.

Just as with the European nations the ancient polities of the East turned to archaeology as they became conscious of themselves as modern states. The Japanese adopted archaeology as part of the process of westernization and soon reached a high level of proficiency. China was rather later in the field, but when the republican régime was firmly established archaeological activity of a scientific character soon began. For generations China had been the despair of archaeologists. Quite apart from the difficulty of western scholars working in the interior, archaeological excavations of an open character would have been strongly opposed by the peasants as unpropitious, likely to jar the susceptibilities of the spirits and interfere with the fertility of the soil. This meant that the demand for antiquities, both in China and in the outside world, had to be satisfied by clandestine robbing of tombs and other ancient sites: a steady stream of ancient objects poured into the cabinets of museums and wealthy collectors all over the world, but information about their provenance was understandably vague, if not entirely lacking. When the country was opened up western scholars were able to make many new discoveries which, taken together, inaugurated the modern era in Chinese archaeology: two French Jesuits, Teilhard de Chardin and Emile Licent, found the first Palaeolithic remains in China on the edge of the Ordos Desert; a Swedish mining adviser, Dr G. Andersson, and an American dental specialist, Dr Davidson Black, were responsible for the discovery of Peking Man; and it was the former who pointed out the significance of the chalcolithic painted pottery of Honan and Kansu. Yet from the beginning China played an essential part in unveiling her own distant past. The National Geological Survey of China and the Official National Research Institute between them carried out most of the field-work and published periodicals like the *Bulletin, Memoirs,* and *Palaeontologia Sinica* of the Survey. Furthermore, there emerged a number of Chinese research-workers, some of whom, like Dr Li Chi, excavator of the Bronze Age city of Anyang, and Dr W. C. Pei, investigator of Chou K'ou Tien enjoy a world fame. Since the communist revolution archaeological activity has been carried on, on an even greater scale, and though the motive is doubtless in part Marxist it is reasonable to think that national sentiment remains an important driving force in the recovery of the Chinese past.

The movement towards independence in the Middle East, where Old World civilization originally developed, has found expression among other ways in the staffing of Antiquities Services by nationals in place of westerners and in controlling more or less rigidly the export of antiquities, which have come to be regarded as an integral part of the national patrimony. It is further noticeable that India, Pakistan, and Ceylon have all maintained or instituted, as the case may be, their archaeological services, and it may be anticipated that as the various African territories enter on a fuller control of their affairs they also will continue and develop services for the excavation, preservation, and publication of the archaeological traces of their past. By the same token the provision of adequate archaeological services is a manifest duty of imperial powers towards their remaining dependent territories. The value of archaeology in lands, in many of which prehistory lasted down to modern times and in which the bulk of the population is still preliterate, hardly needs emphasis.

In a pathological sense the misuse of archaeology is almost equally illuminating. The leaders of National Socialist Germany showed a clear-sighted recognition of the value of archaeology for enhancing solidarity, even if their motives in doing so were nefarious, nor need we find it difficult to admit that some of the research they made possible was of a high technical standard and yielded valid results. Much, on the other hand, was corrupted by doctrines which stemmed directly from Gustaf Kossinna (1858–1931), an ardent exponent of Pan-Germanism and Nordicism. Kossinna cherished the idea, taken from the historian Sybel, that 'a nation which fails to keep in living touch with its past is as near to drying up as a tree with severed roots. We are today, what we were yesterday.'[1] Unfortunately he quite failed and in fact made no real attempt to study the remote past with scientific detachment. His aim was rather to use the archaeological material to demonstrate the 'superiority' of the Germans at all times. His favourite method was so to inflate the chronology of German prehistory that any innovation could be ascribed to a German origin and its diffusion due to the domination by Germans of 'inferior' peoples. He found

[1] G. Kossinna, *Ursprung und Verbreitung der Germanen in vor- und frühgeschichtlicher Zeit*, vol. I, Leipzig, 1926.

no difficulty in recognizing 'more than a dozen spreads of the megalith Indogermans from the North over the whole of Central Europe as far as the Black Sea';[1] gloried in the flint daggers of the Stone Cists,[2] symbols in sober fact of the cultural retardation of the North, as evidence of a noble pride and joy in weapons; and hailed the bronze trumpets of the Nordic Bronze Age as evidence of German superiority in music already in prehistoric times, contrasting their majestic volume combined with gentleness and euphony with the monotone, diatonic melodies of the South.[3]

In all essentials this was the outlook of Heinrich Himmler, the mild connoisseur of prehistory, who defined the subject, doubtless for a thousand years, as 'the doctrine of the eminence of the Germans at the dawn of civilization'. What a deserving and obliging branch of learning and by the same token how convenient was the Third Reich! Writing in 1939, Professor Hermann Schneider of the University of Tübingen was quite lyrical:

'The year 1933 witnessed the victory of an attitude towards the history of the culture of Germany which gave to the Germanic element of all that is German a significance previously unthought of. "The best of what is German", it was declared, "is Germanic and must be found in purer form in early Germanic times." Archaeological research thus found itself faced with the pleasant task of examining and reconstructing the real essence of Germanic life and customs.'[4]

An ostensible outcome of the Second World War has been a further extension of the principle of national self-determination, so that every people outside the area of communist

[1] G. Kossinna, *Ursprung und Verbreitung der Germanen in vor- und frühge-shichtlicher Zeit*, vol. 1, Leipzig, 1926, p. 160.   [2] Ibid., pp. 289 and 302.
[3] G. Kossinna, *Die deutsche Vorgeschichte eine hervorragend nationale Wissen-schaft*, Leipzig, 1912, pp. 29-30.
[4] Quoted from H. Rauschning, *Hitler speaks: a series of Political Conversations with Adolf Hitler on his real aims*, London, 1939, p. 255.

domination has achieved or can look forward to achieving national identity. With this there has been associated, as we have seen (p. 256f), what can only be termed the nationalization of archaeological activities. Yet the realities, even the political realities, are rather different: in terms of economic and military force the number of effective units in the world has in fact been reduced to two *blocs*, and the most pressing problem of world politics is now quite evidently the reconciliation of these and the achievement of a world order. Modern technology has made this possible, and nuclear fission has made it an imperative condition of survival. Intellectually the requirement is clear enough. To realize it in practice is much more difficult, because it involves the emotions of peoples of widely varying traditions, degrees of civilization, and standards of material well-being. In the last analysis the problem is one of creating a frame of mind, a vivid consciousness of belonging to a world society, transcending, but also comprehending regional and even national loyalties.

As we have seen, one of the most potent factors in social integration is history. If people are to be led to feel themselves members of a world society, one way of helping them to do so is to stimulate a consciousness of world history. In other words, the unit of history has to be expanded from the parochial to the universal, from the history of nation or civilization to that of the world. To anyone familiar with the conservatism of the teaching profession this might seem an almost insuperable task— one recalls the almost missionary zeal with which Arnold Toynbee has found it necessary to insist that the 'General History' of our schools deals in reality with the development of only one among many literate civilizations, several of which continue, beneath the apparent uniformity imposed by modern technology, to exercise an important influence down to our own day. But the world is not peopled by academics or even by people wedded particularly to western civilization. Contemporary developments in science and technology have already gone far to transform the social structure of western society as well as to undermine its hegemony: the new world community, if it ever emerges, will comprise, not only all the members—not merely the *élite*—of each of the great civilizations still extant, but in addition all those numerous peoples who until yesterday were prehistoric and preliterate. The vast mass of the world's population is not highly educated in any one of the great traditions, and to that extent involved involuntarily in its defence, but, on the contrary, is so ignorant as to be innocent of any deep attachment to any particular one.

This is not to say that any appeal can usefully be made over the heads, so to say, of the few. The fact that in the free countries of the world modern conditions have favoured the masses as consumers does not alter the fact that ideas come from the comparatively small minority of the highly educated: indeed, the conditions which have discomfited the old leisured class in western society, although entailing a regression in some spheres of culture, have in many ways increased the influence of this intellectual elite; the more open society of our time has made it easier for natural ability to emerge and reach positions of influence; and the growth of a new, scientifically based culture has already greatly enlarged the proportion of those who have received advanced education, a movement which shows every sign of increasing momentum as we move into the age of electronics and atomic power.

The kind of universal history needed, therefore, is one capable of appealing both to the under-privileged and to the growing class of the highly educated; moreover, and above all, it is one that must be addressed to a culture dominated by science and by what may be termed scientific humanism. The situation is much more hopeful than it might have seemed. Science knows no frontiers. The scientific temper, which brought the contemporary world into being and created a situation in which unity is a condition of survival, is at the same time much more conducive to new ideas of history than one dedicated to perpetuating the parochial traditions of a former phase in the history of the world. What is needed is a sense of history universal in time as well as in space.

It would be no answer to comprehend the histories of each of the major civilizations, even if this was possible in the detail needed for sound understanding. The history of each civilization or nation enhances the solidarity of its own members, but it by no means follows that contemplation of the history of all the several civilizations is necessary to or would in fact promote the realization of a world community: on the contrary, the essence of a literate civilization is that it separates its members from other civilizations—it is precisely on account of this exclusiveness that it has proved so valuable in fostering the solidarity of the group. Once settled life was established sufficiently firmly to make possible the growth of civilizations the history of different groups diverged: conversely, the only kind of history common to all civilizations is that which preceded them; that is, prehistory and specifically primary prehistory.

It is the story told by primary prehistory, the tremendous struggle over tens or even hundreds of thousands of years, culminating in the discovery of farming and the beginning of settled life, that reveals the previously hidden foundations on which all civilizations alike were reared. This is the true epic of man, underlying and setting in perspective the histories of all his various civilizations. All men, whatever the colour of their skin and however recently—or long ago—they emerged from prehistory, can recognize in the archaeological traces of their remote prehistoric forebears symbols both of their common kinship and of the glorious fact of human progress.

Yet we must never forget that under conditions of freedom a world-wide order can only be attained through the voluntary association of peoples of every state and civilization, and that the quality of life in any world-wide community will depend very largely on the degree to which each of its members is able to contribute its own distinctive quota to the sum of human experience. It is a fallacy to assume that wider loyalties supersede or even necessarily weaken narrower ones: as we have argued earlier, social integration involves not only an enlargement in the area of historical awareness, but also in its depth, as older loyalties are incorporated in newer, wider ones. One of the main virtues of prehistory from a social point of view is precisely that it enables us to view history in a broader perspective. Citizens of different states and members of distinct civilizations are liable to be better and not weaker adherents of a world order in proportion as they cherish their own histories and the secondary prehistories and protohistories that throw light on the immediate sources of these, provided only that they do so against the background of world prehistory.

If prehistory may be said to serve its highest social purpose in helping to promote human solidarity, one should never forget that societies are composed of individuals, and that it is in reality to these that prehistorians address themselves. It may be that prehistory is a social kind of history in the sense that prehistorians are unable to concern themselves directly with the choices made by individuals; yet it forms the prologue to the kind of history in which the fate of such can be discerned and its own course is marked by a progressive widening in the range of choice open to communities. As we have emphasized earlier in this chapter, prehistory appeals to individuals not merely as members of societies, but as persons, and it finds complete justification if it enriches the experience of men and helps them to live more abundantly as heirs of all ages and brothers to one another.

INDEX

Aamosen, Denmark, 147
Abingdon, Berks, 53
Abington Pigotts, Cambs., 45
Absolon, Professor C., 111
Acheulian culture, 123, 141, 145
Aegean, 164
Africa, 23, 34f., 64, 68, 77–80, 84, 92,
  136, 139f., 162–6, 205, 230, 259
Ahrensburgian culture, 180f.
agriculture, 30, 80, 88, 177f., 188–96,
  209, 212. See also cereals, fields,
  granaries, irrigation, manure, ploughs.
Aichbühl, Federsee, Württemberg,
  114f.
air-photography, 56f., 59–66, 124
Akerman, J. Y., 153
Alaska, 242
Alexander the Great, 23
Allen, Major G. W. G., 60, 63
Altai Mountains, 97
amber, 67, 215f.
America, 24, 36, 60, 64, 77, 83–86, 95ff.,
  106, 157ff., 168, 176, 241f.
amulets, 228
Andamanese, 173f.
Andersson, J. G., 73, 258
Ångerman River, Sweden, 156
Anglesey, 57
Angles-sur-Anglin, France, 204
Anglo-Saxons, 40, 52, 120f., 126, 239
antler, 76, 104, 183, 209
An-yang, China, 71, 73, 258
Arctic Stone Age, 183, 226
ards, 192
Arizona, 84f., 158, 205
Arminghall, Norfolk, 65
armour, 237
art, 19, 42, 57, 192, 197, 204f., 207,
  212ff., 220f., 223–6, 232, 236, 240, 254.
  See also cave art, 213ff.
Arundel, Thomas Howard, Earl of, 27
Aryans, 223
Ashmolean Museum, 27
Asia, 23, 34ff., 57, 64, 71ff., 77, 80–83,
  94f., 97–100, 113, 124f., 150, 162f.,
  165, 204, 207, 230, 233, 257ff.
associations, 137f. See also hoards.
astronomy, 154f., 158, 230f.
Atkinson, Richard J. C., 63, 131n., 167n.
Atreus, 67
Aubrey, John, 29, 68

Aurignacian culture, 123
Australasia, 23, 36, 173, 242
Austria, 216, 245
Avebury, 29, 74
Azilian culture, 123

baleen, 96f.
Ballinderry crannog, County Westmeath, 159
balloons, 57
Baltic region, 67, 143, 151, 157, 189
Bann Valley, North Ireland, 51
barbarians, 28, 164f., 236. See also Celtic
  peoples, Scyths, Teutonic peoples.
bark, 92, 104
barrows (tumuli), 29f., 43f., 57, 64, 66,
  69f., 91f., 97ff., 102f., 117ff., 128f.,
  148f., 192, 243. See also cairns.
Darcy Docks, 55
Basket-maker culture, 83ff.
basketry, 79f., 83, 87
battle-axe cultures, 214
beads, 67, 165–8
Beazeley, Colonel, 56
Beck, H. C., 165n.
Beresovka, Siberia, 94f.
Bible, 78
Bird, Junius, 86
Birket-Smith, Kaj, 95
bison, 227
Black, Davidson, 73, 258
boats, 49f., 93, 96, 120f., 186, 212f., 215.
  See also canoes, paddles.
bogs, 44, 46, 57, 86, 93, 146–9, 192,
  234, 239
bomb-damage, 58
bone, 76, 96, 104, 183, 209. See also
  fauna, fluorine tests, human remains.
boundaries, 191, 236, 238. See also
  palisades.
bows, bowmen, 82, 87, 213
Breuil, Abbé H., 33, 53
bricks, 74f., 108
Brigg, Lincs., 50
Britain, 27ff., 39–47, 49–55, 57f., 60–70,
  135, 153f., 159f., 194, 220, 235, 242,
  256. See also England, Scotland, Wales.
British Museum, 49, 78
broch, 57
bronze, 53f., 75, 134f., 137f., 201, 226,
  236

Teutonic peoples, 205, 239, 250
Téviec, Morbihan, 197
textiles, 78, 82f., 85ff., 92, 98, 204, 210f.
  See also cotton, linen, silk, wool.
Thames, river, 40, 54
Thomsen, C. J., 30f.
Thule culture, 96f.
Thurnwald, R., 173
tin, 216
tinder, 88
Tingstade Trask, Lake, Gotland, 159
Tollund, Jutland, 93, 196
tomb-robbing, 70, 98f., 109, 120
tombs. See burials.
Toynbee, Arnold, 261
toys, 96
trade, 48, 137, 163-8, 205, 209, 214-18,
  221, 236, 248
tradition, 70f.
transport, 211-15, 217, 236. See also boats,
  canoes, chariots, skis, sledges, wagons,
  wheeled vehicles.
traps, 183, 187f.
treasure-seeking, 26, 70
treasure trove, 42
tree-lopping, 191
trees, 145, 149, 158f. See also forest
  clearance, tree-lopping, wood-work.
Trent, river, 53
trepanation, 246
Tripolje culture, 190, 202f.
Trobriand Islanders, 174
Trois Frères, Ariège, France, 228f.
Troy, 67, 124, 193
Trundle hill-fort, Sussex, 61
Turkey, 67, 124, 193, 257
Tutankh-Amen, 78f.
typology, 134-7

Ur, 113, 124f., 163, 165
urnfield, 67

Vallois, H. V., 245
varve analysis, 156f.
Västerbjers, Gotland, 205f., 220
Vedda, 173
vegetation, 64ff., 77, 81, 87f., 95, 102.
  See also cereals, forest clearance, trees.

Veneti, 215
Vinča, Yugoslavia, 40
volcanic activity, 102
votive offerings, 138, 213, 234f.

Wady el-Mughara, Mount Carmel,
  Palestine, 150
wagons, 212ff.
Wales, 43, 45, 54f., 57, 195
war, warriors, 55ff., 222, 235ff., 248.
  See also defensive works, hill-forts,
  weapons.
Wasserburg Buchan, Württemberg, 88ff,
  197
Waterbolk, H. T., 148
water-supply, 198
weapons, 85, 92, 96, 98, 179, 181-5, 187,
  220, 235ff., 246. See also bows.
weaving appliances, 87, 210f., See also
  textiles.
Wessex Bronze Age, 167
Weymouth, W. D., 168n.
weights and measures, 218, 230
wheeled vehicles, 91, 191, 212f. See also
  chariots, hearses, wagons.
Wheeler, Sir Mortimer, 127f., 151n, 244
wheel-tracks, 214
Wiegand, Dr Theodore, 56
wine, 167, 196
Wisley, Surrey, 50
Woodhenge, Wilts., 66
wood-work, 76, 79-83, 85-93, 96-100,
  102, 104ff., 109ff., 126, 187, 195,
  200f., 210
wool, 86, 92, 98, 205f., 209
Woolley, Sir Leonard, 113, 124
Works, Ministry of, 57
written records, 20ff., 52, 67f., 73, 81, 85,
  176, 236f., 239, 244, 253. See also
  papyri.
Wurmius, Olaus, 28f.

Yetts, W. Perceval, 97n., 98
Yugoslavia, 257

Zalavrouga, Carelia, Russia, 213
Zeuner, Professor F. E., 138n., 155

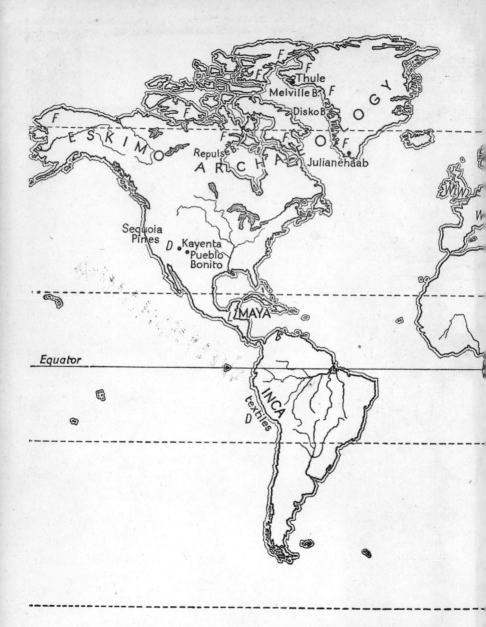

F = Frozen sites   W = Waterlogged sites

ARCHAEOLOG